# BASEBALL EXPLAINED

# BASEBALL EXPLAINED

Mike Shatzkin

Pelham Books

First published in Great Britain by
Pelham Books Ltd
27 Wrights Lane
London W8 5TZ
1987

© 1987 by Mike Shatzkin
Diagrams by Bob Carroll

Printed and bound in Great Britain by
Butler & Tanner Ltd, Frome and London

All Rights Reserved. No part of this publication may be reproduced, stored in a retrieval system, or transmitted, in any form or by any means, electronic, mechanical, photocopying, recording or otherwise, without the prior permission of the Copyright owner.

ISBN　0　7207　1781　7

# CONTENTS

| | |
|---|---|
| Introduction | 7 |
| 1. **American Baseball in Britain:** a brief report of a scant association. | 9 |
| 2. **The Rules and Objects of Baseball:** the laws of the game. | 11 |
| 3. **Playing Baseball:** the practices and tactics of the game. | 25 |
| 4. **Baseball Statistics**: analysing the game. | 53 |
| 5. **Thumbnail History of Baseball:** origins, organization, great players and teams, expansion and change. Baseball's place in Americana. | 63 |
| 6. **Following Baseball Each and Every Day:** satisfactorily, from Britain! | 73 |
| **Appendices** Reader's guide to appendices. | 90 |
| 1. The American League | 91 |
| 2. National League | 107 |
| 3. National League All-Stars | 125 |
| 4. American League All-Stars | 145 |
| 5. Championship Teams 1901–1986 | 158 |

# INTRO-
# DUCTION

# BASEBALL EXPLAINED

In the summer of 1958, when I was eleven years old, I was lucky enough to visit Britain for ten days with my parents. By that time a baseball fan for just two years, my first wish was to see a cricket match. A visit to Lord's was engineered for me.

Of course, I had no idea what was going on in the match between Somerset and Middlesex. Immediately afterwards I found a book – *The Laws of Cricket* – to read before I got one more chance to see a match, at the Oval. The book of rules and regulations was predictably unsatisfactory; a dry recitation of the rules to a game doesn't tell even an adult much about the essence. It was a losing battle for an eleven-year old. My day was saved by the niece of family friends who *did* know the game and explained what I was seeing as we watched at the Oval.

In the years since, I've had the opportunity to introduce baseball to a number of foreign friends, mostly British, in ballparks all over America. The game seems well-suited to the British temperament, which doesn't seem to mind its ambling pace and can appreciate its richly-documented history.

Now that broadcast and print deliver America's national pastime to a worldwide audience, this book is written with the hope that nobody will have to learn baseball the way I tried to learn cricket: from a book of rules.

The chapters entitled 'The Rules and Objects of Baseball' and 'Playing Baseball' are necessarily dry but, I hope, precise and clear. If you already have watched a game or two with some satisfactory guidance, you might skip lightly over these, just taking in enough to fill the gaps in your knowledge. The chapter entitled 'Statistics' tries to offer a view of baseball's special subtleties and will, it is hoped, give some insight into what makes the game 'tick'.

Bob Carroll, one of the most impressive sports historians I've encountered in Britain or US, has written the team summaries and player profiles for the appendix of this book. Bob is from the heartland of America – an hour outside of Pittsburgh – and I asked him to present this information in an authentic American baseball style. Some of the information he covers dates quickly: indeed, when he wrote, we didn't know where major stars like Lance Parrish and Tim Raines would play this year; they hadn't signed 1987 contracts yet although Spring Training had begun. These sections were written to make it easier for the non-American to pick favourite teams and players, even at a distance.

It is hard to explain the 'reasons' for love, but I think my own endless fascination with baseball stems from two aspects that separate it from all other sports:

The *game itself* builds in the complications. In American football, for example, the *object* of the game is simple and similar to soccer, rugby, hockey, basketball: advance to the goal the opponent defends. The complications are created by coaches. There is no real distinction between *situations*, which you will see is the key to baseball.

Baseball has a meaningful *history*; what happened in 1907 or 1927 could suddenly have relevance in 1987. The statistics tie the eras together; knowledge of them ties generations of today's fans together with their predecessors.

We Americans have got a lot from the British: from the roots of our democracy to the music of the Beatles. There hasn't been much of a cultural quid pro quo. Maybe baseball will be it.

# 1 AMERICAN BASEBALL IN BRITAIN

Only twice before the Channel 4 telecasts of 1986, had the professionals of American baseball brought their game to Britain: in the last century (1889) Albert Spalding led a touring group, and just before World War I (1914) Charles Comiskey and John McGraw brought a group of major leaguers playing as the Chicago White Sox versus the New York Giants.

Spalding was the president of the now-defunct Chicago White Stockings of the National League – he became much more famous later for the sporting goods company that bore his name – when he led the nineteenth-century contingent. Baseball had not yet taken all its present dimensions and basic rules: a game programme of the time reveals that the distance from pitcher to hitter was 50 feet where today it is standardized at 60 feet, 6 inches. A few noteworthy players made that trip with Spalding, including Adrian (Cap) Anson and John Montgomery Ward. Ward was an unpopular figure with the baseball ownership of the time for being in the forefront of early unionization attempts for the players. In 1890 he went into open warfare with Spalding by forming a Players League, which had a very brief history.

Comiskey was the owner of the Chicago White Sox – then and now members of the American League – and McGraw was the manager of the New York (now San Francisco) Giants of the National League when they led their group. Comiskey was one of baseball's early owners and the stadium the White Sox have occupied on Chicago's South Side since that time is still called Comiskey Park. (It is scheduled to be replaced by a newer stadium in the next few years.)

McGraw is a legend of baseball history, having played for the Baltimore Orioles of the 1890s, considered the best of the clubs of the pre-modern (pre-1900) era. He managed the Giants for the first third of the twentieth century, winning 10 league pennants and 5 world championships in that time.

The teams in both those early tours played on cricket grounds, football stadiums, and racetracks – hardly the most satisfactory way to present a game where the shape of the field is as important as it is in baseball. Both teams were in Britain as the last stop of a round-the-world tour.

Now baseball comes to Britain again on television and in print. And this time – and in this way – it has probably come to stay.

# 2 THE RULES AND OBJECTS OF BASEBALL

BASEBALL EXPLAINED

Major League Baseball – the fourteen clubs in the American League and the twelve clubs in the National League – is played between two teams of nine hitters opposing nine fielders on a field of live or ersatz grass, whose precise shape varies from ballpark to ballpark.

*This diagram shows the essential elements of a major league ballpark with the standard positioning of the defensive players. It is not drawn to scale (outfield walls would be considerably further from home plate).*

## THE PLAYING FIELD

**Fair territory** is a wedge of 90 degrees, extending from **home plate**, bounded by the **foul lines** and the arc of the outfield fences. The **foul poles** rise perpendicular to the field where the foul line meets the outfield fence.

**Foul territory** is the area of the playing field outside the foul lines.

The distance from home plate to the outfield

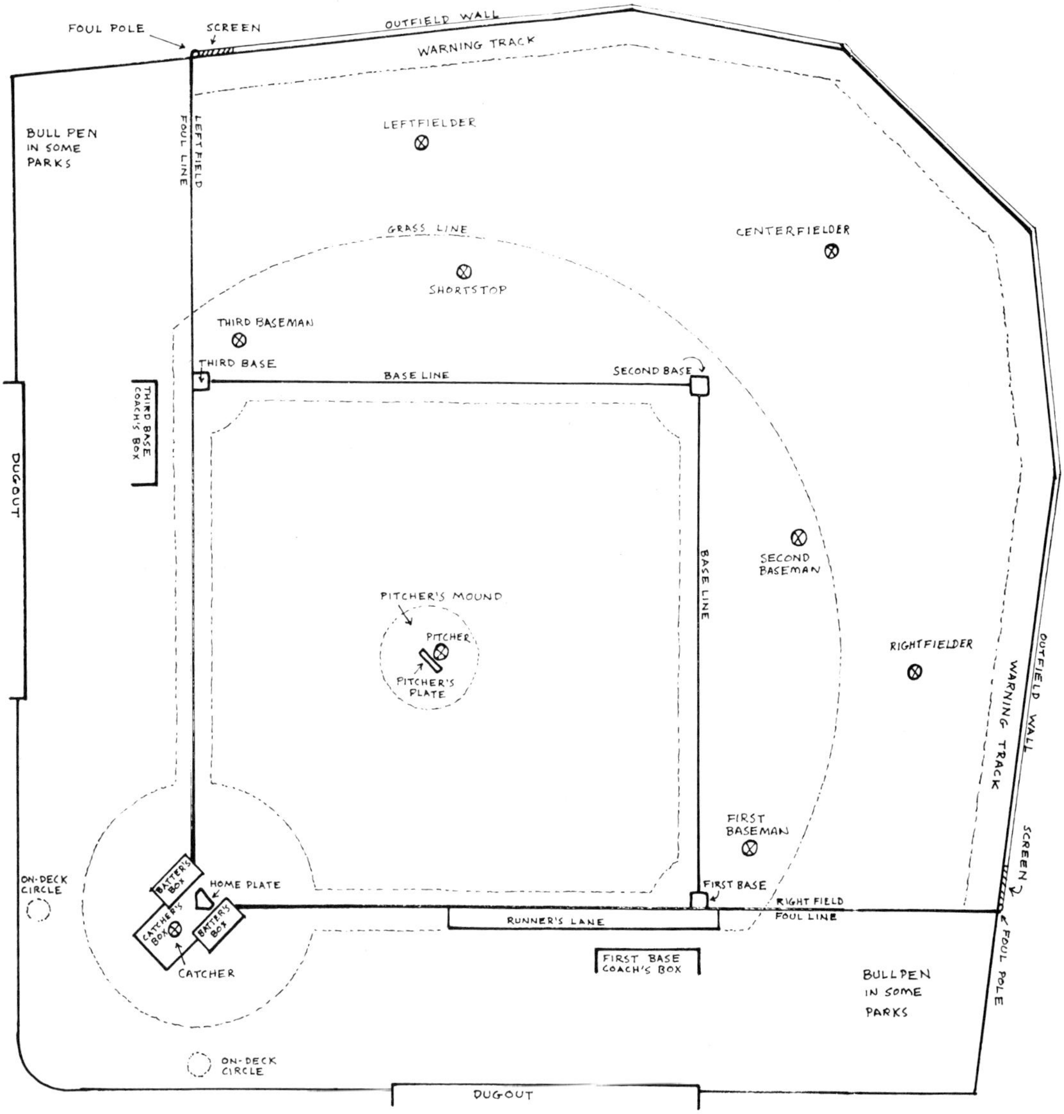

fences and from fair territory to the stands in foul territory differs with every ballpark.

**Home plate** – which is actually a squared-front pentagon-shaped disc of hard rubber with a 90 degree pointed side abutting the junction of the foul lines – is the cornerstone of play.

The player **at bat** takes a position with both feet within a batter's box (the two rectangles marked in chalk in foul territory alongside the parallel edges of home plate). **Righthanded batters**, positioning themselves with their left foot forward, the bat held behind the right ear, looking towards the pitcher by looking to their left, occupy the batter's box to the *left* of home plate, while **lefthanded batters** (with the **stance** reversed) occupy the box to the *right*, as viewed from behind the plate.

The catcher, effectively the on-field director of action for the team **in the field**, takes a position in the **catcher's box**, a rectangle marked in chalk below the pointed side of the plate.

**Runs** are scored by players who return to home plate after having successfully and in sequence touched the other bases.

Home plate is at the corner of the **diamond**, or **infield**, a 90-foot square bounded by the bases. The **first base line**, or **rightfield line**, extends anti-clockwise (or to the right, from a vantage point behind home plate) until it ends at the foul pole at the rightfield fence. The **third base line**, or **leftfield line**, extends clockwise (or to the left, from a vantage point behind home plate) until it ends at the foul pole at the leftfield fence.

Along the rightfield line, at a distance of 90 feet from home plate, is a white sack – **first base**. Along the leftfield line, at a distance of 90 feet from home plate is a white sack – **third base**. Completing the symmetrical infield diamond is a third white sack, **second base**, 90 feet from first and third.

Centred between first base and third base, but slightly closer to home than second, inside the diamond, is the **pitcher's mound**, a slightly-raised circle of dirt. Inside the mound, at a distance of 60 feet 6 inches from home plate, is **the rubber**, a slab which preserves the consistent distance between the pitcher and home plate.

The area inside the bases is the **infield**, the area within fair territory outside the bases is the **outfield**.

On natural grass fields (as in the majority of major league stadiums), the infield area is grass and a dirt arc (the **infield dirt**) extends from foul line to foul line, before the **outfield grass** begins. On artificial turf fields, there is usually a solid carpet of turf covering the entire field, except that there are dirt cut-out areas immediately around the bases themselves, the dirt arc sometimes being painted on. (Defensive players use the dirt arc – though it has no mandated dimension – as a guide to their positioning.)

The teams are stationed in **dugouts** (covered benches) along the first and third base lines. Between the dugouts and home plate are the **on-deck circles**, dirt circles where the next batter to hit stations himself while awaiting his turn.

**Coaches' boxes** are long rectangular dirt cut-outs immediately outside fair territory next to first base and third base. The team at bat puts one coach in each box to relay signals from the manager on the bench to the batters and baserunners and to help baserunners with judgements about fielding plays taking place behind them.

The **warning track**, a running-track type of surface, encircles the entire field between the turf and the grandstands. Its purpose is to alert a player tracking down a batted ball that he is nearing a fence.

## BASIC RULES OF PLAY AND OBJECTS OF THE GAME

Major league baseball is a game of **nine innings**. An inning is completed when both teams have hit, the visiting team first (in the **top of the inning**) and the home team last (in the

BASEBALL EXPLAINED

bottom of the inning). Tied games continue with **extra innings** until the tie is broken.

When the home team is leading and the visiting team has completed all its innings, the home team will not take its final at-bats. Thus the home team does not bat in the bottom of the 9th inning unless they trail or the game is tied.

A game may be delayed, interrupted, postponed, or cancelled by precipitation, cold, darkness, local curfew ordinances, or unplayable grounds. In order to count in the league standings as an *official game*, 5 innings (or $4\frac{1}{2}$ if the home team is leading) must be completed.

The team in the field (the home team to start the game) stations nine defensive players, all wearing leather gloves on their opposite-to-throwing hand.

The **pitcher** works from the pitcher's mound inside the diamond.

The **catcher**, the only player to wear heavy protective gear, crouches in the catcher's box behind home plate.

The four **infielders** spread across the arc of the infield dirt: the **first baseman** and **second baseman** between first base and second base, the **shortstop** and **third baseman** between second base and third base.

The three **outfielders** spread across the outfield: the **leftfielder** nearer the leftfield line, the **centrefielder** in the middle behind second base, the **rightfielder** nearer the rightfield line.

The **team at bat** sends one **batter** (or, more optimistically, **hitter**) to bat at a time, according to a **batting order** announced before the game. Batters must appear in turn.

Traditionally, the nine men in a team's batting order were the same nine men fielding the positions. In 1973, the American League introduced the **designated hitter**, a batsman to take the place of the *pitcher* in the team's

*Longtime star Bob Boone in catching regalia; his mask and helmet are in his right hand.*

batting order. Since pitchers are generally the weakest hitters (because they are not selected for hitting ability and because they get less batting practice or coaching than position players), this was an attempt to add more offence to the game. To this day, the designated hitter is used in the American League and not in the National League. Minor professional leagues and various levels of amateur baseball are split in their use of this device. The upshot is that American League teams, in effect, start a 10-man line-up, eight of whom hit and field, a pitcher who doesn't hit, and a designated hitter who does not play the field.

Major league teams play with 24- or 25-man rosters and may make substitutions at any time **the ball is dead** (between pitches.) A substitute batter is a **pinch-hitter**, a substitute baserunner is a **pinch-runner**, a replacement pitcher is a **relief pitcher**. Once a player has been removed for a substitute, he may *not* re-enter the game.

There are generally four **umpires** in a major league game, one behind home plate, the other three at the three bases. In post-season championship games there are two additional umpires stationed down the left- and rightfield foul lines.

The team in the field must get three **outs** to retire the team at bat and complete the half-inning. The 'out' is the basic unit of defensive accomplishment, what the defence counts to measure its progress throughout a game.

The team at bat tries to score **runs** before three outs are recorded. The team scoring the most runs in nine innings wins the game. The 'run' is the unit of offensive accomplishment.

A batter will complete his turn at bat either by being out in some way or **reaching base safely** in some way. If he reaches base safely, he becomes a **baserunner**, attempting to advance in sequence counterclockwise from first base to second base to third base and back to home plate.

Only one baserunner may occupy a base at a time, so there are a maximum of three runners on base at any one time, a situation called **bases loaded**.

If a baserunner completes the circuit before there are three outs on his team, a run is scored. If three outs are recorded before the circuit is completed, the runner is **left on base** and has no further value to his team. Each team's turn at bat begins with the **bases empty**; baserunners do not carry over to the next inning when the team bats again.

## FIRST CONFRONTATION: PITCHER VERSUS HITTER

Play is initiated by the pitcher. With one foot in contact with the pitcher's rubber, he throws the ball (a **pitch**) for the hitter to **take** (allow to go by without attempting to hit) or **swing at** (attempt to hit the ball thrown by the pitcher.)

THE STRIKE ZONE
From batter's armpits to his knees and over the plate

The umpire will **call** every pitch *taken* a **ball** or a **strike**. A strike is a pitch which the umpire sees to cross the plate between the batter's armpits and the top of his knees. A ball is a pitch not swung at by the batter which is outside that defined **strike zone**.

A hitter who has four balls called in one time at bat is **walked**, and goes to first base (becoming a baserunner) while the next hitter comes up to bat. If a teammate was already a runner at first, the teammate moves on to second, and so on, so that a hitter who walks with the bases loaded will **force in a run**, moving each baserunner around so that the one on third crosses home plate. (Note: baserunners must be **forced** to advance on a walk; if a hitter walks with a runner on second but no runner on first, the runner on second does not advance.)

If the pitch hits the batter before it hits the bat, he has been **hit by the pitch** and takes first base. This is a faster (and for the hitter, more painful) version of a walk (or **base on balls**).

A hitter who has three strikes called in one time at bat is **struck out**. He returns to the bench. If his out is the first or second, the next hitter comes to bat. If it is the third, the **side is retired** and the half-inning is over.

The number of balls and strikes on a hitter in his current turn at bat is called **the count**, two numbers with the ball count stated first. A 3-and-0 pitch, therefore, is thrown when a batter has three balls and no strikes on him. A **full count** (commonly called the **pitch of decision**) is a 3-and-2, when one more ball completes the walk and one more strike completes the strikeout.

If the pitch is swung at by the hitter and missed, the umpire will call a strike. If the batter already had two strikes on him, he is out.

It is not always clear whether a batter has swung at a pitch or not; if he starts to swing and stops – **checking his swing** – and the pitch was

A CHECKED SWING

# THE RULES AND OBJECTS OF BASEBALL

FAIR OR FOUL?
A FAIR: *Any ball leaving the park fair is a fair ball.*
B FOUL: *Any ball leaving the park foul is a foul ball.*
C FAIR: *A ball that lands fair after passing a base is a fair ball even if it later bounces into foul territory.*

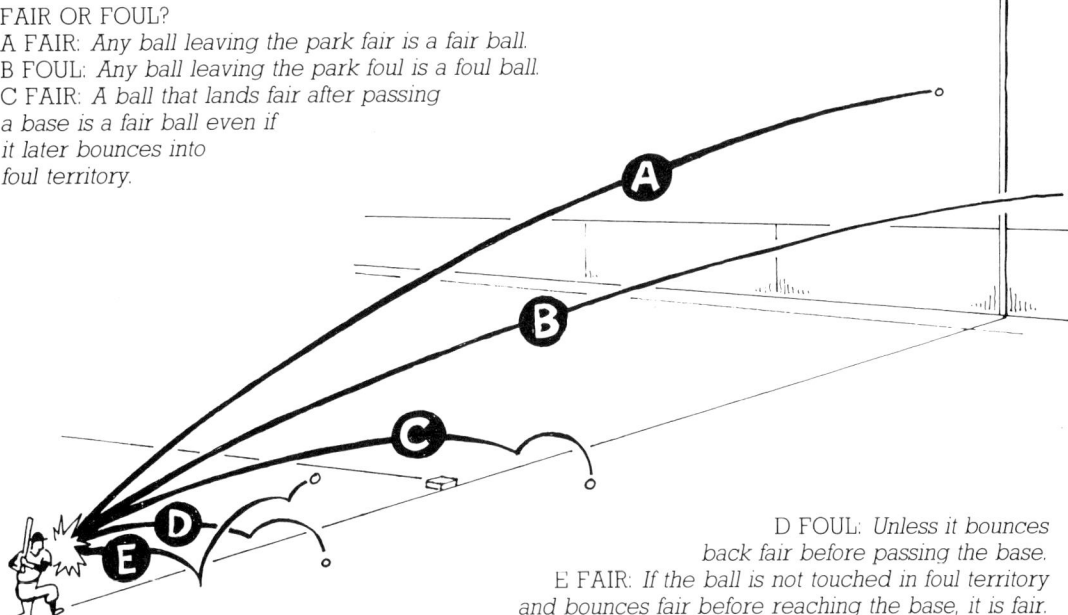

D FOUL: *Unless it bounces back fair before passing the base.*
E FAIR: *If the ball is not touched in foul territory and bounces fair before reaching the base, it is fair.*

not in the strike zone it is up to the umpire to rule. This is the home plate umpire's call, but he will sometimes ask for help from the line umpire opposite the batter – the first base umpire for righthanded batters and the third base umpire for lefthanded batters. The baseline umpires can often see more clearly than the plate umpire whether the batter **broke his wrists** or whether the **bathead went across the plate**, two key determinants for a swing-or-check decision.

If the pitch is hit within the playing field – **fair or foul** – it is **in play**.

**A foul ball** is a ball which never touches the ground in fair territory, or – if it does – crosses over to foul territory after hitting the ground but *before* passing first or third base or being touched by a **fielder**. Fly balls above foul territory are foul.

**A fair ball** is a ball hit – on the ground or in the air – within the two foul lines.

Once a ball goes into the outfield (beyond the bases) as a fair ball or is touched by a defensive player anywhere in fair territory, it remains a fair ball even if it later bounces or is thrown into foul territory.

Once a ball is touched by a defensive player as a foul ball, it cannot become a fair ball again.

Like a fair ball if a foul ball is caught before it hits the field by a defensive player, the batter is out.

If a batted ball hits the ground foul, it counts as *the first or second strike* on the hitter. A foul ball not caught which was hit by a batter who already has two strikes is no play. The batter continues with the count unchanged and the baserunners still at the bases they occupied when the foul ball was hit.

If the batter hits the pitch in fair territory, he and any teammates on base will try to advance and the defensive team will try to get him and his teammates out and to minimize the advancement of baserunners towards home.

A fair ball caught before it hits the ground puts the batter out and the baserunners may leave the base they occupied only *after* the ball is caught. Therefore, a runner on second who started to advance on a hit ball then finds that it was caught, must *return* and **tag up** (retouch second base) before he can proceed. If the defence gets the ball to the base originally occupied after the catch and before the runner tags up, the runner is also out (a form of the **double play**).

A fair ball which strikes the ground before it is caught can be a **fielding chance** (a legitimate opportunity for the defence still to record an out) or a **hit** (giving no chance for the defence to stop the batter from reaching base safely.)

When a ball is hit fair, the batter is *obliged* to try to reach first base before the defensive team can recover the batted ball and get *it* to first base. If the ball beats the batter, he is out and leaves the field; if the batter beats the ball, he is safe and remains on base while the next hitter takes his turn. (Of course, the batter could have been put out by the batted ball having been caught, in which case the defence would not attempt to get the batter out at first.)

Because the batter *must* try to occupy first base after he hits a fair ball, a runner occupying first will be *forced* to second, runners on first and second will be forced to second and third, while all runners are forced if the bases are loaded. The defensive team earns an out by getting the ball to *any* base ahead of a runner forced to that base.

*FORCE: When the batter hits a fair ball that touches the field, the runner (or runners) immediately ahead of the batter is 'forced' to advance. The runner will be out if the base is tagged by a fielder (in possession of the ball) before the runner arrives.*

*NO FORCE: The runner (below, trying for a two-base hit is not 'forced' to advance to the next base. To be put out, he must be tagged. If a runner is on second and first is empty, he is not forced to go to third on a batted ball.*

# THE RULES AND OBJECTS OF BASEBALL

In a bases-loaded situation, a batted ball can be turned into an out beating the runner to *any* base (home included). But note that once an out is recorded, it *changes* the force situation. If the defensive team responds to a bases-loaded ground ball by throwing to second and successfully recording an out, from that moment there is *no longer a force* on the runners who previously occupied second and third (the runner on first who forced them having been retired.) Similarly, if the batted ball is caught in the air for an out, there would be no force plays at any base, since the batter is out and the obligation of the batter to go to first generates *all* force situations. However, after a caught ball, the *tagging up* requirement, very similar to a force, does apply.

To create an out when there is no force, the defensive team must **tag** (touch) the runner with the ball or a fielder's hand holding the ball while the runner is not touching a base. Tag plays are also legal when there is a force. The defence handles a runner trying to tag up after a caught ball like a force; there is no need to tag the runner, only to beat him to the base with the ball.

*The 'force play' begins with a ground ball; here Marty Barrett of the Red Sox fields one.*

# BASEBALL EXPLAINED

When the third out of the inning is recorded on a caught fly ball or a force play, no run can score – even if a baserunner successfully crosses home plate before the out is actually recorded. If the third out is generated on a tag play or on a runner who has failed to properly tag up after a caught fly, then the baserunner's run will count if he crossed the plate before the out was actually recorded.

## DEFINITIONS, WRINKLES, REFINEMENTS AND EXCEPTIONS

When a batter hits a ball that permits him to reach first base safely through no miscue by the defence, it is a **basehit** or a **single**. If the basehit permits reaching second base without a defensive error, it is a **double**; reaching third base is a **triple** and completing the circuit is a **home run**.

A batter may, for tactical reasons we will explain later, try to **bunt** (try to hold the bat in place so that the ball strikes it) rather than **swing away** (take a full swing at the ball.) A ball bunted foul with two strikes puts the batter out on strikes; a full-swing landing foul with two strikes does not change the count.

To complete a strikeout (*except* on a bunted third strike), the catcher must catch the pitch before it hits the ground. If he fails to do so, he may complete the strikeout by tagging the batter or getting the ball to first base before the batter can get there. (A batter is forced to first by a dropped third strike as he would be on a ball batted fair.)

A batter may get a very small piece of the ball – a **foul tip** – which alters the direction of the pitched ball very slightly. A tip landing foul by a batter with two strikes **gives the batter a life**; it is a foul ball and not a strikeout. A tip caught with *less than two strikes* is not an out; a foul ball must go over the catcher's head to qualify as a fly ball to be caught as an out. A tip caught *on the third strike* is a strikeout.

Baserunners are not obliged to remain on the base they occupy. They may attempt to advance *at any time*, including while the pitcher holds the ball between pitches or while the pitch is being made to the plate. Runners trying to advance without benefit of a batted ball are **attempting to steal**. The defence must stop them by tagging them with the ball when they are not on a base (there is no force). In the classic case, the runner on first tries to steal second as the pitcher delivers the ball to the plate; the catcher must catch the pitch and throw it to second base where the second

NO RUNNERS ON BASE:
FULL WIND-UP

baseman or shortstop (depending on tactical considerations) will have **covered** – come from fielding position to receive the throw. If the baserunner is tagged before he can reach the base, he is **caught stealing**. If the baserunner tags and holds the base before the ball is placed on him, he has a **stolen base**.

Note that there is no force in a stolen base situation, so the baserunner has the option of turning round and going back towards the base from which he came. This can result in a **rundown play** or **pickle**, in which the defensive team needs several throws before placing a fielder with the ball close enough to the runner for a tag play to be completed.

It is normal for a baserunner anticipating the next pitch to take a position *off* the base occupied and *towards* the next base. This is the runner's **lead**. A bigger lead is an aid in stealing bases and also makes it harder for the defence to force that runner at the next base.

To make it more difficult for runners to steal

*The time it takes to complete a full wind-up would permit any runner to steal. The shorter delivery from the set position is generally less effective against the batter, but it gives pause to a would-be basestealer when the pitcher stops at the belt.*

RUNNER ON BASE: STRETCH, SET, THROW.

bases and to cut down on the baserunners' lead, pitchers change their delivery motion with runners on base. Whereas normally a pitcher will swing both arms over his head and throw himself (and the ball) towards home plate in one continuous motion, with runners on a pitcher will come to a **stop** with his hands at his waist (**the set position**) and **check the runner**. He may then choose to throw to first base to try to get the runner out (a tag play, not a force) instead of making a pitch. This threat keeps the runner honest. There is then a shorter delivery time to the plate after the check.

The pitcher is not permitted to engage in overtly deceptive changes in delivery to fool a baserunner, such as starting to deliver to the plate and suddenly stopping. Such deception is a **balk**, which permits each baserunner to advance one base. There is no balk with the bases empty.

Two other wrinkles protect the runners from deception by the fielders.

With baserunners in *any* force situation with less than two out, the requirement that the catcher not drop a third strike for the strikeout to be recorded is waived. Were it *not*, with a runner on first base for example, the catcher could deliberately drop a third strike. That would force the batter to first and the baserunner to second, creating a double play (two outs on one pitched ball) opportunity for the defence. Once there are two out, the requirement of catching the third strike is reinstated regardless of the baserunners.

The **infield fly rule** takes effect with runners on first and second, or first, second and third and less than two out. In that situation, a high fly ball which the umpires judge can be caught by an infielder is ruled an infield fly. The batter is *automatically out*, whether the ball is successfully caught or not. This removes the force for the runners at the next base. (The force would be created by the necessity of the batter running to first.) Before this rule was invented, a quick-witted infielder would deliberately drop such a fly. The baserunners would need to remain near their original bases in case the ball were caught (remember the rules on *tagging up*). By throwing to third base and then to second, two baserunners would be forced and the fly ball turned into a double play.

Unlike the dropped third strike rule, the

*The INFIELD FLY RULE protects the runners on first and second with less than two out. Without it, the second baseman would drop the ball, throw to the third baseman (to force the runner at second), who would then go back to second base (probably to the shortstop covering the base) to force the runner from first. Calling the batter out automatically removes the force on a dropped ball.*

infield fly rule does *not* take effect with a runner on first base only, since it is only called by the umpires on a ball hit high enough to permit the batter sufficient time to run to first base before a double play could be completed. On an intentionally dropped third strike the defensive play would begin with the batter still in the batter's box and the 'protection' needs to be extended to the batter as well as the baserunners.

When a batter attempts to reach first base on a batted ball, he is required to run in the 3-foot-wide **lane** which is defined by a line parallel to the first-base line for the last 45 feet of his journey, or he risks being out for **interference** if he is hit by an infielder's attempt to throw to first.

A batter may **overrun** first base without being tagged out after he crosses the bag, as long as he makes no attempt to turn towards second. A baserunner may *not* overrun second or third base without risk of being tagged out while not in contact with the base. After a baserunner crosses home safely, he has scored and can no longer be put out.

## ADDITIONAL DEFINITIONS AND CONTEXT

Most of the time, plays occur on batted balls. The *most* successful strikeout pitchers get 8–10 of their 27 outs (3 in each of 9 innings) on strikeouts; pitchers with the least **control** typically walk no more than 4–6 per game.

**Grounders**, or balls which first hit the field only a few feet from the batter, must be handled by the infield: the infielder in position to **field** the grounder will generally throw it to another infielder covering a base where there is a force before the forced runner reaches the base. A ground ball hit **through the infield** will almost always be a base hit.

**Fly balls**, or balls which are hit in a parabolic arc, are considered **pop-ups** if they are short enough to be handled by the infield. Longer fly balls must be caught by outfielders to secure an out. Fly balls which hit the ground before they are caught are said to have **dropped safely** and are almost always hits.

A **line drive** is a ball hit in the air but on a much flatter arc. Line drives permit much less time for a fielder to react to them and field them successfully; generally hitters try to hit line drives whenever possible.

A ball hit beyond the outfield fence in fair territory before it hits the ground is a home run, permitting the batter (and any baserunners **ahead of him**) to complete the circuit and score. A home run may be achieved **inside the park**, by hitting the ball so that it can't be retrieved and a play made on the hitter before he has completed the circuit. This is one of the rarer plays in baseball.

A home run hit with one runner on base is a **2-run homer** (both the runner and batter score); with two on base it is a **3-run homer**; with the bases loaded (three runners on) it is a **grand slam** and scores four runs. Home runs hit with the bases empty score one run and are called **solo homers**.

A ball which hits the ground within the playing field and then bounces over the fence is generally a **ground-rule double**.

The foul lines and foul pole are in *fair territory*. A batted ball hitting the foul pole on a fly is a home run.

Recording two outs on one pitch is a **double play**. It can occur in a variety of ways, but the most common are:

A ground ball to the infield with a runner on first, permitting a force play at second followed by one at first on the batter.

A strikeout with a runner on base attempting to steal on that pitch; catching that runner stealing is a **strike-'em-out-throw-'em-out** double play.

A line drive hit to an infielder with a runner on base will sometimes permit the defence to get the ball back to the occupied base before the runner can tag up. This happens particularly when a runner has a big lead or when he starts to advance thinking the ball will go through the infield.

*The most common double play: the shortstop (1) comes in to field the ground ball (2) and shovels it (3) to the second baseman coming over from his position (4). As the runner coming in from having occupied first base attempts to upset him, the second baseman (5) 'pivots' and throws on to first base (6) to retire the batter for the second out on the play.*

Recording three outs on one pitch is a **triple play**. This is rare; it happens only a handful of times each season and it almost always occurs when two baserunners get trapped on a caught infield line drive. A triple play can *only* occur with two (or more) runners on base and nobody out.

There are certain umpire calls which require a request by either team to be made, the **appeal plays**:

If a batter appears at the plate out of turn, the umpire will make no attempt to stop him from hitting. If, after the out-of-turn hitter is pitched to and *before* one pitch is thrown to the next hitter, the fielding team appeals, the umpire will rule the out-of-turn hitter out.

If a runner advances a base on a ball caught for an out, the umpire at the base he advances to will call 'out' or 'safe' when he arrives. If the runner left his previous base *before the ball was caught*, it requires an appeal by the fielding team to the umpire at that base before one pitch is thrown to the next hitter for the offending baserunner to be called out. The appeal is made by a defensive player touching the base while holding the ball.

If a runner advances from first base to third, but neglects to touch second base on his way, it requires an appeal by the fielding team to the umpire at the missed base (second, in this case) before the first pitch to the next hitter for the offending baserunner to be called out.

While the umpires make all the decisions about play – calling balls, strikes, outs; foul balls and fair; granting time-out to players' requests; calling balks – the **Official Scorer** creates and controls the official record of the game. The Scorer is usually a local sportswriter, paid by the league for his services, and he decides, for example:

When a batter reaches base whether he did so on a hit or an error (usually this is clear; sometimes it is a matter of interpretation).

When a baserunner advances because the pitch gets by the catcher without being hit by the batter, whether the pitcher should be charged with a **wild pitch** or the catcher with a **passed ball**.

# 3 PLAYING BASEBALL

BASEBALL EXPLAINED

## PITCHERS VERSUS HITTERS: THE BASIC SET-UP

The centrepiece of baseball is the battle between the pitcher and the batter. Each defensive player and baserunner has a role to play, but it is within the context of the pitcher–batter battle.

Pitchers are either right- or lefthanded – almost never does a 'switch-pitcher' occur at any level of the game. Greg Harris of the Texas Rangers is reputed to have the ability to pitch both ways, but so far he has been used exclusively as a right-handed pitcher in the major leagues.

A righthanded pitcher executes his **pitching motion** by pivoting with his right foot on the pitcher's rubber, a lefty does the opposite. When a lefty is in the stretch position, holding baserunners close, he faces first base. That permits him to look directly at a runner on first (the most common baserunner situation), whereas a righthander has to look over his left shoulder to check the runner. This generally permits lefties to hold runners better – making stealing bases more difficult and permitting easier infield double plays.

Some great basestealers have claimed that they can work more easily against a lefty, because their clear view of the pitcher's hands

*A lefthanded pitcher can hold a runner closer to first base than a righthander because he will not have to turn to throw to first.*

*Righthander Mike Witt of the Angels delivers with his left foot in contact with the rubber.*

# BASEBALL EXPLAINED

*A righthanded batter is at a disadvantage against a righthanded pitcher: the pitch starts from slightly behind him and a righthander's curve breaks away from him. Lefthanded pitchers have a similar advantage over lefthanded batters.*

and arms gives them a greater advantage than the pitcher's direct view gives him. This is definitely a minority position.

Lefthanded pitchers (and, by now, lefthanded people) are called **southpaws**, a term with a logical baseball derivation. Ballparks are almost always laid out so that the sun sets behind the plate into the outfielders' eyes and safely out of the hitter's. First base is, therefore, towards the south. Lefthanded pitchers throw 'by way of' first base from the batter's point of view, so a long time ago lefties began to be called southpaws.

Batters are also either left- or righthanded. A righthanded batter stands in the box on the left side of home plate (looking from behind the plate), a lefty batter does the opposite. Batters who are capable of hitting both ways are called **switch-hitters**, and they are fairly common. Most major league line-ups feature at least a couple of switch-hitters.

The lefty hitter is a couple of steps closer to first base than the righty, presenting a small advantage – particularly for a fast runner – in **beating out** infield ground balls for base hits.

A righthanded pitcher has an advantage against a righthanded hitter, a lefty pitcher an advantage against a lefty hitter. A switch-hitter will almost always choose to bat opposite the pitcher: lefthanded against a righthanded pitcher, righthanded against a lefty. This advantage is not speculative; it is a fact verified over and over again in baseball statistics for almost every batter. Even though there are occasional situations where, for example, a righthanded batter hits a particular righthanded pitcher exceptionally well, almost no righthanded batter hits righties in general better than lefties in general.

There are two reasons for this:

A righty pitcher to a righty hitter, or a lefty to a lefty, is releasing the ball from a spot somewhat behind the hitter's head. A hitter facing an opposite pitcher has the entire pitcher's motion and release point in front of him.

The most common **breaking pitch** (a pitch thrown deliberately to deviate from a straight line from pitcher to catcher) is the **curve ball** (others will be discussed later.) A righty's curve ball breaks away from a righty hitter, in towards a lefty hitter (with a lefty's curve ball the opposite occurs.) It is easier to hit a pitch breaking towards you.

An important, but usually unspoken, element of the battle between hitter and pitcher is *fear*. Major league pitchers routinely throw a very hard ball towards the batter at 80–95 miles per hour. Ninety miles an hour is about 130 feet per second; the front of home plate is 60 feet 6 inches from the pitcher's rubber. A pitcher releases the ball somewhat closer to the plate than the rubber, so a batter has 4/10ths of a second or less to make a decision as to *whether* to swing and *then* to successfully hit the ball.

The only major leaguer in history who died directly from being hit in the head with a pitched ball (Ray Chapman of the Cleveland Indians hit by Carl Mays of the Yankees in 1920), was killed before batters wore protective helmets. But many batters since have suffered serious, even career-ending, injuries when struck by a pitch.

The pitcher seldom wants to hit a batter – remember the rules treat a hit batter like a walk and he takes first base – but every pitcher wants to keep the batter considering the possibility of being hit.

## A FEW WORDS ABOUT BALLPARKS

A unique feature of baseball is that each ballpark is different in ways that sharply affect the game.

Minimum distances to outfield fences are mandated in the major leagues (325 feet from home plate to the foul poles and 400 feet to centre field for all stadiums built after 1958) but the precise dimensions differ in every park. And while symmetrical designs (uniform distances to equivalent places in left- and rightfields) have been the seldom-excepted

# BASEBALL EXPLAINED

rule in ballparks built since the 1950s, many of the older ballparks survive with exotic outfield shapes that were inspired by a variety of circumstances.

Lansdowne Street was already there before the ballpark was built, so Fenway Park in Boston has 'the Green Monster': a high leftfield wall that looms much closer to the hitter than the outer barrier in most stadiums. (The dimensions of the rightfield wall are much more typical.) Fenway generally favours powerful righthanded hitters, except that a hard line drive 20 feet off the ground that might go beyond a longer outfield fence is stopped by The Wall and can be held to a long single by alert outfielding. The influence of The Wall – from the practical problems for an outfielder trying to predict how balls will come off of it to the psychological ones for the hitter trying to aim for it and the pitcher trying to stop him – is felt on almost every pitch thrown at Fenway Park.

Yankee Stadium in New York has an opposite bias, a shorter-than-normal rightfield. This was done intentionally when the Stadium was built to favour the great Yankee slugger, Babe Ruth. Ruth was a lefty hitter whose power was to right and Yankee ballclubs since have been constructed with an eye to powerful lefties who can use Ruth's advantage. Leftfield in Yankee Stadium is abnormally *long*, which handicapped the performance of legendary righthanded hitter Joe DiMaggio.

The shape of the outfield is the most obvious and important variation among the ballparks, but there are others. Artificial turf fields are 'faster' than natural grass, so balls hit **into the gaps** between outfielders are harder to cut off. Clubs that play on turf generally sacrifice power for speed. The prevailing wind at Candlestick Park in San Francisco blows across the outfield from leftfield to right, so righty-pull hitters fight the wind and lefties are helped by it. Oakland Coliseum has vast foul territory which means that fouls out of play in most ballparks can be caught for outs in Oakland.

## PITCHERS: THE TYPES AND THEIR TOOLS

The two extreme types of pitchers – although many fall in between – are **power pitchers** and **finesse** or **junk pitchers**.

A power pitcher throws hard – fast balls above 90 miles per hour – and often strikes a lot of batters out. A junk pitcher throwing slower pitches finds it more difficult to make a

batter miss completely. He tries to fool the hitter and throw him off stride so the batter does not hit the ball hard.

A power pitcher is relying on strength, throwing pitches with so much speed and movement that the batter is literally overpowered; this allows a certain margin of error in **control**, or placement of the pitch. Junk pitchers who must rely on guile to fool hitters must have excellent control.

A power pitcher can often get by with only two different pitches; a junk pitcher is almost always required to have four or five to maintain the necessary level of deception.

Branch Rickey was the greatest thinker in baseball history, a mediocre player and manager who became the game's most innovative executive and team-builder. Rickey said that pitchers could fool batters in two ways with a pitch: the *place* and the *time*. In other

*Veteran relief ace Dan Quisenberry of the Royals is a 'submarine' pitcher.*

words, by varying the speed and location of pitches – against what the batter has been seeing and against what the batter expects – the pitcher can fool the batter into a tentative swing or into less-than-total contact between the bat and the ball.

The single most important facet of pitching is control. If a pitcher can't throw strikes, batters can simply wait for walks. If a pitcher can't throw *certain pitches* for strikes, the batter can look for specific other pitches. While the pitcher is trying to make the batter hit a pitch that is either out of the strike zone or in the strike zone in a spot the batter doesn't expect, the batter is trying to guess correctly for speed and location – swinging hard if he's right and taking the pitch if he is wrong.

A pitch close to the batter is said to be **inside**, a pitch away is **outside**. In the nomenclature: 'a fastball inside' would be a ball, 'a fastball on the inside corner' would be a strike.

The pitcher is limited to four balls (or the batter walks) and the batter is limited to three strikes (or he is out). This puts an outer limit on the pitcher's ability to get by without throwing the ball where he intends to and on the batter's ability to take a pitch that fools him.

Since 1920, major league pitchers have been prohibited from applying a 'foreign substance' to the ball. Before that time the application of grease or tar, cutting the ball or spitting on it, or otherwise defacing it from a nearly-round shape so that it would follow a less-than-straight path, was common practice. Some pitchers still get away with illegal pitches – occasionally somebody is caught, fined, suspended for a few games and told not to do it again. But a wide variety of legal pitches are employed.

**The fastball** is the basic pitch for most pitchers. It may have a gentle break, but it is meant to be thrown straight and hard. It is the easiest pitch on a pitcher's arm, and also easiest to control. It is also the easiest pitch for a batter to hit if it is *not* thrown where the pitcher wants it.

**The curve ball** is the basic breaking pitch. By spinning the ball off his fingers, the pitcher makes the ball break – or move from a straight path – generally down and away from a same-sided hitter. There are varying types of curve balls, ranging from big arcs (**rainbow curves**) to those that break more suddenly (**sharp-breaking curves** which are often said to **fall off the table**). Pitchers may have one or more different types in their arsenal. The curve is harder to control than the fastball. If a curve doesn't break it is said to **hang**, and a hanging curve is one of the easiest pitches to hit. A curve is employed by a pitcher in two ways: to look good to the batter and then break out of the strike zone to a difficult spot to hit, or to look bad to the batter who gives up on it and watches it break over the plate for a strike.

**The slider** is faster than a curve with a smaller break, usually a late break. The deception is usually achieved by how much a slider looks to the batter like a fastball, until it is too late.

**The sinker** is a breaking ball that moves down. Sinkerball pitchers make batters hit ground balls and can be more useful than a power pitcher when the defence is looking for an infield grounder to make a double play.

**The knuckleball**, which is actually thrown with a finger-tip grip achieved with long and strong fingernails, is a very slow pitch thrown without any spin, so that it breaks (it almost darts) unpredictably. This is a very difficult pitch to control (most knuckleball pitchers just throw for the middle of the strike zone and hope it will end up somewhere else), very hard to hit, and a nightmare to catch. Not too many pitchers throw it, but those who do can pitch for a long time because it takes very little arm or leg strength.

**The split-finger fastball** is a cousin of **the forkball**, thrown out of the webbing between the first and middle fingers. The forkball was traditionally a breaking pitch, discernible as one to the batter because it was slower than the fastball. Recently, some major league pitchers have developed the split-finger fastball variation, which is devastating if thrown with control. It looks like a fastball and breaks very sharply, like a much more difficult variation of the slider.

**The screwball** is a reverse-break curve; that is, a righty's screwball breaks down and in to a righthanded batter. The motion of throwing the screwball is usually hard on the arm, so it is not a common pitch. Those who throw it can foil the usual tendency of opposite-sided hitters to be most effective.

**The change-up** is the most dramatic example of what the best pitchers do almost all the time; a variation of speed to fool the hitter. The classic change-up is thrown with the full exertion of a fastball motion, but it comes to the plate very slowly. (A good major league fastball is 90 miles per hour; a very good change-up for a 90 miles per hour pitcher would be 60 miles per hour). The change-up's utility is entirely in contrast to the speed of the fastball.

**The palm ball**, with the ball gripped deep in the palm rather than with the fingers, results in a change of speed and, sometimes, a break as well.

**Stuff** is the sheer quality of a pitcher's pitches: a very fast fastball, a sharp-breaking curve. Power pitchers have 'great stuff'. A pitcher who 'has his stuff' is getting his best in velocity and break on his pitches.

As well as there being a variety of pitches, with different combinations in every individual arsenal, pitchers throw with different motions.

**Overhand pitchers** – the classic and most common motion – release the ball with their throwing arm extended straight over their head.

**Sidearm pitchers** throw with what baseball players call a **buggywhip** motion, with the throwing arm extended 90 degrees out to the side of the body, parallel to the ground. Sidearm pitchers exaggerate the effect of throwing from *behind* same-sided hitters, and sidearmers with good control can drive same-sided hitters crazy. On the other hand, they present much less mystery to opposite-sided hitters.

**Submarine** or **underhand pitchers** release the ball with the throwing hand coming up in an arc from behind them.

**Three-quarters pitchers** – almost as classic and common as overhand – throw with a motion that describes an arc between overhand and sidearm.

Most pitchers throw consistently with one of the foregoing motions, although overhand and three-quarters pitchers **drop down** to throw an occasional sidearm pitch.

Each pitcher has a different set of **tools**: different pitches with different **command** of each pitch (ability to control it). The catcher **calls** the pitches, does the thinking about what each pitch should be and hand-signals to the pitcher from the crouch so that the batter and base coaches can't see it. (Sometimes the manager calls the pitches by signalling to the catcher.) The pitcher **accepts** the sign or **shakes it off**, asking for the catcher to communicate a different choice. The catcher gives the pitcher a **target**, often the catcher's glove but sometimes a part of his body.

Although the catcher gives the sign, the pitcher has the ultimate control. How much patience a manager or catcher will have for a pitcher frequently shaking off the catcher's sign depends on the pitcher's age, experience, and success. What is never tolerated is for the pitcher to **cross up** the catcher: throw a pitch different from the sign that was accepted.

The signs from the catcher are picked up by the shortstop or second baseman and communicated by signals to the rest of the team. That way, the fielders know if the pitch will be fastball – harder for the batter to **pull**, or hit to his power field – or a breaking ball. Some fielders will actually move slightly from their fielding position as the ball is pitched because they know what the batter will see.

When a baserunner is on second, he can also see the catcher's signals and can tip off the

batter as to what to expect. Defensive teams try to foil signal-stealing by complicating the code from what it is if only their own players can see it. This usually (not always) frustrates the batting team's attempt to anticipate the pitches, but it can also result in confusing the pitcher or the fielders on their own team as well.

## HITTERS: THE TYPES, STRENGTHS AND WEAKNESSES

Hitters are also in two extreme categories with many in between: **power hitters** and **spray hitters**.

Power hitters generally are a greater threat to hit home runs but, because they swing harder, are more likely to strike out.

Spray hitters tend to **hit the ball where it is pitched**, so that the hit ball may go anywhere on the field. Power hitters tend to **pull the ball**, or hit it to the same side of the field as the batter's box they occupy: lefty hitters to rightfield and righty hitters to leftfield.

The way a batter stands at the plate is called his **stance**. Some hitters have their front foot closer to the plate than their back foot, a **closed** stance. If their front foot is further away, so that they *face* the pitcher, they have an **open** stance. As the ball is pitched and the batter swings, the front foot generally **strides** towards the pitcher. Hitters trying to hit for power will often stride towards the power (pull hitting) field, which can make the hitter vulnerable to a ball breaking over the outside part of the plate.

Some hitters keep their stance very consistent: home run king Roger Maris used to smooth the dirt in the batter's box after each pitch to monitor his stride. Some hitters change their stance regularly; others do it when they are in a streak of bad hitting, a **slump**.

Hitters also vary in their **eye**, or accurate perception of the strike zone. It is harder for a pitcher to get a hitter with a good eye to swing at a pitch that is not a strike.

The smartest and most experienced hitters **work the count**: they know that the pitcher might have to sacrifice **stuff** for control when the batter is **ahead on the count** (usually 2-balls or more, 1-strike or fewer). That puts the odds of a correct guess in the batter's favour (the pitcher must throw whatever he can best control) and permits the batter to take the pitch without severe consequences if he guesses wrong.

Of course, the smartest and most experienced pitchers also work the count. They try to **get ahead of the hitter**, getting strikes early in the count so that they can put the batter in a defensive position, needing to get his bat on the pitch if it is in the strike zone.

Batters also tend to be **low-ball hitters** or **high-ball hitters**. For reasons nobody has ever satisfactorily explained, lefty hitters tend to be low-ball hitters and righties high-ball hitters.

Each pitcher also tends to be more effective either high or low. The best fastball of many power pitchers tends to rise, or **hop**, so they are often more effective high in the strike zone. Junk pitchers, particularly sinkerballers who try to get ground balls, have to be low in the strike zone to be effective. A sinker that starts high can end up at the waist, great hitting territory.

Most batters have areas of the strike zone that are tough for them to **handle**. Of course, for accomplished major league hitters this is a relative thing; if they know what a pitch will be and where it is going to be, they can hit it.

A batter's power and **bat control** can be affected by where he places his hands on the bat. If a batter holds the bat at the bottom of the **handle**, he gives himself the most possible useable bat surface and the greatest bat speed. He also requires himself to move the greatest amount of *weight* through the strike zone. This is how power hitters usually hold the bat.

If the batter moves his hands up the handle, leaving some of the bat below his hands, he is **choking up**. Choking up cuts down power, but increases control, and it is a technique often employed by spray hitters. Sometimes hitters

*Mike Marshall of the Dodgers is one of the top power hitters in the game.*

will move up the handle when the count reaches 2-strikes, willing to sacrifice power for control when the next missed swing would result in an out.

## THE BATTLE BETWEEN THEM

Before each and every major league game, the pitcher and catcher (sometimes with the manager or a coach) **go over the line-up**, analysing the strengths and weaknesses of each opposing batter and how that pitcher should **work** each hitter. Usually a pitcher has a particular **out pitch** – the type of pitch he would like to get the batter to hit. Sometimes the out pitch can vary with the hitter, particularly if a pitcher has an array of pitches.

Within each time at bat, a battle of wits is going on between the pitcher and the hitter. In the major leagues, where most confrontations occur between batters and pitchers who know each other and know that the other knows them, expectation is almost as important as reality.

A pitcher may know that a particular batter usually takes the first pitch to get a 'look' at each at-bat. Does the pitcher throw a fastball down the middle to get ahead on the count, or does he fear the batter's awareness of the pitcher's knowledge makes that too dangerous?

A pitcher who normally has good control of a curveball hasn't got it on a particular day. Does the batter guess fastball on a 2-and-2 pitch, risking a feeble swing or a called third strike if he guesses wrong?

A major league pitcher does not try to get the batter out with every pitch; an unhittably-inside fastball is often the tool to **back the hitter off the plate** to set up an out on the next pitch, which will be a curve low and away from the batter. A pitcher with a mediocre fastball who has been frustrating a hitter with off-speed pitches throughout a game, may **show the fastball** just outside the strike zone and tempt the batter to go for a bad pitch.

There are established 'pitching patterns' which have proven their effectiveness over the years. The classic fastball/curveball 'stuff' pitcher will keep the fastball 'high and tight' and the curve 'low and away', alternating them to keep the batter off balance. Power pitchers with a **hop** on their fastball will go 'up the ladder', throwing progressively higher pitches that the batter will chase up the strike zone.

Batters are also trying to influence the pitching pattern; **forcing a pitcher to come up** by refusing to swing at pitches low in the strike zone (particularly if the ball moves down); **sitting on the fastball** (waiting for it) if the pitcher has erratic control of his curve.

## RELIEF PITCHERS, PINCH-HITTERS AND PINCH-RUNNERS

Pitching is an activity which puts enormous strain on the arm. There are absolute limits on how many pitches a man can throw in a day or a week.

A starting pitcher in the major leagues is expected to complete six or more innings in each start. The starting line-up and batting orders are also set with that expectation. After six innings, sheer armweariness can begin to tell on a pitcher's effectiveness. And after two or three at-bats, batters can begin to **time a pitcher**, get enough of a rhythm with the pitcher's deliveries to make him easier to hit.

Different pitchers show tiredness in different ways. A sudden loss of control is a common symptom for all types of pitchers. Overhand power pitchers will tend to **come up**; their pitches will be higher than they intended. Curve balls that don't break (hang) are another common sign of fatigue. Sometimes a fastball pulled foul will tell a manager that a pitcher is losing his speed.

When a starting pitcher gets into trouble late

*Cecil Cooper of the Brewers uses an extremely 'open' stance; note the shin guard on the right leg to protect him against foul balls hit straight down.*

in a game, or when the manager *thinks* he's about to get into trouble, or when the pitcher leaves the game for a pinch-hitter, he is replaced by a **relief pitcher**.

Though starting pitchers are 'scheduled' for a lengthy apperance, relief pitchers usually are not. Most managers have one **closer**, their best relief pitcher. The closer is seldom called upon to pitch more than two innings in one game. Between the starter and the closer are **long- and short-relief pitchers**. In a close and important game, a very active manager might change pitchers for two or three consecutive batters, to get particular match-ups.

The closer is also sometimes called the **bullpen ace** or the **stopper**. The stopper is also a term used for an exceptionally reliable starting pitcher.

Starting pitchers work in 4- or 5-man rotations, depending on the personnel and the manager's philosophy. Since baseball is played virtually every day, that provides three or four days' rest between starts. Starting pitchers seldom appear between starts (a change between baseball today and baseball 30, 40 and 50 years ago.)

The balance of the usually 9- or 10-man pitching staff pitches relief. Relief pitchers can appear on consecutive days, sometimes for three or four if each stint is short. Even so, a regular starting pitcher will throw more innings than the most hard-working relief pitchers, usually more than double during the course of the season. The special challenges of relief pitching are the frequency of pressure situations (so often they come in *because* there is trouble) and the strains of being called on to warm up and possibly pitch several days in a row. The special challenge of starting pitching is to develop a cycle of readiness-and-recovery that permits maximum effectiveness on a regular basis. A starting pitcher who is ineffective has to wait nearly a week to redeem a bad performance.

A team's batting order is created to attack a particular starting pitcher and to balance the defensive requirements as well. (Remember, except for the designated hitter in the American League, the batting order is made up of players who must also play defensive positions.) When a team is losing in the later innings of a game, it is sometimes necessary to sacrifice defensive considerations to get additional hitting. A **pinch-hitter** is employed in these situations.

A pinch-hitter is chosen from the five or six position players who did not start the game in the field (rarely are pitchers used for pinch-hitters; usually – in the National League where there is no designated hitter – they are the weak hitter the pinch-hitter has replaced). Once a pinch-hitter is used, the player he replaced at bat is out of the game; a pitcher would be replaced by a relief pitcher (whose entrance puts the pinch-hitter out of the game) and a fielder could be replaced by the pinch-hitter or another of the position players on the bench.

There are pinch-hitting **specialists**, although not every team has one, who rise to the special challenge of one pressure at-bat in a game.

A pinch-hitter might be employed because the righthanded starting pitcher has been replaced by a relief pitcher who is lefthanded.

A team may choose to start a stronger-*fielding* player at a particular position, but replace him with a stronger hitter when they are behind in late innings.

A **pinch-runner** is a substitute for a baserunner employed to get more speed on the bases. A pinch-runner is often employed after a pinch-hitter, particularly a specialist who could be an older and slower player, gets on base.

## RUNNING THE BASES

If a batter successfully hits a pitch over an outfield wall, he gets a **home run** and can trot from first base to second to third and to home at his leisure. Since major league line-ups produce less than a home run per game on average, **advancing runners** after they reach safely with less than a home run is an important component of the game.

Runners on second or third base are said to be in **scoring position**, so-called because they can score on almost any **hit** to the outfield. (Remember, a 'hit' means a *safe* hit, on which a batter reaches base. The terminology gets confusing: 'a ball hit to the outfield' might be in the air and be caught for an out, but 'getting a hit' – or 'getting a basehit' – means the batter reaches base.)

**Singles** (1-base hits) are much more common than **extra base hits**, so baserunning tactics are usually predicated on the idea of advancing on *singles or outs*.

If the third out of an inning is recorded on a strikeout, a force or a caught fly ball, no run can score. But a runner on third base with less than two outs can often score on an out. (Although the correct syntax is, of course, 'fewer than two outs', baseball nomenclature uses 'less' far more often.) This situation is a pressure point for the hitter and the pitcher; the team at bat is *expected* to score.

If the infield plays at **normal depth**, a baserunner on third will score on a ground ball hit to the infield. The infielder would not have the time to get the ball home ahead of the runner leading off third, even though there is sufficient time to throw to first to beat the batter for an out.

If the defence plays **the infield in** – at the edge of the infield grass rather than behind the infield dirt – they *can* beat the runner on a play at the plate when the batter hits a ground ball. In that situation, the runner would probably **hold at third** on an infield grounder (unless being forced by a bases-loaded situation). The defence would earn an out and no run would score. The danger in this situation for the defence is that it is much easier for a batter to get a ball **through a drawn-in infield**. A grounder that might be an out with the infield at normal depth can be turned into a basehit. (NB: With less than two out and a runner on first, the infield will play at **double play depth**, halfway between 'normal' and 'infield in', with the **middle infielders** (shortstop and second baseman) 'cheating' towards second.)

On any ball hit reasonably deep to the outfield, a runner on third will score **after the catch**, by leaving third base after the outfielder touches the ball. Depending on how deep the fly ball is and how strong the outfielder's throwing arm is, this attempt can result in a very exciting play at home plate.

The **intentional walk** is sometimes employed in this situation: creating a force at second (at least) and the potential for an inning-ending double play (on which a runner coming in from third would not score). The intentional walk is accomplished by the pitcher throwing four pitches far enough outside for them to be unhittable. It is also used to avoid a dangerous hitter in key situations.

The only way to stop a runner on third with less than two out from scoring without the infield in, an outstanding outfield throw, or an infield double play is for the pitcher to get a **strikeout** or a **pop fly** to the infield.

When a team gets a runner on first – particularly its **leadoff batter** in an inning – getting the man into scoring position is often the next object.

A runner can **steal second**, advance while the pitcher is throwing to the plate. The best basestealers (Vince Coleman of the St Louis Cardinals, Rickey Henderson of the Yankees) are a **threat to steal** almost every time they are on base. Some runners are never a threat to steal.

The team can **start the runner** and oblige the batter to swing at the pitch. This is called the **hit-and-run** play. Since either the shortstop or second baseman will have to move to **cover** second when the runner starts to steal, the batter will have a **hole** in the infield to shoot for, if he can guess correctly which middle infielder will be covering. Hit-and-run plays are usually called with the batter ahead in the count (for example, 2-balls-and-0-strikes or 2-and-1) so that the pitcher is likely to throw a

*INFIELD: 'IN'*

*INFIELD: NORMAL DEPTH*

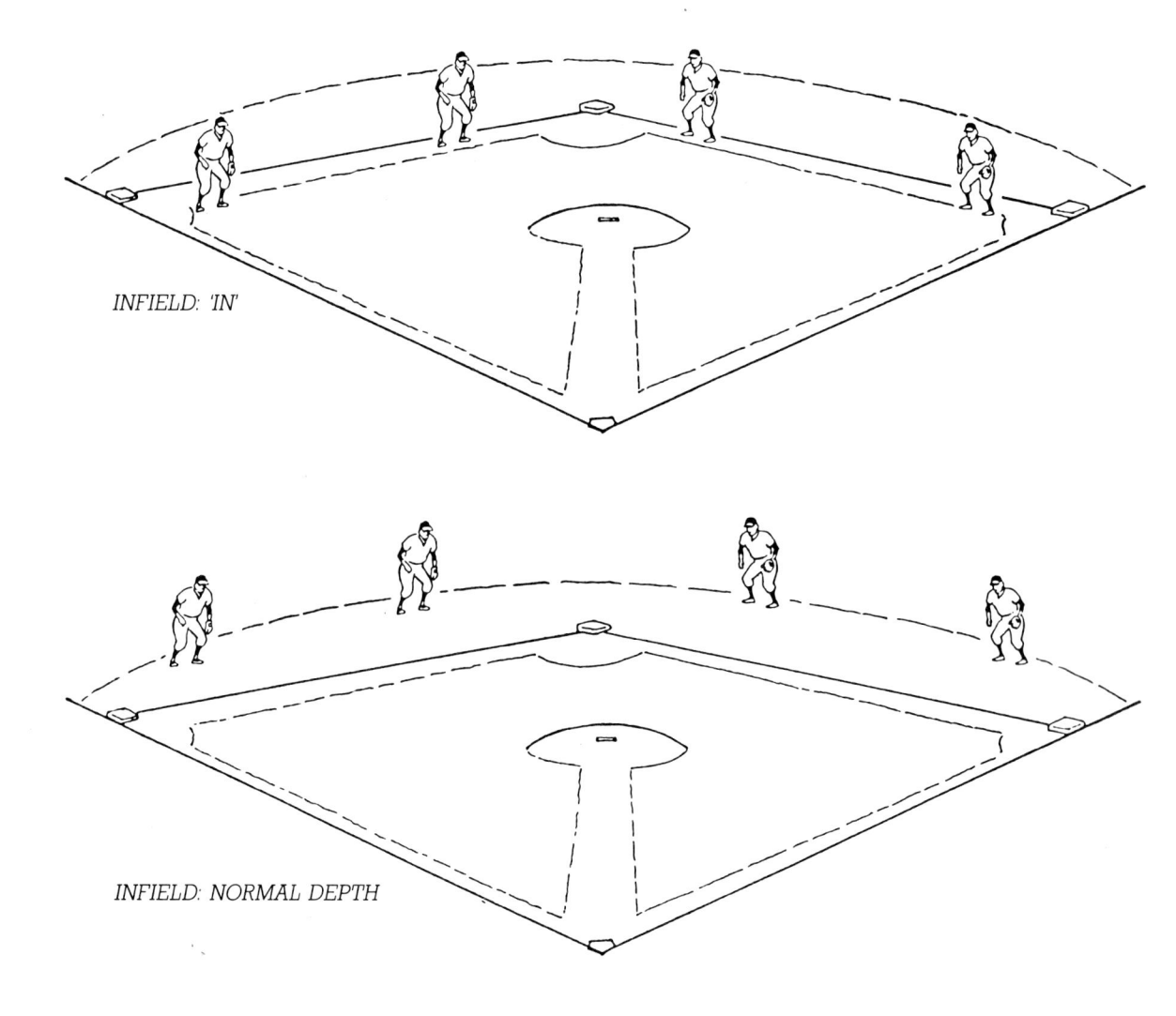

Baseball mythology says that a batter's average is 100 points higher with the infield in, because grounders and line drives are easier to get past the fielders playing closer to the batter. Teams bring the infield in because, at normal depth an infielder would not be able to challenge a runner trying to score from third.

strike. If the batter misses a hit-and-run play, the baserunner is often **caught stealing**, thrown out at second base. A hit-and-run is also used to **keep out of the double play**; a grounder fielded by the infield must be played to first because the started runner would beat the play at second. (NB: With a runner on first and no runner on second, less than two out, the first baseman will 'hold the runner on', moving from normal position off the line and well back of first base to a spot with one foot on the base itself. This further increases the 'hole' a righthanded batter can shoot for with the second baseman covering.)

Because most batters *pull* more often than **hitting to the opposite field**, the shortstop will usually cover against lefthanded hitters, the second baseman against righthanded hitters.

A batter on a hit-and-run will usually try to hit to the opposite field.

A team can **sacrifice**, have the batter **bunt** the ball (tap it gently within the infield). A good bunt will force the defence to throw out the batter, allowing the runner to advance.

Messages from the manager to the batter or baserunners are relayed by **signs** from the first- or third-base coaches. They will **flash** signs for the 'steal' to the baserunner, for the 'hit-and-run' to the batter and baserunner, to 'take' or 'okay to swing away' (**green light**), or to *bunt* to the batter.

Hitters often need a green light to permit swinging at a 2-and-0 or 3-and-0 pitch; managers may require them to 'take' to try to force the pitcher to give up a walk. What hitters may do 'on their own' varies with the ballclub, sometimes with the hitter.

Normally, batters are free to swing on 2-and-0 and 3-and-1 and told to take on 3-and-0.

Top basestealers may be free to go on any pitch except if specifically signalled *not* to steal; most players attempt to steal on managerial instruction.

Base coaches disguise their signs to avoid tipping off the defence. They usually do that by running through a long set of movements and hand motions: touching each hand to their uniform shirt or their cap, hitching up their belt, moving from one end of the coaches' box to the other, clapping their hands. Some of these gyrations have significance; most of them don't.

An important baserunning technique is **sliding**, going into a base on the side of one leg or head first on the belly. Runners slide to present a lower and smaller target for a tag and to be sure they will not go **beyond** the base they have been running towards. Some particularly good baserunners have sliding techniques (the **hook slide**, the **stand-up slide**) that refine the craft.

When a team gets a man on *second* with nobody out, there is a high payoff in advancing him to third with the first out. The runner can score from third base on the second out.

One way to achieve that advance is with the sacrifice bunt, and this is often used if there is no runner on first creating a force play at third.

A **ground ball to the right side** (to the first or second baseman) can also advance an unforced runner from second; the long throw to third for a tag play is a poor risk for the defence. A reasonably long fly ball to rightfield can move the runner after the catch.

In this situation, the pitcher will be trying to get the batter to hit to the left side, the batter will be trying to go to the right side.

In general, a runner on first will advance the same number of bases as the batter earns on a hit: that is, a runner on first would get to second on a single, to third on a double, score on a triple or home run. It is fairly common for a runner to go from first to third on a single to rightfield (where the outfielder has a longer throw to get him), or on any outfield single when the runner was **going on the pitch** (hit-and-run or stealing). Similarly, a runner will *sometimes* score from first on a double and, very rarely, on a single.

## RESPONSIBILITIES BY DEFENSIVE POSITION

The **pitcher** plays only the balls hit in front of him. Most of the time, infield pop-ups are handled by everyday infielders, even if they come down very near the pitcher's mound. The pitcher does **back up** plays on almost every ball hit to the outfield, stationing himself in foul territory to retrieve an overthrow by an outfielder. The pitcher **covers first** on ground balls that require the first baseman to pursue the batted ball rather than going to cover first base.

The **catcher** must field pop fouls hit behind home plate and handle batted balls hit directly in front of the plate (often these are bunts). The catcher also handles the throws to home plate

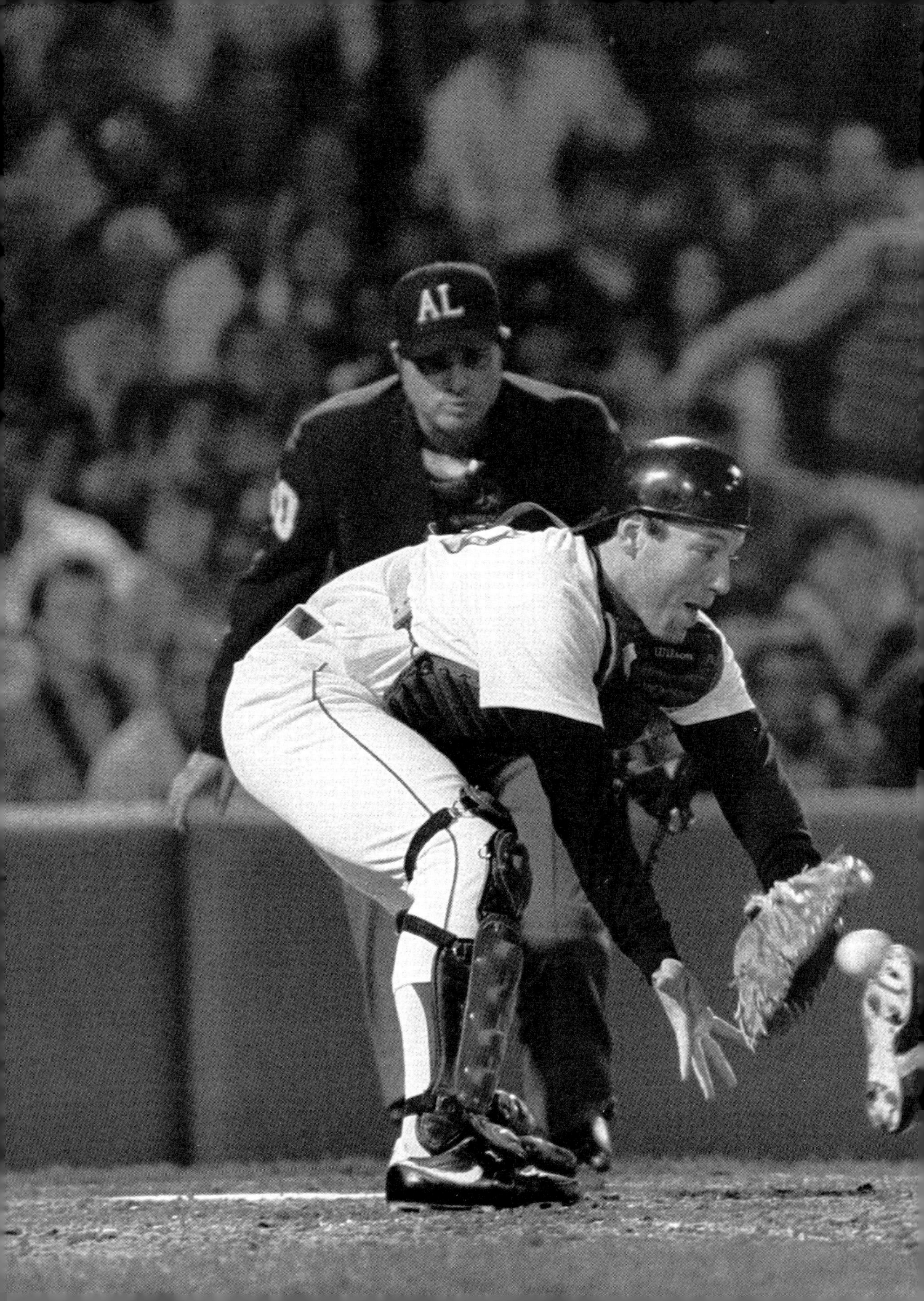
AL
Wilson

*Catcher Rich Gedman is about to catch a throw from a teammate to tag a Milwaukee Brewer out at the plate (which you can see behind Gedman, who is trying to block it from the runner). The umpire is in position to call 'out' or 'safe.'*

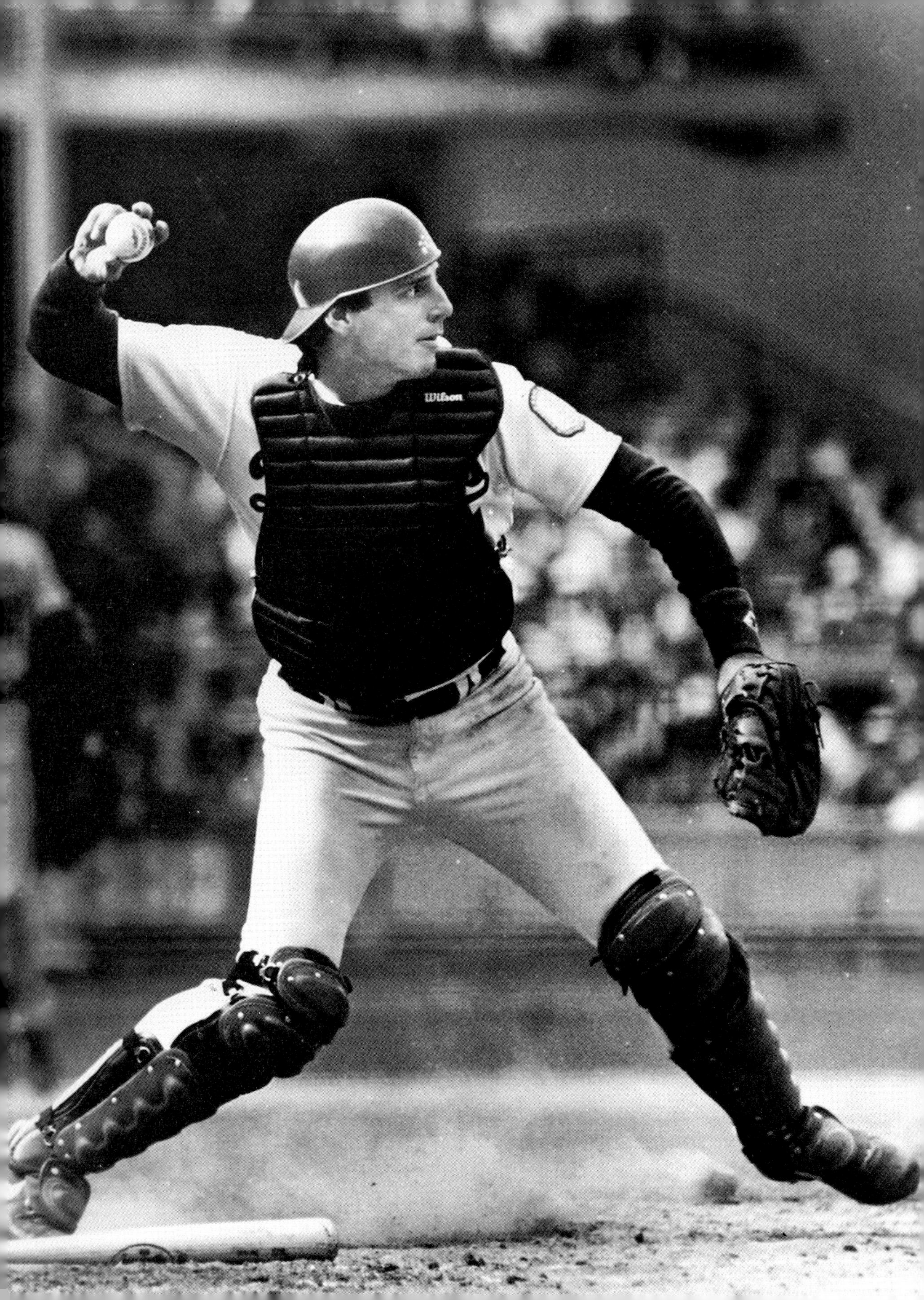
Wilson

to **get a runner**, although plays at the plate are not an every-game occurrence. The catcher also backs up the first baseman on every infield ground ball (running down to first outside the foul line behind the batter who hit the ball). Because the rest of the defence face the catcher, he also is responsible for letting an infielder know where to throw the ball when there could be some doubt. Catcher is the most physically punishing defensive position, going in and out of the catcher's crouch and being struck repeatedly by stray pitches and foul tips.

The most demanding play for a catcher is throwing out a runner attempting to steal second base. The fastest major league basestealers make the dash in slightly over 3 seconds and if they get a **jump** – a running start as the pitcher is throwing to the plate but *before* he actually releases the ball – the catcher can have under 2 seconds to catch the pitch, spring out of his crouch, and make the long throw to second base. Statistics on runners caught stealing are often a misleading indication of a catcher's proficiency, since a catcher is at the mercy of pitchers: how well they hold runners on base, how quickly they release the pitch, and whether they throw fastballs or junk. (One of the hidden effects of a fast baserunner is that his presence on the bases encourages the pitcher and catcher to use *fastballs*, which give the catcher a better chance to stop an attempted steal. Of course, the hitter knows this.)

The **first baseman** must catch the balls thrown by infielders with his foot in contact with first base to record the outs on infield ground balls, often as many as half the outs in a game. The most important skills are his **footwork around the bag** and the ability to **scoop** a low throw from an infielder. He must also catch the balls hit in his area of the infield. First base is the best position to 'hide' a bad throwing arm; seldom does a first baseman have to make a long and accurate throw.

A first baseman has an advantage in being lefthanded. Wearing the glove on the right hand permits him to **slap** a tag onto a baserunner taking a lead that his pitcher is trying to hold close to first, and makes it easier to reach for an infielder's throw that is towards the batter coming from home plate. Throwing lefthanded from first to second or third is easier and more natural than righthanded, which requires turning your body.

The **second baseman** has the single most challenging regular assignment of the infielders, **making the pivot** on the groundball double play. He will handle the throw from the shortstop or third baseman on a ball hit to the left side and then have to turn and throw back across his body to first base to complete the play. Meanwhile a baserunner from first is bearing down on him trying to **take him out** with a hard slide. Second basemen are often small and nimble, and can sometimes get by without a strong throwing arm if they are quick and accurate. The throw to first is shorter than from the left side of the infield.

The **shortstop** is the key man in the infield; since most hitters are righthanded, more balls are hit to the shortstop than to any other defensive player. The shortstop has the longest throws to make to first base from **deep in the hole** (the area between the shortstop and third baseman), so he must have a strong arm. And the shortstop also has a double-play pivot to make (somewhat less difficult than the second baseman's since he is facing the baserunner coming at him and the base he is throwing to), so he must be nimble. As kids grow up, the most talented are made pitchers and shortstops.

The **third baseman** plays the most dangerous infield position; third is called **the hot corner**. Because he must protect against bunts, he must play closer to the batter than any infielder except the pitcher on a regular basis. The throw to first base is long, requiring a strong and accurate arm.

*Mike Scioscia of the Dodgers making a throw to second after a bunt.*

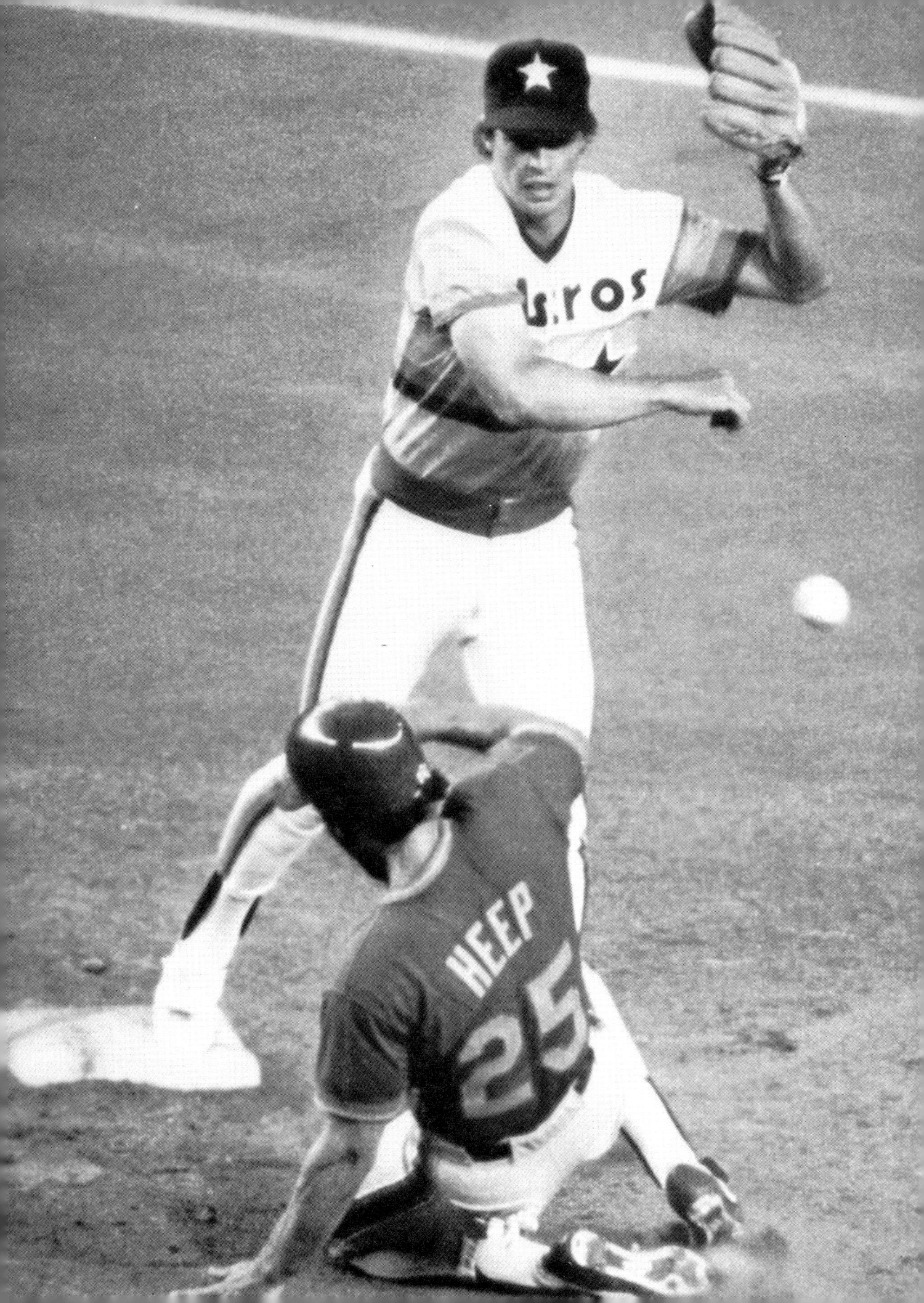

HEEP
25

*Second baseman Johnny Ray of the Pirates has to leap over a sliding runner to complete his double play.*

*OPPOSITE PAGE: Second baseman Bill Doran of the Astros turns a double play with Danny Heep of the Mets sliding into him.*

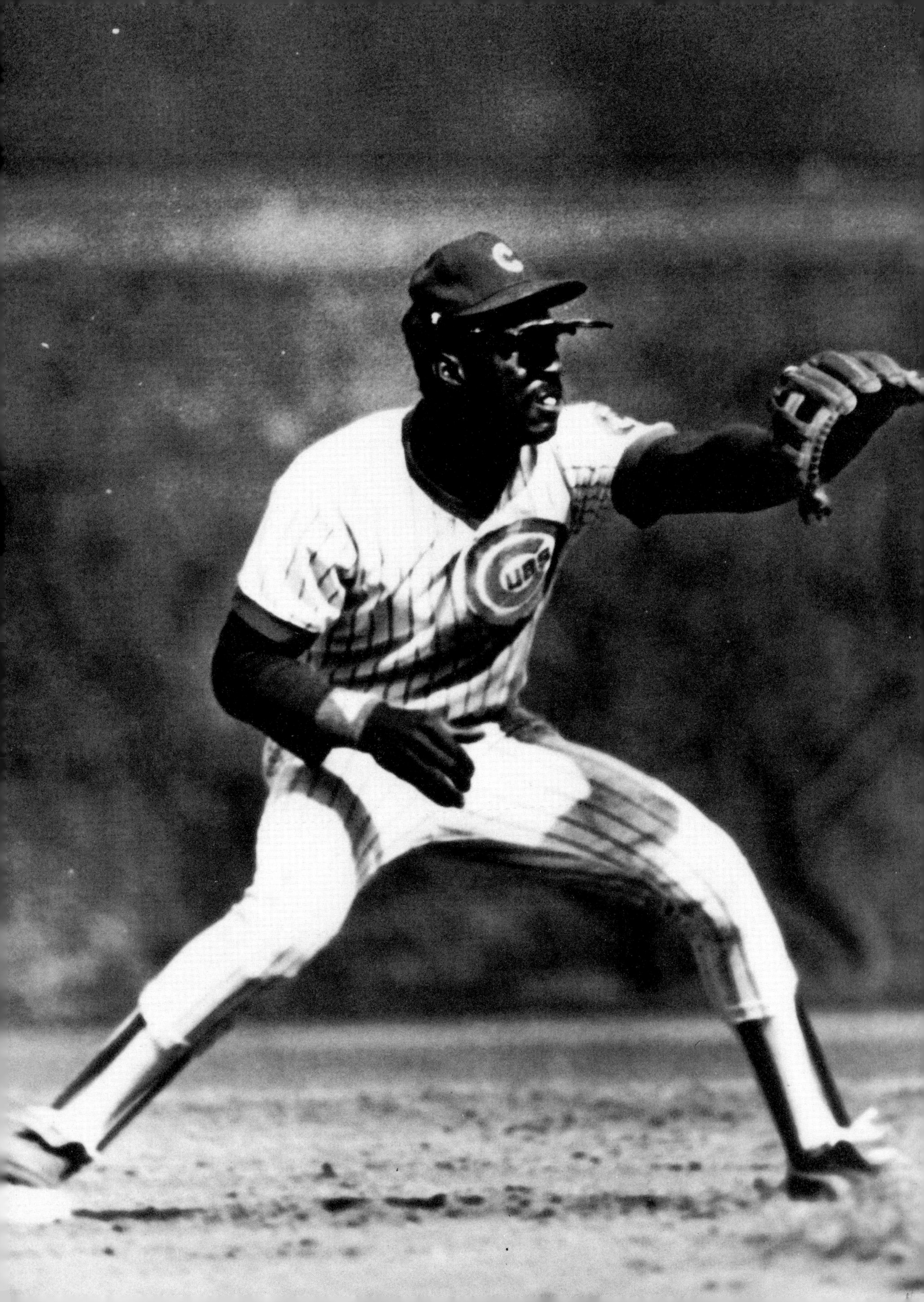
UBS

Catchers, second basemen, shortstops, and third basemen are *always* right-handed. It is easy to see why for the infielders, whose most common requirement is a throw to first base – often on the dead run or after having fielded a ball in an awkward position. While it is true that the catcher throws to third more often than to first, one must wonder whether the absence of lefthanded catchers has a logical explanation that hasn't been articulated yet.

Don Mattingly, the lefthanded Yankee first baseman whom many consider the best player in baseball, filled in at third for a few games in the 1986 season. While he made no errors during his time there, the inherent awkwardness of the situation – even for as graceful a player as Mattingly – was evident.

The **outfielders** must be fast enough to run down fly balls and long hits, reliable enough to catch them every time, and strong-armed enough to discourage baserunners from **running on them**. Outfielders, more than any other defenders except the pitchers, live with the variation in each ballpark and must adjust to each different setting.

The **leftfielder** has the least need for a strong arm since he is closest to third base, where many of the plays on balls hit to the outfield occur.

The **centrefielder** requires the most speed of the outfielders, since he has the most ground to cover. The centrefielder always has the right to **call off** the left- and rightfielders on balls hit between them.

The **rightfielder** must have a strong and accurate throwing arm to keep runners from going from first to third on singles to right.

The diagram of the field showing positioning is the most normal alignment, referred to as **straightaway**. Playing a hitter **to pull** means the fielders shift towards the power field, towards the rightfield line from normal position for a lefty hitter and the opposite for a righty.

*Shortstop Shawon Dunston of the Cubs is looking toward the oncoming runner as he awaits this throw.*

When power- and pull-hitting Ted Williams was terrorising the American League for the Red Sox, player-manager Lou Boudreau of the Cleveland Indians devised a special **shift** for use against Williams with the bases empty, placing the shortstop on the rightfield side of second base and leaving the third baseman alone on the left side of the infield. This defence virtually *gave* Williams a basehit if he were willing to hit to left, but doing so would sacrifice his power. Most homers are hit to the 'pull' field. The 'shift' has been employed since, but it is rare.

Beyond the primary responsibilities of each defensive position, there are others which occur on **relays**.

When a ball is hit into the right-centre gap (between the centrefielder and rightfielder), the second baseman will go into the outfield to receive a throw. He in turn will throw it to a base to try for an out on the batter or a baserunner, or to stop any further advance.

When a fly ball is hit to rightfield with runners on first and third and one out, the first baseman will place himself in the direct line of the throw from the rightfielder to home plate so he can **cut off** the throw to home if there is no chance to stop the runner from scoring. The cutoff – and even the *threat* of the cutoff – can prevent the runner who started on first from advancing to second on the same fly ball.

Almost every player has relay, cutoff, or backing-up responsibilities when a ball is hit with runners on base.

## THE MANAGER

Baseball teams have a **manager** who directs the onfield activity. He is assisted by some three to six coaches, who often supervise a particular aspect of play: all teams have a **pitching coach** to coordinate the pitching staff and a **hitting instructor** to keep daily tabs on the batters.

The manager, in consultation with his boss the **general manager** (who negotiates the con-

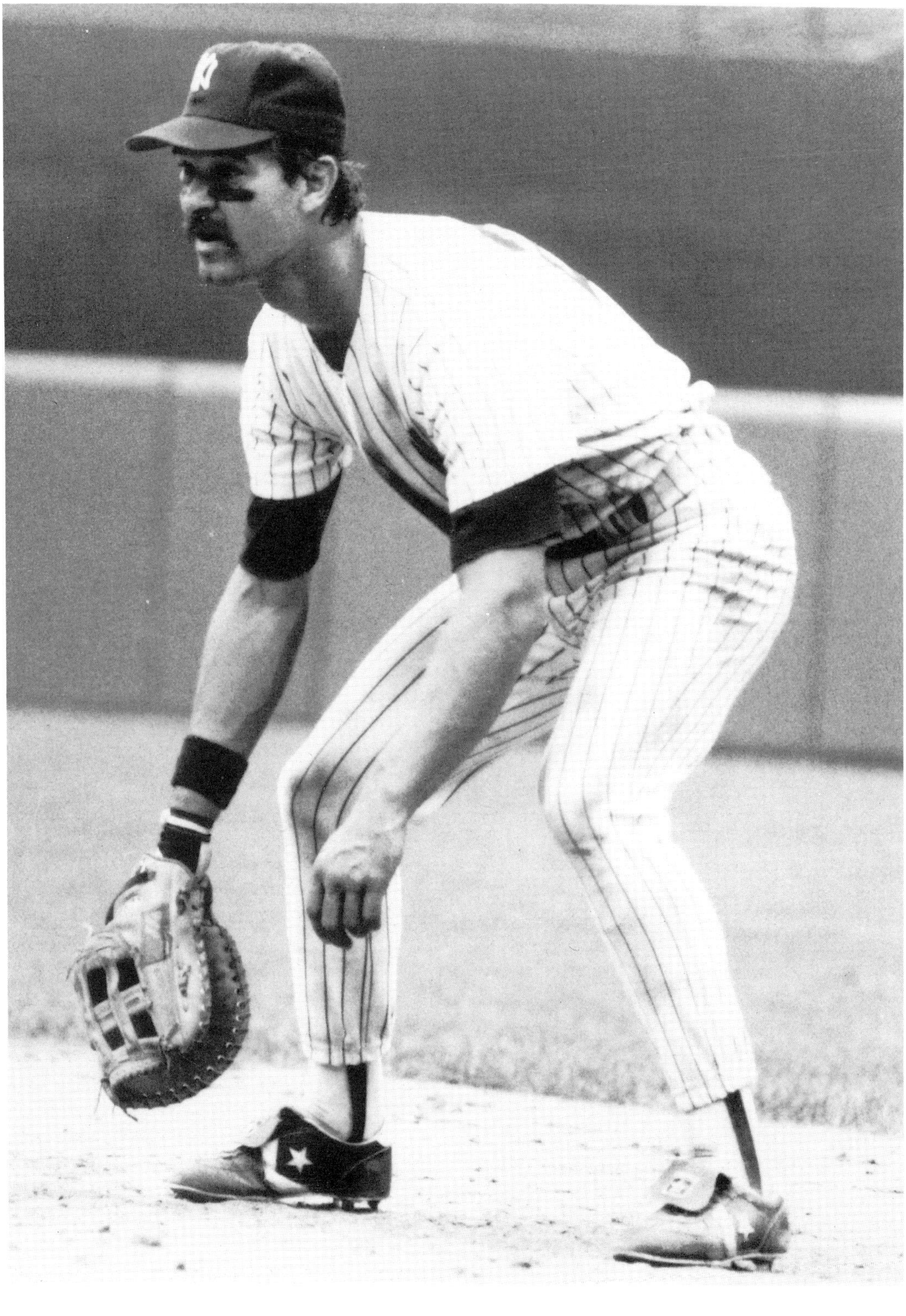

tracts, acquires the players, and hires and fires the manager), selects his **roster** of major league players from all the players under contract to the organization. The others remain in the **minor leagues**, available to the major league **parent club** if they are needed during the season.

Often through the pitching coach, the manager makes the decisions on the pitching staff: which pitchers are in the **rotation** and which are in the bullpen and, consequently, who is starting each game and who is available for relief.

Rotations are predictable anyway, but starting pitchers are announced before each game (and their names are in the newspaper for casual fans and bettors) with reasonable accuracy. The manager will make a **starting line-up** each game, considering the pitcher he is facing, the pitcher he is using, the ballpark he is playing in, and any other factors he cares to consider.

After he has selected the players he wants to use, he has to create a **batting order**, probably the single most important decision of the day.

Before each game, the **pre-game meeting** takes place at home plate among the four umpires and one representative from each team, usually the managers. Line-up cards are exchanged and the 'ground rules' – rules specific to that ballpark – are reiterated. At that point, the line-ups become official. Managers don't play tricks on each other because major league teams meet some thirteen to eighteen times each year, and a breach of ethics would surely be returned in very short order.

In the pre-game meeting, the umpires also review the **ground rules** with the managers, detailed rule refinements required by the particular ballpark which usually have to do with permissible baserunning advances on balls thrown in the stands. After the exchange

*Lefties shouldn't play third base, but Don Mattingly of the Yankees is a magician at his normal first base assignment.*

of line-ups, the play-or-postpone decisions provoked by the weather pass from the home team to the umpires.

Some managers go with a **set line-up**, the same position players, and often the same batting order, on an everyday basis. Other managers **platoon**, switching starting line-ups according to the opposition, usually based on whether they are facing a right- or lefthanded pitcher.

The manager has decisions to make – if he likes – on virtually every pitch of the game. (There are usually 100–150 pitches thrown by each team in a regulation 9-inning game.)

The manager might call the pitches for his side, although this is usually left to the catcher.

The manager will position his defence. Sometimes this is a broad strategic decision, like whether to play the infield in or back early in a scoreless game when the opposition gets a runner on third with one out. Sometimes it is a subtle tactical decision, like moving an outfielder slightly to the right and back because a pitcher or hitter looks a little stronger or weaker than usual.

The manager will make line-up changes: pinch-hitters and pinch-runners, relief pitchers, and defensive substitutes.

## BASEBALL AS A 'GAME OF SITUATIONS'

The key to watching baseball – and the key to enjoying it – is anticipation. When a ball is hit on the ground to the infield with nobody on, you need to know that the infielder reaching the grounder will throw it to first. If a man is on first with less than two out when the ball is hit, you need to know that the likely play is to second to start a double play.

When you know these things, you will almost always see the play develop; when you don't, given the optical challenge of seeing the wide expanse of a baseball field, you may often miss it.

Before *each* pitch, you need to analyse the

situation, bringing to bear as much information as you have:

The basic situation is the score, the inning (the visiting team bats in the **top** of the inning, the home team in the **bottom**), the batter and pitcher, the count, the number of outs, and the location of runners on base. Any baseball fan walking in on a started ballgame will ask: 'What's the situation?' Tell him: '3–2, Yankees leading, bottom of the sixth, Mattingly facing Morris with 2 outs and the bases empty and a count of 0-and-2' and he is substantially located in the ballgame.

Knowing the whole situation is the key to anticipation: with a runner on first and nobody out in the *first* inning of a scoreless game, a sacrifice bunt is very unlikely. The same situation in the *eighth* inning and only the best batters will be permitted to swing away.

Knowledge of the situation can be very sophisticated and detailed: knowing the speed of the baserunner, the strength of the catcher's arm, the ability of the pitcher and the hitter and their previous records against each other, the tendencies of the manager, whether the bullpen ace is tired or ready. All affect what the fan and manager anticipate.

The situation changes with *every pitch*. A baserunner on first is far more likely to attempt a steal with two strikes on a strong batter than with one; a 3–2 pitch with two outs is an **automatic start** situation for all forced baserunners (there are *no* potential adverse consequences from **going on the pitch** in that situation).

# 4 BASEBALL STATISTICS

The most distinctive feature of baseball is its statistics: virtually every pitch of every game, every ball hit and caught, is covered by them.

## MEASURING THE HITTERS

Each time a player completes a trip to the plate – making out or reaching base in any way – he has a **plate appearance**.

For the purposes of figuring **the batting average**, certain plate appearances are not charged as **a time at bat**. These are sacrifice bunts and sacrifice flies, walks and being hit-by-the-pitch, and reaching base on catcher's interference with the swing.

Each time a player reaches base on a batted ball, he is credited with a **hit**, or a defensive player is charged with an **error** if the batted ball should have been turned into an out. (If a batted ball is turned into a force on a baserunner, it is a **fielder's choice** and is not credited as a hit for the batter.)

There can be a hit *and* an error, or more than one error, on a single play. If the batter hits a single to rightfield and the outfielder juggles the ball long enough to allow the batter to reach second base, a hit would be credited and an error charged. The **Official Scorer** determines how to **score** a play; there will often be a judgment required – as in this play – as to whether the rightfielder should have been expected to make the play or whether the batter should be given a **double**.

A player's batting average is a fraction expressed as a decimal to three places, computed by **dividing hits by times at-bat**. The batting average is the most commonly-employed measurement of a hitter's skill: the leading **hitter for average** is considered the **batting champion** in each major league.

The 'perfect' batting average – never achieved – is 1.000. A major leaguer is considered very proficient if he bats .300 or better – achieving 3 hits in each 10 charged at bats – with walks and sacrifices, the extra advantages of **extra-base hits** (doubles, triples, home runs) and the excess damage of hitting into double plays disregarded.

Batting averages have risen and fallen throughout baseball history. They were generally highest before 1920, when **Babe Ruth** of the New York Yankees and a new, 'livelier' ball introduced the home run as a frequent weapon which encouraged batters to sacrifice control in their swing for power.

**Ty Cobb** of the Detroit Tigers holds the **highest lifetime batting average** in modern (post-1900) history at .367. **Ted Williams** of the Boston Red Sox (.344), **Stan Musial** of the St Louis Cardinals (.331), and **Rod Carew** of the Minnesota Twins and California Angels (.330) have the highest lifetime averages posted since World War II. **Wade Boggs** of the Red Sox and **Don Mattingly** of the Yankees are the only active players who appear now to threaten those levels.

A batting average of .400 or better was achieved about a dozen times during the period 1900–1924, but only twice since: a mark of .401 in 1930 by **Bill Terry** of the New York Giants and, the last time, .406 by **Ted Williams** in 1941. The best runs to .400 since were by Williams in 1958 – when he was 40 years old – and Carew in 1977, both at .388, and by the still-active **George Brett** of the Kansas City Royals in 1980 at .390.

In the current era, a batting average of .350 will usually take the batting crown in either league.

Although **plate appearances** are not actually employed to compute the batting average, the minimum standard for a batting championship is 3.1 plate appearances for each game the team plays, or 502 for a full major league season. The old standard was expressed in at-bats. This could be unfair, such as when it denied a batting crown to Ted Williams because he walked frequently in 1954. The rule was changed in 1967.

The batting average reveals something about the subtlety of baseball and the very fine line between stardom and mediocrity. A .300 hitter is a star; a .250 hitter is mediocre. The

*George Brett lifts his front foot to begin his stride, showing the stance that let him hit .390 in 1980, the highest batting average since 1941.*

difference between the two is about one hit a week during a major league season: one hit in about six games. But certain hitters routinely get that extra hit – not just week in and week out but year in and year out.

An eye-catching display of hitting consistency is the long **hitting streak**, when a batter gets a hit for many consecutive games. DiMaggio holds the record – a 56 consecutive game streak in 1941. In most seasons, nobody achieves a 25-game streak; anything above 20 creates real interest.

Interestingly enough, 1941 is also the year of the last .400 season, Williams hitting .406. Williams' accomplishment is understood when one considers that DiMaggio's average was .407 *during the streak*.

Although the batting average is the most common measurement of a hitter's proficiency, it doesn't truly measure the ability to get on base (because it leaves out walks) and it also reveals nothing about **power** – a hitter's ability to get doubles, triples, and home runs.

Doubles, triples, and home runs are counted and tracked; home run hitters have their totals watched as carefully as the averages are for batting leaders.

Counting a single as one base, a double as two and so on, gives a hitter's **total bases**. The **slugging percentage is total bases divided by times at-bat**. A 'perfect' slugging percentage would be 4.000 – a home run and four bases in each charged at bat. The greatest slugging percentage ever achieved was .847 by Babe Ruth in 1920. Among active players, only **Mike Schmidt** of the Philadelphia Phillies, **Jim Rice** of the Red Sox, and **Eddie Murray** of the Baltimore Orioles had lifetime slugging percentages above .500 after the 1984 season.

The number of home runs hit is the most frequently employed measurement of a player's power.

Only seventeen times in major league history has a batter hit more than 50 home runs in a season – about one every three games. The record is 61 by **Roger Maris** of the Yankees in 1961. Twelve of those power seasons were achieved by five players: **Babe Ruth**, who did it *four times* topped by 60 in 1927, **Mickey Mantle** of the Yankees (52 in 1956 and 54 in 1961), **Jimmie Foxx** (58 for the Philadelphia A's in 1932 and 50 for the Red Sox in 1938), **Ralph Kiner** of the Pittsburgh Pirates (54 in 1949 and 51 in 1947), and **Willie Mays** of the NY/San Francisco Giants (51 in 1954 and 52 in 1965).

**Hank Aaron** of the Milwaukee/Atlanta Braves holds the lifetime record of 755 major league home runs. Ruth hit 714, Mays hit 660, and about a dozen other hitters hit 500 or more.

The record for a team in a season is 240 home runs, by the Yankees in 1961 (the year Maris hit 61 and Mantle 54 – the record performance by teammates). The Twins in 1963 hit 225, and the 1956 Cincinnati Reds and 1947 Giants each had 221.

The most powerful major league teams usually hit a little better than one home run for each of the 162 regular season games – or about 160–180 for the full season.

Each time a player crosses home for his team – no matter how he got on base or advanced – he is credited with a **run scored**. The mark of excellence is to score 100 runs in a season.

Each time a player's at-bat results in a *teammate* scoring a run without a fielding error, the hitter is credited with a **run batted in**, usually called an **RBI**.

A hitter is credited with an RBI if a run scores when he makes an out, as long as there was no double play or fielding error which itself allowed the run. A fly out to score a runner from third is a **sacrifice fly**, which is an RBI and also not charged as a time at-bat.

The three important hitting statistics usually presented by radio or television announcers as each hitter appears – current to the last at-bat – are batting average, home runs, and RBIs (presented in that order.)

Complete batting statistics published ubiquitously in America (and now substantially available in *USA TODAY* in Britain) also include: number of times walked and struck out, **on base percentage** (which adds walks back into the batting average), sacrifice hits and flies, successful stolen bases and times caught stealing.

## MEASURING THE PITCHERS

Starting pitchers and relief pitchers use largely the same statistical measurements, but they are interpreted differently.

This is apparent in comparing the statistical record for starters and relievers for **games** and **innings pitched**. Regular starters today will usually appear *only* in the games they start, so 'working regularly' through a season will yield 33–36 game appearances. Since the starters are supposed to go 6-or-more innings, a regular starter can pitch well over 200 innings, often over 250, sometimes over 300.

Top relief pitchers will appear in many more games – 60 or 70 is not uncommon – but pitch far fewer innings, almost always under 150 and usually under 100.

In each game, one pitcher from the winning team is **credited with the win**, and one pitcher from the losing team is **charged with the loss**. This determination is made by the Official Scorer, but he follows guidelines:

A starting pitcher must pitch 5 innings or more to be credited with the win. There is no minimum for a starting pitcher to be charged with the loss.

Generally, the win will be credited to the pitcher in the game when his team scores the runs that put them ahead to stay; the losing pitcher is the one charged with the runs that put his team behind to stay.

A save can be credited to one relief pitcher in each game who successfully protects a lead for his team, provided certain standards are met: the 'tying run in the on-deck circle' when the reliever comes in or pitching a minimum of 3 innings protecting the lead. A relief pitcher must *finish* the game to *earn* a save.

Being credited with the win or charged with the loss is 'getting the decision' – credit for a save is not.

Saves are usually earned by a team's **closer** or **stopper**, the dominant relief pitcher brought in to pitch the last inning or two to protect a slim lead. Top stoppers get 25 or more saves a year, with the league leader generally in the 30s. The record is 46 by **Dave Righetti** of the Yankees in 1986.

A pitcher's **won-lost record** is expressed in writing as two numbers separated by a hyphen, wins followed by losses. Orally, the word 'and' is inserted for the hyphen. (The pitcher's 7-3 record is called 'seven-and-three'.)

A pitcher's **winning percentage** or **won-lost percentage** is the number of **wins divided by total decisions**.

The starting pitcher's equivalent of hitting .300 is being credited with 20 wins. **Twenty game winners** occur in most baseball seasons, but not all, and they are always starting pitchers.

The leading winner in the majors will usually have 20–25 wins. Winning 30 is like hitting .400, a virtually extinct species. **Denny McLain** of the Detroit Tigers last did it in 1968 (31–6); the last before that was by **Dizzy Dean** of the St Louis Cardinals in 1934 (30–7).

Top relief pitchers seldom win in double figures; they are used by their teams to come into games to *protect leads*; they can, therefore, only earn a win by first allowing the game to become tied – not what they are paid for.

The top winning percentage is usually over .700 (7–3, 14–6, 21–9), rarely over .800, only over .900 twice (by relief pitchers) in the past forty years. The winning percentage leader must have 15 decisions to qualify for the crown.

The other carefully watched statistic for all pitchers is the **earned run average**, commonly called the **ERA**.

An **earned run** is charged to a pitcher when the opponents score through no misplay by his teammates or fielding error on his own part. It is the Official Scorer's job to call runs earned or **unearned**.

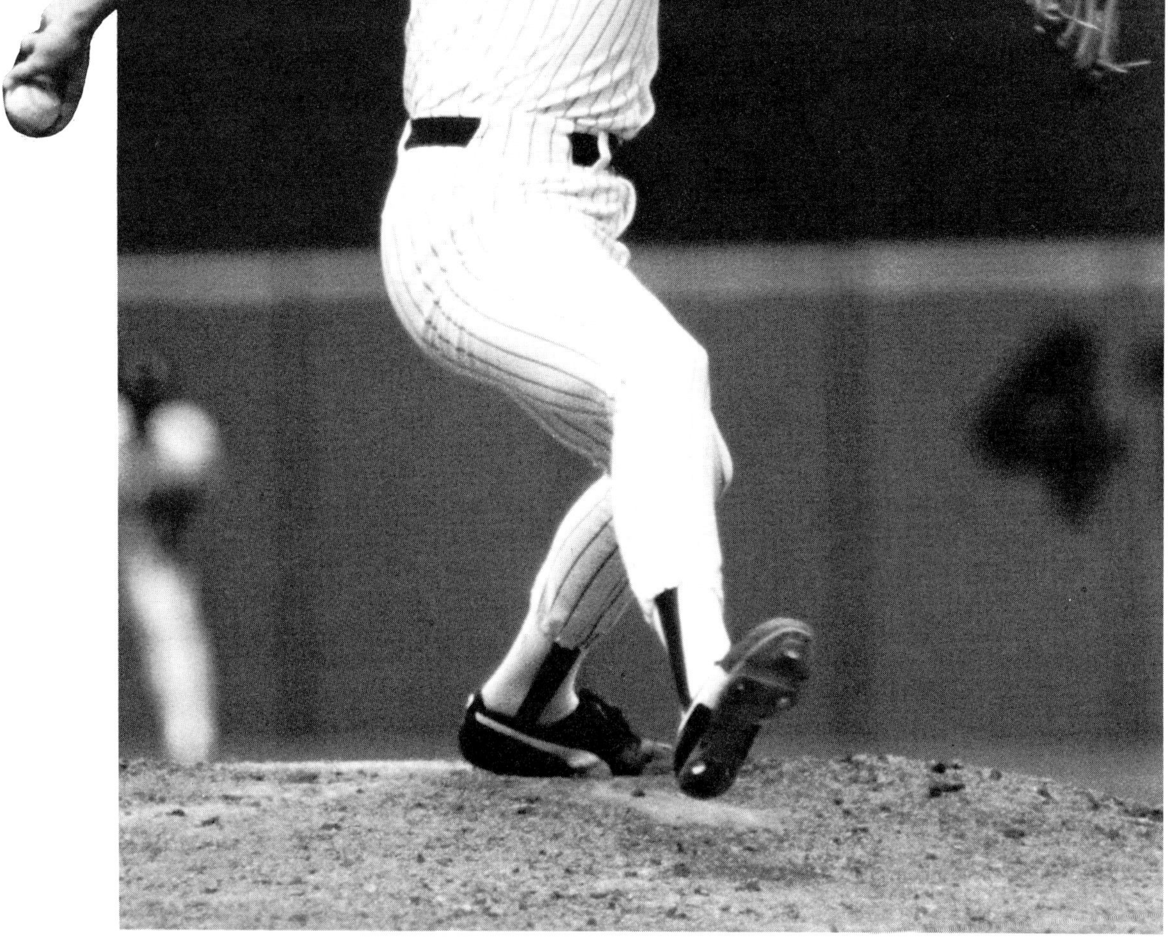

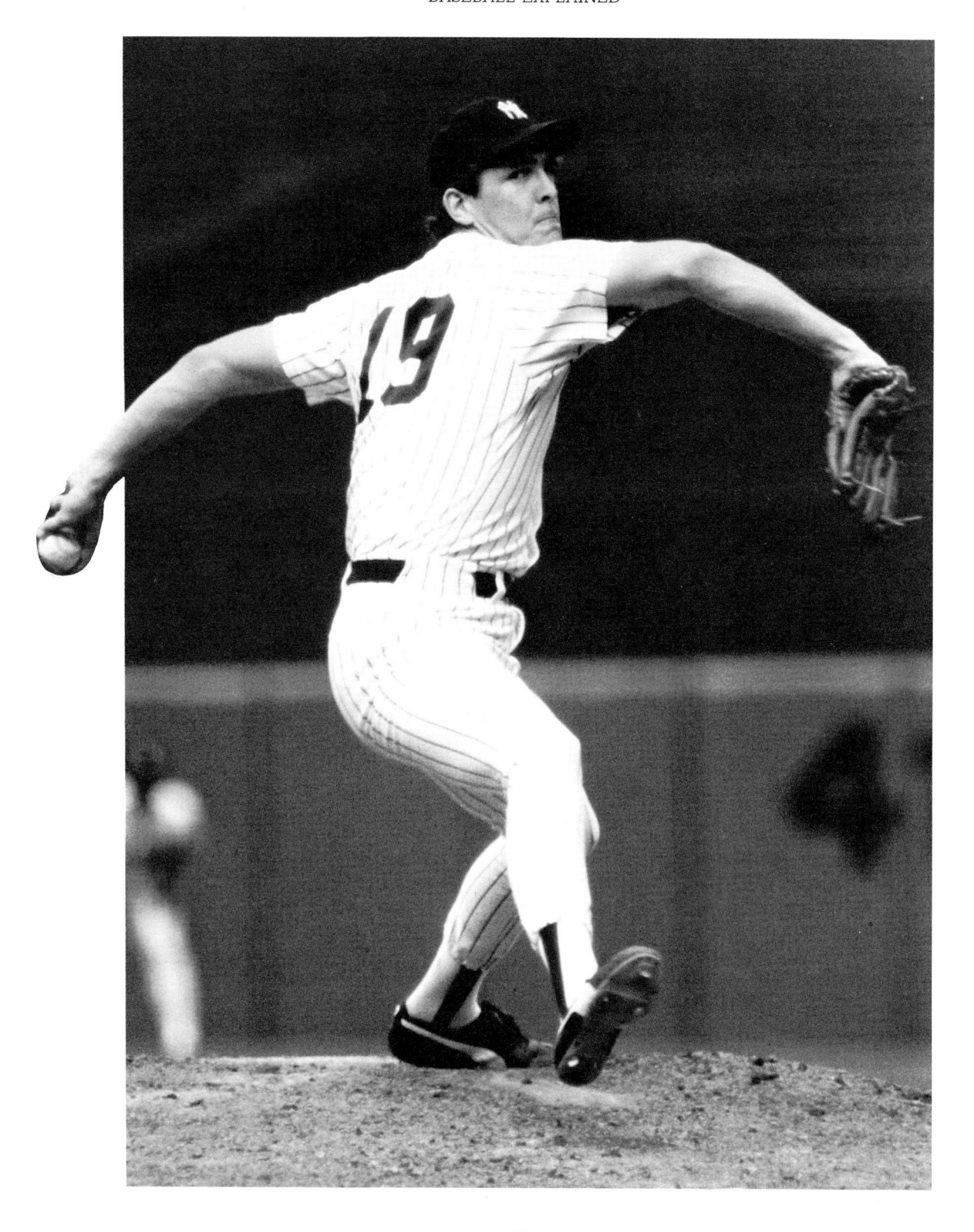

If a pitched ball gets by the catcher and allows runner(s) on base to advance, the Scorer will charge a **wild pitch** to the pitcher or a **passed ball** to the catcher, depending on fault. Runs which score due to a wild pitch are earned; runs which score due to a passed ball (like any other fielding error) are not.

In figuring earned and unearned runs, the Scorer tries to analyse what would have happened with no misplay. Therefore, if an error has **prolonged** an inning, all runs scored after three outs would have been made without the error are considered unearned. This can lead to a pitcher being pummelled but his ERA escaping unscathed.

The .300-hitting, 20-game winning standard for ERA is 3.00 – allowing an average of three earned runs (or fewer) per game, or nine innings pitched.

The ERA is computed by **multiplying earned runs allowed by nine and dividing the product by innings pitched**.

Innings pitched are credited by **thirds of an inning**, or after each out. A pitcher getting one out in an inning is credited with $\frac{1}{3}$ of an inning pitched. Innings pitched are sometimes expressed with abuse of the decimal point: $8\frac{1}{3}$ innings pitched can appear as 8.1.

When a runner reaches bases safely, he is **charged** to the pitcher who allowed him to do so. If he later scores, even when a relief pitcher is working, the run is charged to the pitcher who allowed him to reach base.

A relief pitcher's ERA should be lower than a starter's because relief pitchers throw more partial innings; it is somewhat less likely that a pitcher will permit a run in a one- or two-out stint than in a complete inning.

The ERA champion must pitch one inning for each game his team plays, or 162 in a normal major league season. Relief pitchers very seldom qualify. The ERA champion will generally have a mark of 2.20–2.60. An ERA under 2.00 is outstanding and is seldom

*Lefty relief ace Dave Righetti of the Yankees bears down in a late-inning pressure situation.*

achieved by a starting pitcher. It has been achieved recently: by **Dwight Gooden** of the New York Mets in 1985 and **Ron Guidry** of the Yankees in 1978. The best ERA in the modern era was by **Bob Gibson** of the Cardinals in 1968 at 1.12.

Pitchers are also watched for their **walks** and **strikeouts** (also called **'K's'**, for the scoring notation for strikeouts). The top strikeout pitchers **fan** over 200 per season, hovering near an average of one an inning. The best control pitchers walk between one and two batters per nine innings.

Strikeouts have been on the rise for the past forty years, even though batting averages have maintained fair stability during that time. The two top strikeout pitchers in history, **Nolan Ryan** – currently of the Houston Astros and formerly with the Mets and the California Angels – and **Steve Carlton** of the Cards and Phillies and now with the Cleveland Indians are both active in 1987.

Only fifteen times in major league history has a pitcher struck out more than 300 batters in a season: *five times* by Ryan. **Sandy Koufax**, the great Dodger lefthander of the 1950s and 1960s, did it three times. Carlton is one of the seven others to do it once.

Sophisticated fans also watch the strikeout-to-walk ratio, looking for a hard thrower to achieve at least 2-to-1. This is not a measurement of importance with all pitchers; many pitchers achieve great success with very few strikeouts. But it is useful to track the progress of a young pitcher with a strikeout pitch and poor control.

Another barometer of a pitcher's effectiveness – perhaps the best indication of how **overpowering** a pitcher can be – is **baserunners permitted per nine innings**. This is computed by adding hits allowed and walks and dividing the total by innings pitched. Any pitcher near 10 batters per game reaching safely is having a great year. ( Although this is a very useful stat, it is not computed for publication as often as many others. It can often be figured from the stats that are published.)

*Fireballing righthander Nolan Ryan is the greatest strikeout pitcher in the game's history.*

## MEASURING THE FIELDERS

Each time a ball is hit by the batter or thrown by fielders to get an out, fielding statistics are generated.

A fielder gets a **fielding chance** each time he achieves a **putout** (by catching a fly, tagging a base ahead of a forced runner, tagging the runner himself, or – in the catcher's case – completing a strikeout by catching the third strike) or an **assist** (by throwing the ball on a play leading to a putout), or makes an **error** (misplays a ball resulting in an out lost or a base advanced).

If a ball is hit or thrown to a fielder which he should handle and does not (in the opinion of the Scorer); or if the fielder throws the ball badly, and as a result the batting team gets a runner on base, fails to get an out, or a runner advances a base; the fielder is charged with an error.

The **fielding average** is the **chances handled successfully** (putouts and assists) **divided by total chances** (putouts, assists, and errors.) The fielding average has an obvious flaw in analysing fielding proficiency, since it does *not* account for the difference in **range** – how a player uses quickness and positioning to get to more batted balls – one of the most important assets of a good fielder.

On the other hand, the fielding average demonstrates perhaps better than other statistics how subtle baseball is. What is an acceptable fielding average varies by position, with remarkable consistency within very narrow parameters.

Catchers and first basemen should have the highest fielding averages, because they have the highest number of fairly easy chances: catchers recording a strikeout and first basemen handling the throws on infield grounders. Although a catcher's percentage can be skewed downward by a staff with few strikeouts and poor technique holding runners close – which leads to more throws to second base for steal attempts, relatively error-likely plays – most of the time the major league leaders will show percentages of .995 or better for both positions. This is a success rate of 99.5 per cent.

Outfielders also have a high percentage of 'routine', or easy, plays when they catch fly balls. Most outfield errors are made on throws attempting to get runners looking for extra bases. Very seldom does a major leaguer drop a fly ball. They also approach the .995 standard. Occasionally an outfielder will field 1.000 for the season.

Second basemen, shortstops, and third basemen handle the tough chances – often being asked to catch *and* throw the ball to earn a single assist on an infield play. (There can be two chances credited on one play: a second baseman 'turning the pivot' on a double play will get the putout at second and the assist on the out at first.) Second basemen, with the shorter throws, can approach the .990 range, although usually they are nearer .970–.980. Shortstops and third basemen do well to field .980, often they are nearer .960–.970. So their success rate 'drops' to 96–97 per cent.

This difference, between .960 for a third baseman and .995 for a first baseman (the difference between 96 per cent and 99.5 per cent), is consistent and palpable. A third baseman who managed to field .995 would be checked for magnets (or accused of shying away from any ball that was tough to handle); a first baseman at .960 would have to hit a ton of homeruns or he'd end up a minor leaguer.

## USE OF STATISTICS BY THE FAN

Baseball statistics have two important applications for the fan: they shed light on baseball history and they reveal important facts about the 'situation' of every game played every day. All discussion of baseball history makes reference to the stats and there are some that every fan knows.

Cy Young is the pitcher who won the most games in his career: 511, but he began pitching in 1897 before the 'modern era' began in 1901.

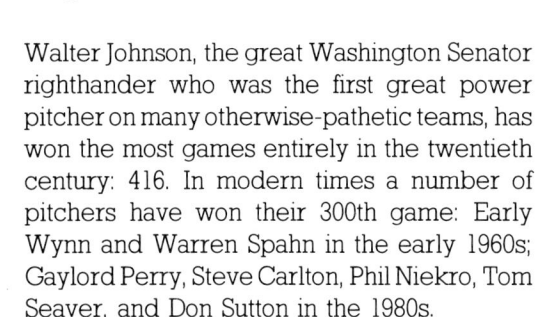

Walter Johnson, the great Washington Senator righthander who was the first great power pitcher on many otherwise-pathetic teams, has won the most games entirely in the twentieth century: 416. In modern times a number of pitchers have won their 300th game: Early Wynn and Warren Spahn in the early 1960s; Gaylord Perry, Steve Carlton, Phil Niekro, Tom Seaver, and Don Sutton in the 1980s.

Babe Ruth was the first great home-run king; his marks of 60 in a season and 714 for his career stood for many years. Roger Maris hit 61 in 1961 (but had fewer than 300 in his career) and Hank Aaron finished his career with 755 in the early 1970s (but never hit 50 in a season.)

The Chicago Cubs of 1906 won 116 games (of 152) and the Cleveland Indians of 1954 won 111 (of 154) and both lost in the World Series. In many seasons no team wins 100 games. Last year (1986) the New York Mets won 108.

Today's baseball fan never saw Babe Ruth, Walter Johnson, or Cy Young – let alone the 1906 Cubs. But we all saw the 1986 Mets, Carlton, Niekro, Sutton, and Seaver; most of us saw Perry, and many of us saw Maris, Aaron, and at least some of the players from the 1954 Indians. The statistics tie them together in a way that makes history very real.

We know who the hot hitters on an opposing team are by looking at their batting averages; we know that if a season is one third over and a pitcher has won 7 games then he may be on his way to 20 wins – great success. The devoted fan watches the statistics – *the historical measurement* – move perceptibly with every at bat, every out, every hit, every run.

The raw data are endlessly analysable by the mathematical zealots, who are plentiful among baseball people. Some managers work with the batting average of each hitter against each pitcher, or in each park, or over the last ten days (whether with or without the mathematical sophistication to know how many occurrences provide a representative sample) in an effort to make the right batting order or to select the right pinch-hitter or relief pitcher.

A recent article in the SABR (Society for American Baseball Research) Research Journal analysed the effect of the count on batting averages and likeliness to walk or strike out. The research, of course, confirms that a hitter is very dangerous on a 2–0 or 3–1 pitch, that he is deeply in a hole on 0–2 or 1–2. But it also *quantifies* that difference. For years, baseball people have repeated the rule of thumb that bringing the infield in (a defensive tactic to cut off a runner from third with less than two outs) effectively raises the batter's average 100 points (i.e. makes a .300 hitter into a .400 hitter). Nobody to my knowledge has ever proved that, but it seems reasonable. Expressing that hitter's advantage in that way is understandable to every baseball fan. Now it has been proven that a 2–0 count is worth *more* than 100 points more than 0–2.

Watching baseball with statistical knowledge permits a fan to *feel* the difference between 30 per cent of the time and 25 per cent of the time (a .300 hitter versus a .250 hitter), *appreciate* the difference between 95 per cent of the time and 99 per cent time (a third baseman's fielding average compared to a first baseman's). The process makes one sophisticated and instinctive about weighted averages, just knowing how much a good day or good week can move a batter's average in May when he has had 100 at bats, versus in August when he's nearer 500.

In May of every baseball season, there are a lot of good hitters hitting .220, bad hitters over .300, and many others doing some statistically unlikely things: averaging over .400 or a home run every two games. The numbers come back to normal most of the time by July – almost always by October. Baseball provides a reaffirmation of how the world really works and, more important, a daily reminder.

# 5 THUMBNAIL HISTORY OF BASEBALL

## PRE-'MODERN' BASEBALL: THE NINETEENTH CENTURY

One way or another, Americans made baseball out of rounders. Some folk historians credit American Indian games or variations of rounders from other countries to baseball's development – and those influences may be there – but given the predominance of Britain's cultural influence on the early United States, it is safe to say Americans made baseball out of rounders.

For years, the dominant American folklore claimed baseball was invented by Abner Doubleday – a Union general during the Civil War whose extended family founded the Doubleday Publishing Company – in Cooperstown, New York in 1839. That folklore has been discredited, despite the fact that the National Baseball Hall of Fame and Museum (along with many of baseball's best scholars and certainly its best library) is in Cooperstown.

The first recorded game between two organized teams was between the 'New York 9' and the 'Knickerbockers' on the Elysian Fields, Hoboken, New Jersey on 19 June, 1846. The New York 9 won, 23–1.

The first professional team was the Cincinnati Red Stockings, who barnstormed to a 56-win, 1-tie record in 1869. In 1871, the first professional league – the National Association – was formed, joined in 1876 by the National League. A variety of leagues competed for the remainder of the nineteenth century, but the National League survived and is one of the two major leagues today.

In the late nineteenth century the game evolved into the form we know today. By 1900, four balls was a walk, three strikes an out, the catcher was dressed in his heavy gear and stationed immediately behind the batter, and fielders all wore gloves to help them catch the ball. Agreement on these points did not exist in 1876.

## THE STRUCTURE IS ESTABLISHED

In 1901, the American League was formed and in 1903 the first World Series between the leagues' pennant winners had the Boston Red Sox defeating Pittsburgh. The rival leagues' conflicting agendas prevented a World Series in 1904, but in 1905 the tradition returned to stay, uninterrupted by war or greed, until this day. (The New York Giants salvaged the 'Senior Circuit's' honour by beating Connie Mack's Philadelphia A's in 1905.)

The World Series is a best 4-out-of-7 game series, with Games 1, 2, 6 and 7 (if necessary) played in the home park of one team, Games 3, 4 and 5 (if necessary) at the other. The first World Series and those of 1919–21 were 5-out-of-9.

By 1905, both leagues were playing a 154-game schedule with franchises that would remain in place until the 1950s. The team nicknames sometimes shifted a little bit in the early days, but this list is accurate for geography from 1901 and for nicknames from the 1920s.

| National League | American League |
| --- | --- |
| Chicago Cubs | Chicago White Sox |
| St Louis Cardinals | St Louis Browns |
| Boston Braves | Boston Red Sox |
| Philadelphia Phillies | Philadelphia Athletics |
| New York Giants | New York Yankees |
| Brooklyn Dodgers | Washington Senators |
| Pittsburgh Pirates | Cleveland Indians |
| Cincinnati Reds | Detroit Tigers |

This roster of 'major league' cities is almost shockingly small, concentrated in the northeast and exclusively (except by about a mile for the Cardinals and the Browns) east of the Mississippi River. 'Brooklyn' is politically and effectively the same as 'New York', so only five of the sixteen major league franchises had a monopoly in a market and only ten cities had major league teams.

'Modern' major league baseball is dated from 1901, with records compiled before the turn of the century not considered 'modern' records. When the 'major league record' is referred to, statistics from the nineteenth century are ignored.

## THE DEAD BALL ERA

The period from 1901–1919 is called the 'Dead Ball Era'. Baseball of that time was characterized by durable pitchers and very little long ball hitting. The ball was indeed – by later standards – 'dead': less hard, less truly spherical. They used fewer of them in a game (half-a-dozen or fewer compared with sixty or more today), so the ball in use was dirtier and dented from previous play. This all worked to the advantage of the pitchers: the softer ball couldn't be hit for distance, the dirtier ball was harder for hitters to see, and the dents and scrapes gave pitchers various tools to throw hard-to-hit breaking balls.

As baseball came into prominence at that time, the modern ballparks necessary to accommodate tens of thousands of fans were built. Some of the ballparks built then – Fenway Park in Boston, Comiskey Stadium and Wrigley Field in Chicago, and Tiger Stadium in Detroit – are largely unchanged and still the site of major league action today. All of those parks were built near city centres (this being before the mass-market automobile) where the availability of land would work its influence on the ballpark's shape, and thus the dimensions of the playing field itself and, ultimately, on the history of the game.

Pittsburgh, Chicago, and New York were the dominant National League teams of the Dead Ball Era. The Pirates were led by their greatest-ever shortstop, Honus Wagner; the Cubs by their slick infield; the Giants by their matchless pitcher, Christy Mathewson, and their feisty manager, John McGraw. The most stunning of the early National League pennant races was won by the Miracle Braves of 1914, who were dead last at the halfway point of the season and came on to win the pennant.

In the American League, Detroit, Philadelphia, and Boston enjoyed the most consistent success. The Tigers were led by Ty Cobb, the dominant player of the era, who won 12 league batting championships. Philadelphia was built by owner/manager Connie Mack into a powerhouse champion with a '$100,000 infield' (a label of luxury in 1914, the price of a back-up second baseman today). After winning several pennants, Mack sold off his star players, consigning himself to over a decade of heavy losing. (Strangely enough, he repeated the cycle in the 1930s.) Boston was led by outfielders Tris Speaker and Harry Hooper, joined in 1915 by pitching (and later hitting) star Babe Ruth.

In the mid-1910s, the major league establishment was challenged by the Federal League, which recruited some major league stars with high bonuses and salaries. But the challenge failed quickly, restoring economic control to the major league owners. By the end of World War I, baseball was strongly established as America's 'national pastime'.

## BABE RUTH, COMMISSIONER LANDIS, AND BASEBALL AS WE KNOW IT

Two things changed baseball irrevocably in 1919. First, in Boston, Babe Ruth was made a parttime pitcher so he could be a nearly-fulltime outfielder. He hit 29 home runs, nearly doubling the previous major league record and catching the fancy of fans all over the country. This encouraged the ownership to make the ball more lively to add more home runs to the game. The lively ball created the balance of runs, hits, home runs, and outs that has existed pretty consistently from 1920 to today.

Second, eight players from the Chicago White Sox were charged with having accepted bribes from gamblers to throw the 1919 World Series to the Cincinnati Reds, an incident for ever known as the Black Sox scandal. Fearing that the scandal would discredit and financially injure the game, the leagues and individual owners consented to a strong central Commissioner of Baseball. Judge Kenesaw Mountain Landis was elected to the post and provided a strong image of probity which helped protect baseball's goodwill after the Black Sox scandal broke. (Babe Ruth's home runs were probably the more important ingredient of the increased fan support.) The commissionership itself reduced feuding among the clubs and between the leagues to everyone's benefit.

After the 1919 season, Red Sox owner Harry Frazee sold Ruth to the New York Yankees for $125,000 and a $300,000 loan he desperately needed to sustain some Broadway show investments. In this ironic transaction, New York won twice: gaining the benefit of the Broadway investments and the presence of baseball's greatest star. In 1920 Ruth raised the home run record to an astonishing 54 while leading the Yankees to a 3rd place finish. In 1921 they won the League pennant, starting a record of success that is unapproached by any other franchise.

The 1920s were a hitter's era, although other home run stars comparable to Ruth were slow to develop. George Sisler, a first baseman for the St Louis Browns, compiled a .401 batting average through a five-season stretch early in the decade. Since 1930, .400 has been topped only once, by Ted Williams (.406) in 1941.

In 1925 powerful first baseman Lou Gehrig joined Ruth in the Yankee line-up to cement the New Yorkers' dominance: they won pennants in 1921, 1922, 1923, 1926, 1927, and 1928. In 1927, Ruth hit 60 home runs and Gehrig 47: no other *team* hit more than 56! Connie Mack had rebuilt the Athletics into a powerhouse by the decade's end and they beat out the Yankees in 1929, 1930, and 1931.

But when Mack once again sold off his great players – sluggers Al Simmons, Jimmy Foxx, and Mickey Cochrane and pitcher Lefty Grove – the path was cleared for the Yankees' reign to resume.

## BRANCH RICKEY: THE INTRODUCTION OF INTELLIGENT MANAGEMENT

Another subtle revolution of the 1920s was fostered by general manager Branch Rickey of the St Louis Cardinals, who built the first successful 'farm system' of minor league teams in support of a major league franchise. Before Rickey – a mediocre catcher and manager who made his mark as a baseball executive – minor league teams existed independently of the majors. The owners of teams in the minors gained much of their income selling the players they discovered and developed to major league teams. (Young George Herman Ruth was discovered in a Baltimore reform school by Oriole owner Jack Dunn. 'Dunn's Babe' was sold to the Red Sox and the nickname stuck.)

Rickey had the idea of putting a much larger number of players under contract to the parent major league club and then having 'working agreements' or owning minor league teams to develop the talent. He was encouraged in this effort by his contract with the Cardinals, which gave him a share of proceeds from sales of ballplayers to other teams. By the end of the 1930s, all the teams had farm systems, but the Cardinals had established a pattern of success for themselves that persists to this day.

The first great Cardinal teams were in the 1930s; led by third baseman Pepper Martin and pitcher Dizzy Dean, they were a rambunctious group known as the Gas House Gang. The Cardinals, Giants, and Cubs were the leading National League teams of that decade. The Yankees overcame the retirement of Ruth and the tragic illness and death of Gehrig (after Gehrig had established a record of 2,130 consecutive game appearances, one baseball record that will almost certainly never be broken) to sweep four World Championships, 1936–39. The new New York hero was centrefielder Joe DiMaggio, who came to the Yankees from his hometown San Francisco Seals in 1936 and dominated the scene until 1951.

The Yankees and the Cardinals remained the leading teams through the years of World War II, when baseball continued its full schedule despite other restrictions on travel and entertainment. Many of baseball's heroes were in the service and the lifetime records of a number of great players (DiMaggio, Ted Williams of the Red Sox, Stan Musial of the Cardinals, pitcher Bob Feller of the Cleveland Indians) were truncated by the lost playing time.

Also during the War, Branch Rickey left the Cardinals and became general manager of the Brooklyn Dodgers. The Dodgers had broken a twentyone-year drought by winning the National League pennant with a fairly senior team in 1941, but Rickey wanted to establish the kind of enduring excellence the Yankees had attained through their superstars and the Cardinals had achieved through their farm system.

Rickey did two things none of his competitors did. First, he signed a number of young ballplayers who, because they were about to be drafted, couldn't play baseball until the war ended (which none of the more 'thrifty' owners were inclined to do). Much more dramatically, he laid the groundwork to break the colour line in baseball, introducing non-white talent into the game for the first time in the 'modern' era.

Because only white ballplayers were permitted in the majors – by covert rather than open agreement of the owners – Negro Leagues had developed parallel to the big leagues. Rickey by-passed the established Negro League stars, notably pitcher Satchel Paige, to sign young infielder Jackie Robinson as the first Negro in 'organized baseball' (the generic name given to the major and minor leagues under the Commissioner). Rickey knew that the first Negro in baseball would face difficult challenges: baiting, pitches thrown at his head, challenges to fight from opposing players. He picked the college-educated, ex-military officer because of his background and character. Robinson signed with the Dodgers shortly after the war ended in 1945, and spent the 1946 season at the Brooklyn farm club at Montreal. He made his debut in the majors in 1947 and starred with the Dodgers for ten years. Rickey and Robinson not only changed baseball for ever; they accelerated the pace of racial change in American society.

Robinson was joined by other Negroes (catcher Roy Campanella, pitcher Don Newcombe) and the white players signed by Rickey early in the War (outfielders Carl Furillo and Duke Snider, first baseman Gil Hodges) on the powerhouse Brooklyn Dodger teams which dominated the National League from 1947–57, until the franchise moved to Los Angeles. As with the Cardinals, Rickey built an organization to last: even though he was forced out in an ownership battle with Walter O'Malley in 1951, the Dodger organization has remained successful – and an overtly Rickey-inspired organization – to this day.

## THE POSTWAR ERA: NEW YORK DOMINATES

Meanwhile, the Yankees were passing the torch to the heir to the Ruth/Gehrig/DiMaggio legacy: Mickey Mantle came up in 1951 and took over in centrefield from Joe DiMaggio in 1952. With the eccentric Casey Stengel becoming the Yankee manager in 1949, they went on a burst of sustained success that probably will never be matched. The Yankees won the American League championship every year from 1949 to 1964 except *twice* (in 1954 and 1959), and they won the World Series five consecutive times in Stengel's first five years.

The Dodgers won in the National League in 1947, 1949, 1952, 1953, 1955, and 1956. The New

York Giants won in 1951 (after coming from 13½ games behind the Dodgers with two months to go) and in 1954. The Giants were led by their own star centrefielder, Willie Mays, while the Dodgers' flashiest player was centrefielder Duke Snider. World Series games were played in New York in every year from 1947–58; seven times in those twelve years *both* pennant winners were New York teams. And the three most exciting players at one of baseball's most eyecatching positions – Mantle, Mays, and Snider – provided daily thrills to the New York fans.

The addition of the black (and later, Latin) ballplayers, the great success of the teams and the development of glamorous stars in America's media centre, plus the growing availability of the game on television to the entire nation combined to multiply the scope and popularity of the sport. The interest beyond the northeastern quadrant of America could only be satisfied by *live* major league baseball.

Early in the 1950s, not every franchise was prospering. The Boston Braves – despite a pennant in 1948 – were failing in the box office war with the popular Red Sox. The Philadelphia A's and St Louis Browns had been consistent losers for decades and their fans were dwindling.

In 1953, the Braves moved west and set up shop in Milwaukee, almost instantly establishing a pattern of drawing 2 million fans a season when the 'magic number' for box office success was 1 million. (Many of the teams draw 2 million today; the Dodgers have topped 3 million repeatedly, an average of nearly 40,000 per game for 81 games during the summer.) Encouraged by the Braves' success, the St Louis Browns became the Baltimore Orioles in 1954 and the A's moved to Kansas City in 1955.

But all these franchise shifts were by teams failing on and off the field. When the Brooklyn Dodgers and the New York Giants announced that they were moving to Los Angeles and San Francisco, respectively, to start the 1958 season, the shock waves were as transcontinental as the move. The Giants – whose attendance had slipped at their Harlem ballpark, the Polo Grounds – were only three years from their last World Championship. And Walter O'Malley's Dodgers were one of baseball's top teams in the standings and at the box office.

## THE THREAT OF COMPETITION LEADS TO EXPANSION: RICKEY AGAIN

The joint move left New York without National League baseball. (Yankee attendance didn't really benefit from the loss of competition.) The shifts of the 1950s made clear that new markets for major league baseball existed. If the established leagues wouldn't expand to meet the opportunity, perhaps for the first time since the Federal League of World War I a new major league might form.

Branch Rickey, who in his seventies had turned his attention to building the moribund Pittsburgh Pirates after leaving the Dodgers in 1951 (his efforts resulted in a World Championship in 1960) suddenly appeared as the key figure in a new venture: the Continental League. With a team in New York as an anchor for the enterprise and the brilliant Rickey to offer guidance, the threat to the existing establishment was very real. Following on the heels of the new league's announced intention to form, the two existing leagues voted to expand for the first time in the 'modern' era. Two new teams were added to the American League in 1961 and an additional two to the National League in 1962.

Expansion required a change in the schedule which, like the geography, had been virtually unchanged in this century. The eight teams played each of seven opponents 22 times a season in a 154-game schedule, 11 games at each park. The games were played in series of 2–5 games – usually three or four – which meant (normally) four visits by each team to each league city during the season.

# THUMBNAIL HISTORY OF BASEBALL

The expansion to a 10-team league produced a *162*-game schedule, reducing to 18 the number of times teams met and to three the number of visits each team made to each league city.

The increase to 162 games caught immediate attention, because in the first year of the expanded schedule Roger Maris beat Babe Ruth's cherished home run record. The eight extra games on the schedule became an issue when Maris hit his 60th home run after the 154th game and his 61st in the season's finale. Commissioner Ford Frick ruled that Maris's record would be posted with an asterisk, in effect creating *two* records for the different-length seasons. This position has been pretty well ridiculed to death in the years since.

When the American League expanded, it moved into southern California to compete with the Dodgers with the Los Angeles Angels (who have since moved to nearby Anaheim – where Disneyland is – and are called the California Angels). And it added the twin cities of Minneapolis–St Paul by the odd device of moving the Washington Senators (who became the Minnesota Twins) and inventing a *new* Washington Senator team through expansion. This was done to reward longtime Senator/Twin owner Calvin Griffith with an exciting new market; it was a cynical joke on the Washington fans, who were seeing their longtime losers beginning to turn into winners. (The Twins – led by Harmon Killebrew – snapped the Yankees' string of American League pennants in 1965.) The Senators shortly failed again, being moved to Arlington (near Dallas) Texas and becoming the Texas Rangers in 1972.

The National League expansion was to Houston (the team born the Colt .45s and now the Houston Astros) and, of course, back into New York with the Mets. The Mets hired ex-Yankee manager Casey Stengel as their first skipper and a lot of National League stars of the 1950s made up their first squad. The names (Snider and Hodges from the Dodgers, Richie Ashburn of the Phillies, Frank Thomas of the Pirates, Warren Spahn of the Braves) were illustrious; their twilight performances mediocre. Even the imaginative Stengel – still full of vinegar in his seventies – had to resign himself to pleasing the press; this team couldn't win many games. Still, the re-launch of the National League in New York was a resounding commercial success, particularly after the collapse of the Yankee dynasty in 1965.

The second wave of baseball expansion ended the 1960s: both leagues going from 10 to 12 teams in 1969. Earlier, the Kansas City A's had moved on to Oakland and the Milwaukee Braves to Atlanta – the first twice-moved franchises hardly a decade from their first move. The second expansion re-filled those gaps: the Milwaukee Brewers (after one year as the Seattle Pilots) and Kansas City Royals being added to the American League; the Montreal Expos (the first team out of the United States) and the San Diego Padres coming into the National League.

In the second expansion, the leagues also changed their structure. Until that time, there was one set of league standings for the 8, and then 10, teams. When the leagues went to 12 teams they also split into *divisions* – Eastern and Western in each league – and the division champions started to meet in the League Championship Series (LCS) to determine the pennant and the World Series contestants.

The expansion again required a schedule change, but this time the length of the regular season (162 games) was left untouched. Teams played intra-Divisional rivals 18 times and inter-Divisional 12 each.

But the season was really lengthened again, by the addition of the best 3-out-of-5 LCS. The combination of the 1961 and 1969 expansions was to push the World Series back a full two weeks from its traditional slot in the first week of October. In the 1980s it has been pushed a little further by expanding the LCS to 4-out-of-7.

The shift has certainly attracted notice because of the frequency of World Series games played in unreasonably cold weather, particularly since they are now usually played at night. Cynics have a good time contemplating the year that Montreal and Toronto have a World Series in the snow.

What has never been carefully examined is the impact of the calendar change on American politics, where it is axiomatic that public interest in the campaign picks up after the World Series is over. Election Day in the US is always the first Tuesday in November (except November 1st), so the effective length of national campaigns has been incrementally cut in half since 1961. John Kennedy was elected in 1960.

When the divisions were created, the names Eastern and Western were not taken too literally. Chicago ends up Eastern in the National League, Western in the American. Atlanta and Cincinnati, both somewhat substantially east of Chicago, are in the NL's Western Division.

## BASEBALL TODAY

The 1950s were characterized by the first franchise shifts and the 1960s by expansion; the 1970s were the decade when the leagues diverged, for the first time, in fundamental ways.

The American League (in 1973) added the *designated hitter*, a substitute in the batting order for the pitcher. This was an attempt to add more runs to the game, at the expense of the symmetry of having nine men play the game and of some tactical subtleties revolving around the characteristic inability of pitchers to hit. The National League has never followed suit.

In 1977, the American League expanded again (to 14 teams, creating awkward 7-team divisions) by putting the Blue Jays in Toronto and the Mariners in Seattle, where they replaced the 1969 expansion team which moved after one season to Milwaukee. The National League has resisted an additional expansion to this unwieldy number and the difference has existed for the past ten years. A corollary of this difference is a much more sensible National League schedule: National League teams still play 18 games against teams in their division and 12 against each team in the opposite division; American League teams play 12 or 13 games against every other team regardless of division.

One change in the 1970s that affected both leagues was a court ruling ending the 'reserve clause'. That paragraph in standard player contracts effectively protected a team's 'rights' to a player until the team sold or traded the player to another team. With 'free agency', some players could negotiate their own deals with the highest bidder. Salaries escalated dramatically and only recent concerted action by the owners (which may prove to be illegal) has stopped their steady rise. Meanwhile, the average major league salary tops $400,000, with many of today's stars earning $1 million or more per season.

In the 1970s, the Oakland A's won three consecutive World Series (1972–74) and the Yankees won it twice in a row over the Dodgers after losing in 1976 to Cincinnati. Since the second Yankee win in 1978, there has been no sustained dominance, with teams rising in the standings one year and dropping like flies in the next. Although certain teams are often near the top of their division: the Orioles, Yankees, Dodgers, Royals, and Phillies – almost every race has started almost every year without a consensus favourite.

The 1980s have been an exciting time for statistical milestones, highlighted by Pete Rose breaking Ty Cobb's lifetime record for basehits (surpassing 4,191 with a total that may still rise) and having five pitchers win their 300th game (Gaylord Perry, Phil Niekro, Steve Carlton, Tom Seaver, and Don Sutton), a feat that hadn't been accomplished since the early 1960s. Nolan Ryan and Carlton finally beat Walter Johnson's career strikeout mark of 3,508 which had stood since the 1920s; Ryan will hold the record for at least the next generation at well over 4,000.

*Don Sutton won his 300th game in 1986.*

## BASEBALL'S IMMORTALS: THE HALL OF FAME

The National Baseball Hall of Fame and Museum is in Cooperstown, New York – a good five-hour jaunt from the closest major league ballpark. The Hall was established in the 1930s, with the charter group of five players (Ty Cobb, Walter Johnson, Christy Mathewson, Babe Ruth, and Honus Wagner) selected in 1936.

Each year, a group of Hall electors from among the baseball writers in America vote on the eligible players: those who retired five to twenty-five years ago. An 'Old-Timer's Committee' has jurisdiction beyond the twenty-five-year limit and recently a special effort was undertaken to include players from the Negro Leagues who were not permitted to play in the Majors.

The approximately-200 members of the Hall are added slowly; 75 per cent of the writers must place a player on their list of no more than ten (many vote for *none* in any particular year) for the player to gain entry. Only a handful of players make the Hall in their first year of eligibility.

# 6 FOLLOWING BASEBALL EACH AND EVERY DAY

## BASEBALL IS AN EVERYDAY THING

**Opening Day** of the **regular season** is the first Monday in April in Cincinnati and in perhaps a couple of other cities as well. While other teams open at home and on the road in alternate years, Cincinnati retains a privileged place in recognition of its being the birthplace of professional baseball. All the teams are in action on the following day.

In addition to the 'regular season', there is the **pre-season** or **Spring Training** schedule of games in March and the **post-season**: the LCS and World Series games.

Each team plays 162 games, 81 at home and 81 on the road, concluding on the first Sunday in October. Games are played in *series* – usually 2-to-4 games in length between two teams at one park. **Homestands** are generally 2-to-4 series long, as are **road trips**. Teams are at home for a week or two and then on the road for a week or two throughout the six-month season.

Three of the (approximately) 185 days from the regular season's start until its end are taken off for the **All-Star Break**, at approximately mid-season (mid-July). A squad of All-Stars, starters elected by the fans and most selected by the managers of last year's World Series contestants, play the **All-Star Game** during the break; everybody else can rest. That leaves about 180 days to play 162 games.

There are a few scheduled **doubleheaders**, where teams play two games against each other in a single day. (These are bargains for fans, because tickets are sold at the regular price.) Some teams have none, so they play on 162 of the 180 days.

The contract between Major League Baseball and the Players Association requires a team be given a day off after 17 straight days of play. This results in light schedules on Mondays and Thursdays and, rarely, a Monday or Thursday with no games played. On every single other day, every team is scheduled so there are 13 games: 6 in the National League and seven in the American.

Except in Seattle, Minneapolis, and Houston (where there are domed stadiums) games are subject to **rainouts** and cold weather can force postponement of early season games in many major league cities. These games are rescheduled for later in the season, sometimes creating a number of doubleheaders for a team within a short time. This can be murder on a pitching staff.

## STANDINGS AND BOX SCORES IN THE MORNING PAPER

A significant portion of male America *requires* a check of the standings and the box scores in the morning paper before a day during the baseball season can begin. This is a peculiar pleasure of baseball: following the performances of favourite teams and favourite players on a daily basis.

Virtually every newspaper in America carries baseball standings and box scores. Because games are played across the country in four time zones, morning papers in the east sometimes don't carry complete information on night games played on the west coast. Baseball zealots will routinely buy a second paper later in the day if the first one they read did not contain the complete review of the previous day's Major League action.

Because Britain is five hours later than the east coast of the US, and eight hours later than the west coast, printed coverage in Britain is necessarily a day behind. In this section, the illustrative material is what is available on a daily basis in Britain: the standings, box scores, and statistical tables of the International Edition of *USA TODAY*. This is the first time in history that this information has been available worldwide on a daily basis: the *International Herald-Tribune* has never carried anything but **line scores** – the inning-by-inning summary of scoring in a game – and less-complete versions of the standings.

On the morning of Tuesday, 22 July 1986, *USA TODAY* printed the accompanying **stand-**

FOLLOWING BASEBALL EACH AND EVERY DAY

# AMERICAN

AMERICAN LEAGUE BASEBALL NEWS
FROM USA TODAY'S **NATIONAL NEWS NETWORK**

## STANDINGS

| EAST | W | L | Pct. | GB | Last 10 | Streak | Home | Div. |
|---|---|---|---|---|---|---|---|---|
| Boston | 57 | 34 | .626 | — | 5-5 | Lost 1 | 30-19 | 22-16 |
| New York | 52 | 41 | .559 | 6 | 6-4 | Lost 2 | 22-23 | 19-20 |
| Cleveland | 48 | 41 | .539 | 8 | 5-5 | Lost 1 | 25-19 | 15-21 |
| Baltimore | 49 | 42 | .538 | 8 | 6-4 | Won 2 | 23-20 | 16-22 |
| Toronto | 50 | 44 | .532 | 8½ | 6-4 | Won 1 | 26-25 | 25-15 |
| Detroit | 47 | 44 | .516 | 10 | 8-2 | Won 5 | 25-16 | 20-19 |
| Milwaukee | 42 | 48 | .467 | 14½ | 2-8 | Lost 1 | 24-23 | 17-21 |

| WEST | W | L | Pct. | GB | Last 10 | Streak | Home | Div. |
|---|---|---|---|---|---|---|---|---|
| California | 49 | 42 | .538 | — | 5-5 | Lost 1 | 23-20 | 25-13 |
| Texas | 47 | 45 | .511 | 2½ | 3-7 | Lost 4 | 27-20 | 23-17 |
| Chicago | 42 | 48 | .467 | 6½ | 5-5 | Won 2 | 23-26 | 19-19 |
| Kansas City | 42 | 50 | .457 | 7½ | 5-5 | Won 1 | 27-22 | 18-22 |
| Seattle | 42 | 52 | .447 | 8½ | 7-3 | Won 1 | 24-20 | 18-22 |
| Minnesota | 38 | 54 | .413 | 11½ | 2-8 | Lost 2 | 22-26 | 18-20 |
| Oakland | 37 | 57 | .394 | 13½ | 5-5 | Won 1 | 20-22 | 16-24 |

## SUNDAY'S RESULTS

| | WP | LP |
|---|---|---|
| Chicago 8, New York 0 | Allen (7-1) | Shirley (0-4) |
| Baltimore 8, Minnesota 3 | Boddicker (12-5) | Smithson (8-9) |
| Kansas City 4, Cleveland 2 | Farr (7-1) | Noles (2-2) |
| Detroit 4, Texas 0 | King (6-2) | Guzman (8-10) |
| Seattle 9, Boston 5 | J.Reed (2-0) | Sellers (3-5) |
| Toronto 6, California 3 (10) | Henke (7-3) | Corbett (2-2) |
| Milwaukee 7, Oakland 2 (1st) | Higuera (11-7) | Plunk (2-6) |
| Oakland 4, Milwaukee 2 (2nd) | Rijo (4-8) | Leary (6-10) |

## MONDAY'S PITCHING LINE

| Teams | Pitchers | W-L | 1986 season IP | ERA | Career W-L | vs. opp. 85-86 W-L | IP | vs. opp. ERA |
|---|---|---|---|---|---|---|---|---|
| Texas at New York | Witt (R) | 4-8 | 90.1 | 6.38 | 0-1 | 0-1 | 6.2 | 8.10 |
| | Drabek (R) | 1-2 | 41.2 | 5.18 | 0-0 | 0-0 | 3.0 | 0.00 |
| Minnesota at Detroit | Viola (L) | 9-8 | 141.0 | 5.17 | 4-6 | 1-0 | 5.0 | 1.80 |
| | Thurmond (L) | 0-0 | 0.1 | 0.00 | — | — | — | — |
| Chicago at Cleveland | Davis (R) | 4-4 | 104.1 | 4.49 | 0-0 | 0-0 | 19.2 | 4.12 |
| | Oelkers (L) | 1-1 | 29.0 | 0.10 | 0-1 | 0-1 | 4.1 | 6.23 |
| Kansas City at Baltimore | Jackson (L) | 5-6 | 77.0 | 3.97 | 3-2 | 1-0 | 6.0 | 0.00 |
| | Dixon (R) | 9-7 | 120.2 | 4.03 | 2-1 | 1-1 | 13.0 | 4.85 |
| Milwaukee at California | Wegman (R) | 2-8 | 121.2 | 4.96 | 0-1 | 0-1 | 25.0 | 2.16 |
| | Romanick (R) | 5-7 | 101.2 | 5.31 | 6-1 | 0-0 | 8.0 | 2.25 |
| Toronto at Seattle | Cerutti (L) | 4-2 | 61.0 | 4.28 | 0-1 | 0-1 | 2.0 | 13.50 |
| | Huismann (R) | 2-2 | 54.0 | 4.50 | 1-1 | 1-0 | 10.1 | 2.61 |
| Boston at Oakland | Hurst (L) | 5-3 | 77.1 | 2.79 | 9-2 | 1-0 | 10.0 | 1.80 |
| | Young (L) | 6-6 | 90.2 | 3.97 | 0-1 | 0-1 | 13.1 | 4.73 |

Source for standings and statistics: Elias Sports Bureau.

## SATURDAY'S RESULTS

| | WP | LP |
|---|---|---|
| Oakland 3, Milwaukee 2 | Mooneyham (3-3) | Clear (2-4) |
| California 9, Toronto 3 | Candelaria (3-0) | Stieb (2-10) |
| Chicago 8, New York 3 | Cowley (5-5) | Nielsen (2-1) |
| Detroit 5, Texas 3 (12) | Hernandez (5-4) | Harris (3-8) |
| Baltimore 1, Minnesota 0 | Flanagan (4-6) | Heaton (3-9) |
| Cleveland 6, Kansas City 4 | Niekro (7-6) | Bankhead (3-4) |
| Boston 9, Seattle 4 | Clemens (16-2) | Morgan (7-9) |

■ **WEDNESDAY: AL team-by-team statistics**

# NATIONAL

NATIONAL LEAGUE BASEBALL NEWS
FROM USA TODAY'S **NATIONAL NEWS NETWORK**

## STANDINGS

| EAST | W | L | Pct. | GB | Last 10 | Streak | Home | Div. |
|---|---|---|---|---|---|---|---|---|
| New York | 60 | 28 | .682 | — | 5-5 | Lost 3 | 32-14 | 30-10 |
| Montreal | 48 | 39 | .552 | 11½ | 5-5 | Lost 1 | 21-21 | 24-19 |
| Philadelphia | 43 | 46 | .483 | 17½ | 4-6 | Won 1 | 22-18 | 18-24 |
| Chicago | 38 | 50 | .432 | 22 | 6-4 | Lost 1 | 22-18 | 16-24 |
| Pittsburgh | 38 | 51 | .427 | 22½ | 5-5 | Won 3 | 19-27 | 16-25 |
| St. Louis | 38 | 52 | .422 | 23 | 5-5 | Lost 1 | 18-27 | 19-23 |

| WEST | W | L | Pct. | GB | Last 10 | Streak | Home | Div. |
|---|---|---|---|---|---|---|---|---|
| Houston | 50 | 42 | .543 | — | 6-4 | Won 3 | 27-20 | 26-19 |
| San Francisco | 50 | 42 | .543 | — | 5-5 | Won 1 | 28-21 | 25-20 |
| San Diego | 46 | 46 | .500 | 4 | 4-6 | Lost 3 | 28-22 | 24-20 |
| Cincinnati | 43 | 45 | .489 | 5 | 8-2 | Lost 1 | 18-20 | 18-24 |
| Atlanta | 43 | 48 | .473 | 6½ | 2-8 | Won 1 | 22-20 | 22-22 |
| Los Angeles | 42 | 50 | .457 | 8 | 5-5 | Won 1 | 29-22 | 17-27 |

## SUNDAY'S RESULTS

| | WP | LP |
|---|---|---|
| Pittsburgh 4, San Diego 2 | McWilliams (2-5) | Dravecky (7-8) |
| Los Angeles 7, St. Louis 2 | Honeycutt (6-5) | Conroy (3-5) |
| Philadelphia 9, Cincinnati 3 | Hudson (5-9) | Denny (6-9) |
| San Fran. 5, Chicago 4 | Garrelts (8-7) | Eckersley (3-6) |
| Houston 9, New York 8 (15) | Knepper (12-7) | McDowell (7-4) |
| Atlanta at Montreal, ppd. rain. | | |

## MONDAY'S PITCHING LINE

| Teams | Pitchers | W-L | 1986 season IP | ERA | Career W-L | vs. opp. 85-86 W-L | IP | vs. opp. ERA |
|---|---|---|---|---|---|---|---|---|
| San Diego at Chicago | Hoyt (R) | 5-4 | 87.0 | 4.97 | 1-2 | 1-1 | 18.0 | 4.00 |
| | Moyer (L) | 1-2 | 16.1 | 9.37 | — | — | — | — |
| Philadelphia at Atlanta | Carman (L) | 4-2 | 46.2 | 4.44 | 0-1 | 0-0 | 0.2 | 0.00 |
| | Smith (R) | 7-10 | 142.0 | 3.49 | 2-1 | 1-0 | 7.0 | 1.29 |
| New York at Cincinnati | Aguilera (R) | 2-3 | 60.0 | 5.40 | 1-0 | 0-0 | 6.1 | 5.68 |
| | Soto (R) | 3-7 | 77.0 | 3.97 | 9-6 | 0-2 | 12.0 | 5.25 |
| San Francisco at St. Louis | Carlton (L) | 4-9 | 91.0 | 6.23 | 38-13 | 0-0 | 8.1 | 9.72 |
| | Mathews (L) | 4-2 | 57.1 | 3.30 | 0-0 | 0-0 | 4.0 | 0.00 |
| Montreal at Houston | Martinez (R) | 0-2 | 25.2 | 6.66 | 0-1 | 0-1 | 5.0 | 11.80 |
| | Knudson (R) | 1-3 | 24.1 | 3.70 | — | — | — | — |

Only games scheduled
Source for standings and statistics: Elias Sports Bureau.

## SATURDAY'S RESULTS

| | WP | LP |
|---|---|---|
| Cincinnati 5, Philadelphia 2 | Gullickson (7-6) | Rawley (11-6) |
| St. Louis 2, Los Angeles 1 | Forsch (8-6) | Welch (4-8) |
| Pittsburgh 4, San Diego 3 | Guante (4-1) | Lefferts (6-4) |
| Chicago 11, San Fran. 6 | Hoffman (4-2) | Krukow (11-6) |
| Atlanta 7, Montreal 2 | Palmer (6-8) | Tibbs (4-6) |
| Houston 5, New York 4 | Smith (2-6) | McDowell (7-3) |

## MONDAY IN BASEBALL

**1945:** The Detroit Tigers and the Philadelphia Athletics battled 24 innings and ended in a 1-1 tie. Les Mueller pitched 19 2-3 innings for the Tigers.

**1956:** Brooks Lawrence of the Cincinnati Reds had his 13-game winning streak snapped as Roberto Clemente's three-run homer led the Pittsburgh Pirates to a 4-3 victory.

**1975:** Joe Torre of the New York Mets grounded into four double plays in a 6-2 loss to the Houston Astros. Felix Millan had four singles but was wiped out each time.

**Monday's birthday:** Dave Henderson 28.

■ **THURSDAY: NL team-by-team statistics**

ings, **results**, **schedule**, and **pitching line** information for the American and National Leagues.

## EXPLANATION OF THE STANDINGS

At seven o'clock on Tuesday morning, when *USA TODAY* becomes available, Monday's games on the west coast of the US may still be going on. So on this Tuesday morning, we see what America saw on Monday.

In the American League, Boston leads the East with 57 wins and 34 losses, a **winning percentage** of .626. ('This is computed by dividing wins by the sum of wins and losses, as it is for pitchers' winning percentages.) The next column, headed *GB* stands for **Games Behind**.

Games Behind is the number of games a team behind would have to beat a team ahead in order to catch up to them in **games above .500**. (A team is playing .500 when it has an equal number of wins and losses.) In the East, the Yankees would achieve this by beating Boston six times; Boston would then be 57–40 and the Yankees 58–41. In that case, the Red Sox would be in first place by **percentage points**.

Half-games behind result from teams playing unequal numbers of games. Looking at the American League West, we see that if Texas beat California twice, they would still be behind (California 49–44, Texas 49–45); but if they beat them three times, Texas would be ahead (Texas 50–45, California 49–45.)

Uneven numbers of games played can also result in the anomaly of the team in first place being *games behind* the team in second place. Imagine if we had a team that had played five more games than the Red Sox at this point in the season, winning three of them. The standings would then read:

|  | W | L | PCT | GB |
|---|---|---|---|---|
| BOSTON RED SOX | 57 | 34 | .626 | ½ |
| OUR TEAM | 60 | 36 | .625 | – |
| NEW YORK YANKEES | 52 | 41 | .559 | 6½ |

At the end of the season, any games postponed not *previously* decided which would determine the pennant race are played, so that the uneven number of games can never ultimately decide the pennant. (The exception is if there is an interruption by strike or natural disaster. The latter has never occurred; the former affected the seasons of 1972 and 1981.)

In the Western Division, there is a much closer race. California has a slim 2½ game lead over Texas, with Chicago in third place as close to first as the Yankees are in their Division.

The column headed 'Last 10' gives the teams' records for their past ten decisions; a quick scan shows that Detroit (8–2) and Seattle (7–3) have been **hot**, Milwaukee (2–8) and second-place Texas (3–7) have been **slumping**.

'Streak' indicates the recent record of wins since the last loss, or losses since the last win. Detroit has the best **winning streak**, 5 in-a-row; Texas has lost 4 in-a-row.

The last two columns give the teams' records *at home*, where it is almost always better than on the road, and *within the Division*, where they are playing teams with which they directly compete in the standings. The most noteworthy item in these two columns is the Yankees' high standing *despite* a sub-.500 home record.

The previous day's (Sunday's) results give the **winning pitcher** and his season's record and the **losing pitcher** with his. (Because this edition covers the weekend, the Saturday results are published as well.) At this point, about 55 per cent through the season, Mike Boddicker won his 12th game for Baltimore which makes him a realistic candidate to win 20. Toronto beat California in 10 innings (the notation appears after the game score); Milwaukee and Oakland **split a doubleheader**, which means they both get credit for a win and a loss in the league standings.

The schedule and pitching line for 'today's' (Monday's) games follows. The Yankees will try to extend Texas's losing streak and improve their home record, while the Red Sox play much weaker Oakland on the west coast. Western leader California hosts backsliding Milwaukee.

The 'pitching line' gives information on the **scheduled starters** for that day's games. The column with the pitchers' names carries (R) for righthanders, (L) for lefthanders. The next three columns give 1986 season records for won-lost, innings pitched, and earned run average. The next column is the *career* (i.e. *lifetime*) won-lost record against that opponent; the last three give the last two seasons' ('85–'86) record against that opponent.

That information reveals that in the important games on Monday both Texas and the Yankees are starting pitchers with poor records this season, as are both Milwaukee and California. Boston seems to have the most successful starter of the day – Bruce Hurst – who is not only the only scheduled American League starter with an ERA under 3.00, he has beaten Oakland nine times in his career. Frank Viola (Minnesota) and Mike Boddicker (Baltimore) are going for their 10th wins of the year.

In the National League East, the Mets are runaway leaders over the pack, with Montreal in second place the only other Eastern team above .500. In the West, Houston and San Francisco are in a dead heat with the same records; *all* of the West teams are still within striking distance with 70 or so games to go.

Despite their big lead, the Mets have not played well lately; they have a 5–5 record for their last 10 and have just lost 3 in a row. But only the Cubs – a hopeless 22 games behind – have picked up any ground during the slump.

San Diego has just lost 3 in a row, which means they were even closer to the leaders before the last weekend.

The Sunday results show that Atlanta and Montreal were postponed by rain and that the Mets lost in 15 innings.

The scheduled starter for the Mets is their weakest of five: Rick Aguilera has a high earned run average and hasn't pitched too much. (Starters routinely work 200 innings; Aguilera has thrown only 60 in 55 per cent of the season.) Going for the Giants is just-signed veteran lefty Steve Carlton with a poor record and high earned run average. Obviously, it would be a great boost to their pennant chances if he were able to regain a semblance of his great form.

The accompanying illustrations of **League Leader** tables, also from *USA TODAY*, is complete through Sunday, 20 July.

The 'batting leaders' are ranked by *batting average*, hits divided by total at-bats. In the American League, Boggs leads Mattingly by a considerable margin. The columns show the number of *games* in which the player has appeared, the number of *charged at-bats* (which excludes walks and sacrifices), the number of *runs scored*, the number of *hits* (singles through home runs counting the same), and the player's *batting average*.

Underneath the averages table are the standings for *home runs, runs batted in (RBIs), runs scored*, and *slugging percentage*. Slugging percentage does weight power hits with total bases divided by times at-bat. Jose Canseco of Oakland leads in homers and RBIs; Rickey Henderson of the Yankees has a wide lead in scoring runs.

In the National League, note that Hubie Brooks of Expos and Chris Brown of the Giants have played in significantly fewer games than the other batting leaders. In Brown's case this is accounted for by an injury which has healed; Brooks at this point had just gone out for the season. The '3.1 plate appearances' requirement will eventually edit his name from the rolls.

The National League batting race is tight among the remaining competitors: perennial leader Tony Gwynn of San Diego, Tim Raines of Montreal, and Steve Sax of the Dodgers fighting it out with Brown. Mike Schmidt – the leading power hitter of the era in the National League – ends the weekend with narrow leads in home runs and RBIs.

## AL leaders
**Through Sunday**

### BATTING LEADERS

Based on 3.1 plate appearances for each game player's team has played.

|  | G | AB | R | H | PCT |
|---|---|---|---|---|---|
| Boggs, Bos | 84 | 318 | 59 | 116 | .365 |
| Mattingly, NY | 93 | 396 | 64 | 136 | .343 |
| Puckett, Minn | 92 | 399 | 68 | 135 | .338 |
| Rice, Bos | 90 | 362 | 57 | 120 | .331 |
| Easler, NY | 85 | 311 | 40 | 103 | .331 |
| Yount, Mil | 77 | 287 | 46 | 94 | .328 |
| Bell, Tor | 92 | 368 | 63 | 118 | .321 |
| Joyner, Cal | 91 | 365 | 57 | 117 | .321 |
| Fletcher, Tex | 83 | 284 | 48 | 91 | .320 |
| Carter, Clev | 88 | 350 | 56 | 110 | .314 |

**HOME RUNS**
- Canseco, Oak ... 23
- Pagliarulo, NY . 22
- Barfield, Tor ... 21
- Hrbek, Minn .... 21
- Kingman, Oak ... 21
- Parrish, Det ... 21
- Bell, Tor ....... 20
- Joyner, Cal ..... 20

**RUNS**
- Henderson, NY . 87
- Puckett, Minn .. 68
- Mattingly, NY .. 64
- Phillips, Oak .... 64
- Bell, Tor ....... 63
- Hrbek, Minn .... 60
- Boggs, Bos ..... 59
- Barfield, Tor ... 58
- McDowell, Tex . 58

**RUNS BATTED IN**
- Canseco, Oak ... 78
- Joyner, Cal .... 73
- Bell, Tor ...... 72
- Presley, Sea ... 69
- Mattingly, NY .. 68
- Barfield, Tor .. 65
- Hrbek, Minn ... 64
- Carter, Clev ... 63
- Evans, Bos .... 61

**SLUGGING**
- Bell, Tor ...... .565
- Barfield, Tor .. .563
- Hrbek, Minn ... .561
- Puckett, Minn . .554
- Pagliarulo, NY . .551
- Mattingly, NY . .551
- Joyner, Cal ... .540
- Tartabull, Sea . .534

### PITCHING LEADERS

**VICTORIES**
- Clemens, Bos .. 16-2
- Boddicker, Balt 12-5
- Rasmussen, NY 11-2
- Boyd, Bos ..... 11-6
- Higuera, Mil ... 11-7
- Schrom, Clev .. 10-2
- Clancy, Tor ... 10-5
- McCaskill, Cal . 10-6
- Morris, Det ... 10-6

**ERA**
Based on one inning pitched for each game player's team has played
- Clemens, Bos . 2.59
- Higuera, Mil .. 2.75
- Darwin, Mil .. 2.82
- Witt, Cal ..... 3.03
- McCaskill, Cal . 3.26

**STRIKEOUTS**
- Clemens, Bos .. 154
- Morris, Det ... 139
- Witt, Cal ..... 130
- Rijo, Oak ..... 123

**SAVES**
- Aase, Balt ..... 25
- Righetti, NY ... 21
- Hernandez, Det . 18
- Harris, Tex .... 15

## NL leaders
**Through Sunday**

### BATTING LEADERS

Based on 3.1 plate appearances for each game player's team has played.

|  | G | AB | R | H | PCT |
|---|---|---|---|---|---|
| Brooks, Mtl | 78 | 300 | 49 | 101 | .337 |
| Brown, SF | 77 | 280 | 38 | 94 | .336 |
| Gwynn, SD | 91 | 355 | 61 | 119 | .335 |
| Raines, Mtl | 82 | 326 | 53 | 109 | .334 |
| Sax, LA | 88 | 350 | 51 | 114 | .326 |
| Oberkfell, Atl | 85 | 284 | 33 | 89 | .313 |
| Bass, Hou | 91 | 340 | 47 | 103 | .303 |
| Ray, Pitt | 86 | 316 | 37 | 94 | .297 |
| C.Davis, SF | 87 | 303 | 46 | 88 | .290 |
| Hayes, Phil | 87 | 331 | 55 | 96 | .290 |

**HOME RUNS**
- Schmidt, Phil ... 21
- Davis, Hou ..... 20
- Parker, Cin .... 19
- Marshall, LA ... 18
- Horner, Atl .... 17
- Stubbs, LA .... 17
- Carter, NY .... 16

**RUNS**
- Gwynn, SD ..... 61
- Murphy, Atl .... 57
- Schmidt, Phil ... 56
- Carter, NY .... 55
- Hayes, Phil .... 55
- Raines, Mtl .... 53
- Davis, Cin ..... 52
- Doran, Hou .... 52

**RUNS BATTED IN**
- Schmidt, Phil .. 69
- Carter, NY .... 68
- Parker, Cin ... 63
- Davis, Hou .... 62
- Brooks, Mtl ... 58
- Horner, Atl ... 56
- C.Davis, SF ... 55
- Wallach, Mtl .. 54
- Strawberry, NY 52
- Moreland, Chi . 50

**SLUGGING**
- Brooks, Mtl .... .567
- Strawberry, NY .547
- Schmidt, Phil .. .544
- Davis, Hou .... .528
- Parker, Cin ... .500
- Gwynn, SD ... .496
- Raines, Mtl ... .491
- Bass, Hou .... .488
- Horner, Atl ... .482

### PITCHING LEADERS

**VICTORIES**
- Fernandez, NY 12-2
- Valenzuela, LA 12-6
- Knepper, Hou . 12-7
- Ojeda, NY ..... 11-2
- Krukow, SF ... 11-6
- Rawley, Phil .. 11-6

**ERA**
Based on one inning pitched for each game player's team has played
- Ojeda, NY .... 2.13
- Honeycutt, LA 2.15
- Scott, Hou .... 2.34
- Forsch, StL ... 2.44
- Rhoden, Pitt .. 2.45
- Knepper, Hou . 2.61
- Tudor, StL ... 2.64
- Show, SD .... 2.65
- LaCoss, SF ... 2.75
- Darling, NY .. 2.82

**STRIKEOUTS**
- Scott, Hou .... 174
- Valenzuela, LA 142
- Welch, LA .... 113
- Fernandez, NY 110
- Palmer, Atl ... 106
- Smith, Atl .... 105

## READING BOX SCORES AND SCORING SUMMARIES

*USA TODAY*'s International Edition on the morning of Wednesday, 23 July, reports the results of Monday's action in even more detailed form than appears in most US dailies.

In the American League, the Yankees have beaten Texas, both the Red Sox and the Angels have lost.

The scoring summary ('How They Scored') as printed in this edition of *USA TODAY* for all the games (and reproduced here for the Yankee game) appears only if space permits. The baseball fan goes straight to the box score for his analysis of the action.

There are variations of the box score, but the *USA TODAY* version is on the very-complete side of standard.

# Yankees ....... 8
# Rangers........ 4

**HOW THEY SCORED**

**Yankees 1st:** Henderson homered to left. Washington doubled to left. Mattingly struck out. Easler walked. Washington stole third. Winfield struck out. Pagliarulo homered to right, Washington, Easler and Pagliarulo scored. Wynegar popped out to second. **Yankees 4, Rangers 0.**

**Rangers 2nd:** Incaviglia hit by pitch. Ward grounded to second, Incaviglia forced out at second, second to shortstop, Ward safe at first. Parrish doubled to center, Ward scored, Parrish out at third, center fielder to shortstop to catcher to third to first. Slaught doubled to center. Buechele grounded out to second. **Yankees 4, Rangers 1.**

**Yankees 2nd:** Randolph walked. Berra struck out. Henderson popped out to second. Randolph stole second. Washington singled to right, Randolph scored, Washinton to second on throw home. Mattingly flied out to left. **Yankees 5, Rangers 1.**

**Rangers 4th:** Ward flied out to right. Parrish grounded out to second. Slaught homered to left. Buechele homered to right. Wilkerson grounded out to shortstop. **Yankees 5, Rangers 3.**

**Rangers 5th:** McDowell singled to pitcher. Fletcher doubled to left, McDowell to third. O'Brien grounded out to second, McDowell scored, Fletcher to third. Incaviglia struck out. Ward grounded out to shortstop. **Yankees 5, Rangers 4.**

**Yankees 5th:** Russell pitching. Easler singled to first. Winfield singled to center, Easler to second, Easler to third on center fielder McDowell's fielding error. Mahler relieved Russell. Pagliarulo walked, Winfield to second. Wynegar hit sacrifice fly to left, Easler scored. Randolph singled to center, Winfield scored, Pagliarulo out at third, center to first to second. Berra flied out to left. **Yankees 7, Rangers 4.**

**Yankees 7th:** Mohorcic pitching. Easler homered to right. Winfield grounded out to third. Pagliarulo grounded out to first, Wynegar flied out to right. **Yankees 8, Rangers 4.**

| TEXAS | ab | r | h | bi | NEW YORK | ab | r | h | bi |
|---|---|---|---|---|---|---|---|---|---|
| McDowell cf | 4 | 1 | 2 | 0 | Hendersn cf | 3 | 1 | 1 | 1 |
| Paciorek ph | 1 | 0 | 1 | 0 | Washingtn lf | 4 | 1 | 2 | 1 |
| Fletcher ss | 4 | 0 | 1 | 0 | Roenick lf | 1 | 0 | 0 | 0 |
| O'Brien 1b | 3 | 0 | 0 | 1 | Mattingly 1b | 4 | 0 | 0 | 0 |
| Sierra ph | 1 | 0 | 0 | 0 | Easler dh | 2 | 3 | 2 | 1 |
| Incaviglia rf | 3 | 0 | 0 | 0 | Winfield rf | 4 | 1 | 1 | 0 |
| Ward lf | 4 | 1 | 1 | 0 | Pagliarulo 3b | 2 | 1 | 1 | 3 |
| Parrish dh | 4 | 0 | 3 | 1 | Wynegar c | 2 | 0 | 0 | 1 |
| Slaught c | 4 | 1 | 2 | 1 | Randolph 2b | 1 | 1 | 1 | 1 |
| Buechele 3b | 4 | 1 | 1 | 1 | Berra ss | 4 | 0 | 0 | 0 |
| Wilkersn 2b | 3 | 0 | 0 | 0 | | | | | |
| Harrah ph | 1 | 0 | 0 | 0 | | | | | |
| Totals | 36 | 4 | 11 | 4 | Totals | 27 | 8 | 8 | 8 |

| | | | | |
|---|---|---|---|---|
| Texas | 010 | 210 | 000 | — 4 |
| New York | 410 | 020 | 10x | — 8 |

**Game-winning RBI:** Henderson (6).

E: McDowell. DP: Texas 2, New York 1. LOB: Texas 8, New York 6. 2B: Washington, Parrish, Slaught, Fletcher, Ward. HR: Henderson (16), Pagliarulo (23), Slaught (9), Buechele (13), Easler (8). SB: Washington (4), Randolph (13). Caught stealing: Henderson. SF: Wynegar. Struck out: Rangers (O'Brien, Incaviglia 2, Slaught, Wilkerson, Buechele); Yankees (Mattingly, Winfield, Berra).

| | IP | H | R | ER | BB | SO |
|---|---|---|---|---|---|---|
| **Texas** | | | | | | |
| Witt L,4-9 | 2 2-3 | 4 | 5 | 5 | 5 | 3 |
| Russell | 1 1-3 | 2 | 2 | 2 | 0 | 0 |
| Mahler | 1 | 1 | 0 | 0 | 2 | 0 |
| Mohorcic | 2 | 1 | 1 | 1 | 0 | 0 |
| Williams | 1 | 0 | 0 | 0 | 2 | 0 |
| **New York** | | | | | | |
| Drabek W,2-2 | 6 2-3 | 8 | 4 | 4 | 2 | 4 |
| Righetti S,22 | 2 1-3 | 3 | 0 | 0 | 0 | 2 |

Russell pitched to 2 batters in 5th inning, Mahler pitched to 2 batters in 6th inning. HBP: Incaviglia by Drabek, Pagliarulo by Witt. WP: Witt, Williams. Umpires: HP-Ford; 1B-Reed; 2B-Kosc; 3B-Garcia. T: 3:11. A: 20,109.

With the visiting team on the left, the home team on the right, the batting summary gives charged at-bats ('ab'), runs scored ('r'), basehits ('h'), and RBIs ('bi') for each player, with the totals for the teams below the players. The letters after the players' names indicate the fielding position at which they entered the game, with 'ph' for pinch-hitters and 'pr' for pinch-runners who did not play a fielding position.

Underneath the batting summary is the line score, showing the number of runs each team scored in each inning. For the Yankee–Texas game the line score shows that the Yankees took a big 4–0 lead in the first inning, Texas closed the gap to 5–4 in the top of the 5th, and then the Yankees pulled away.

Below the line score appear additional statistical details.

The **Game-Winning RBI** is credited for the run which puts a team ahead to stay. Since runs score without RBIs being credited (on misplays, stolen bases, and double plays), for some games there is *no* Game-Winning RBI.

'E: McDowell' indicates a fielding error by Texas centrefielder Oddibe McDowell.

'DP' shows the number of double plays by each team.

'LOB' is the number of baserunners 'left on base'; runners who reached base safely and who did not score and were not retired when the third out was made and the inning ended. This is a barometer of lost opportunity.

'2B' lists the players who hit doubles.

'3B' *would* list the players who hit triples; in this game there were none.

'HR' lists the players who hit home runs; the number in parentheses after the players' names shows how many home runs they now have this season. If a number appears *before* the parenthetical number, it shows the number of home runs hit in *that game* by the player.

'SB' lists the players who stole bases, with numbers showing game and season totals as with home runs.

'Caught stealing' lists the players who attempted to steal and were thrown out.

'S' *would* indicate successful sacrifice bunts; in this game there were none.

'SF' indicates sacrifice flies; fly balls to the outfield which score a runner from third, saving the batter a charged at-bat and crediting him with an RBI.

'Struck out Rangers ... Yankees' lists the players from each team who were struck out in the game.

Below the foregoing information is the pitching summary listing the pitchers for the visitors first, the home team second, in the order in which they appeared.

The notation 'L' next to Witt's name shows that he was the losing pitcher; '4–9' shows his season won-lost record after the defeat. The 'W' shows that Drabek was the winner. The 'S' shows that Righetti was credited with a save. There is always a 'W' and an 'L'; not always an 'S'.

'IP' is the number of innings pitched; the number of outs achieved divided by 3. *USA TODAY* shows Witt here at 2 2–3 innings; that can sometimes be listed as 2.2. In any case, it means he went out with two outs in the third inning.

'H' is the number of hits allowed.

'R' is the number of runs allowed.

'ER' is the number of *earned* runs allowed.

'BB' is the number of walks (bases on balls) given up.

'SO' is the number of strikeouts the pitcher got.

Underneath the pitching summary is some additional information.

The information about Russell and Mahler pitching to some batters before any outs were recorded helps you 'tie in' all the information in the box score. Without it, you would conclude that Russell – pitching $1\frac{2}{3}$ innings following the $2\frac{2}{3}$ by Witt – retired the side in the 3rd and pitched through the 4th. But he gave up two runs, and the Yankees scored *no* runs in the 3rd and 4th. That is explained by the fact that he pitched to two hitters in the 5th without being credited with any innings.

'HBP' shows players hit by a pitched ball and by which pitcher; the batter got to first base and was not charged with an at-bat. It is not unusual to see – as in this game – one player hit from each team if anybody is hit at all.

'WP' shows which pitchers threw wild pitches.

'PB' *would* indicate the catchers who had suffered passed balls, but in this game there were none.

'Umpires' names the men who officiated at the game and at which base they worked.

'T' is the time passed on the clock from the first pitch to the last out.

'A' is the paid attendance.

The only really badly designed aspect of box scores is the sophistication required to discern the starting line-ups and the substitutes. Before a streamlining of box scores in the 1960s, they listed all pinch-hitters and all the defensive positions any player occupied in a game. That made it much easier.

In the Yankee–Ranger game, the starting line-ups were probably:

*Texas*
McDowell cf
Fletcher ss
O'Brien 1b
Incaviglia rf
Ward lf
Parrish dh
Slaught c
Buechele 3b
Wilkerson 2b

*Yankees*
Henderson cf
Washington lf
Mattingly 1b
Easler dh
Winfield rf
Pagliarulo 3b
Wynegar c
Randolph 2b
Berra ss

with Paciorek, Sierra, and Harrah substitutes for the Rangers and Roenicke a substitute for the Yankees.

## SIGNIFICANT INFORMATION IN THE BOX SCORE

In a manner that might appear Holmesian to the uninitiated, a baseball fan can 'see' a lot of yesterday's game through the box score.

In the Yankee–Texas game, we might note:

Don Mattingly, the league's second leading hitter, was 0-for-four.

Texas manager Bobby Valentine is a big believer in righty-lefty platooning: he pinch-hit righty Paciorek for lefty McDowell against Yankee lefty Righetti, even though McDowell had been 2-for-4.

Yankee second baseman Willie Randolph had only *one* charged at-bat. Since the man behind him in the order (Dale Berra, son of Hall-of-Famer Yogi Berra) had *four* at-bats, Randolph must have had four plate appearances. Since he had no sacrifices, wasn't hit by the pitch, and there is no error by the catcher or other notation (as there might be) of a catcher's interference, he must have *walked three times*. Note that the Yankees had a total of nine walks from the five Ranger pitchers.

Since the Game-Winning RBI is credited to Yankee lead-off man Rickey Henderson, he must have had a home run to lead off the game. The Game-Winner was the first run the Yankees scored, since they were never caught after they took the lead, and they scored four runs in the first inning.

BASEBALL EXPLAINED

# AMERICAN

AMERICAN LEAGUE BASEBALL NEWS
FROM USA TODAY'S **NATIONAL NEWS NETWORK**

## STANDINGS

| EAST | W | L | Pct. | GB | Last 10 | Streak | Home | Div. |
|---|---|---|---|---|---|---|---|---|
| Boston | 57 | 35 | .620 | — | 4-6 | Lost 2 | 30-19 | 22-16 |
| New York | 53 | 41 | .564 | 5 | 7-3 | Won 1 | 23-23 | 19-20 |
| Cleveland | 49 | 41 | .544 | 7 | 6-4 | Won 1 | 26-19 | 15-21 |
| Toronto | 51 | 44 | .537 | 7½ | 7-3 | Won 2 | 26-25 | 25-15 |
| Baltimore | 49 | 43 | .533 | 8 | 5-5 | Lost 1 | 23-21 | 16-22 |
| Detroit | 47 | 45 | .511 | 10 | 7-3 | Lost 1 | 25-17 | 20-19 |
| Milwaukee | 43 | 48 | .473 | 13½ | 3-7 | Won 1 | 24-23 | 17-21 |

| WEST | W | L | Pct. | GB | Last 10 | Streak | Home | Div. |
|---|---|---|---|---|---|---|---|---|
| California | 49 | 43 | .533 | — | 4-6 | Lost 2 | 23-21 | 25-13 |
| Texas | 47 | 46 | .505 | 2½ | 2-8 | Lost 5 | 27-20 | 23-17 |
| Chicago | 42 | 49 | .462 | 6½ | 4-6 | Lost 1 | 23-26 | 19-19 |
| Kansas City | 43 | 50 | .462 | 6½ | 6-4 | Won 2 | 27-22 | 18-22 |
| Seattle | 42 | 53 | .442 | 8½ | 6-4 | Lost 1 | 24-21 | 18-22 |
| Minnesota | 39 | 54 | .419 | 10½ | 3-7 | Won 1 | 22-26 | 18-20 |
| Oakland | 38 | 57 | .400 | 12½ | 6-4 | Won 2 | 21-22 | 16-24 |

## MONDAY'S RESULTS

| | WP | LP |
|---|---|---|
| Cleveland 5, Chicago 2 | Yett (4-0) | J.Davis (4-5) |
| Minnesota 1, Detroit 0 | Viola (10-8) | Thurmond (0-1) |
| Kansas City 6, Baltimore 1 | Jackson (6-6) | Dixon (9-8) |
| Milwaukee 5, California 3 | Wegman (3-8) | Romanick (5-8) |
| New York 8, Texas 4 | Drabek (2-2) | B.Witt (4-9) |
| Oakland 5, Boston 2 | Young (7-6) | Hurst (5-4) |
| Toronto 8, Seattle 3 | Cerutti (5-2) | Huismann (2-3) |

## TUESDAY'S PITCHING LINE

| Teams | Pitchers | W-L | 1986 season IP | ERA | Career W-L | vs. opp. 85-86 W-L | vs. opp. IP | ERA |
|---|---|---|---|---|---|---|---|---|
| Boston at Oakland | Seaver (R) Andujar (R) | 4-7 5-2 | 98.2 50.0 | 4.01 3.42 | 3-1 1-0 | — 1-0 | — 9.0 | — 1.00 |
| Texas at New York | Correa (R) Rasmussen (L) | 6-7 11-2 | 121.1 124.1 | 3.86 3.40 | 9-6 0-0 | 1-0 — | 9.0 — | 0.00 — |
| Minnesota at Detroit | Blyleven (R) Terrell (R) | 9-8 8-8 | 150.2 128.1 | 4.78 4.42 | 10-14 2-1 | 1-2 1-0 | 21.0 13.0 | 6.86 6.23 |
| Chicago at Cleveland | Dotson (R) Candiotti (R) | 7-9 8-7 | 115.0 129.2 | 5.40 3.75 | 6-4 0-1 | 0-1 0-1 | 10.0 7.0 | 6.30 6.43 |
| Kansas City at Baltimore | Saberhagen (R) Davis (R) | 5-10 6-8 | 120.2 100.0 | 4.18 3.33 | 2-2 4-3 | 1-0 1-0 | 9.0 6.0 | 0.00 3.00 |
| Toronto at Seattle | Key (L) Langston (L) | 9-6 9-6 | 123.1 132.0 | 4.31 4.30 | 4-0 1-5 | 2-0 0-0 | 14.2 9.0 | 4.30 6.75 |
| Milwaukee at California | Nieves (L) Sutton (R) | 8-4 8-6 | 122.2 109.2 | 4.04 4.60 | 2-1 2-1 | 2-1 1-1 | 17.1 14.0 | 5.19 3.21 |

Source for standings and statistics: Elias Sports Bureau.

## WEDNESDAY'S GAMES

| | |
|---|---|
| Texas at New York | Chicago at Cleveland |
| Boston at Oakland | Kansas City at Baltimore |
| Toronto at Seattle | Milwaukee at California |
| Minnesota at Detroit | |

## SUNDAY'S RESULTS

| | |
|---|---|
| Chicago 8, New York 0 | Milwaukee 7, Oakland 2 (1st) |
| Detroit 4, Texas 0 | Oakland 4, Milwaukee 2 (2nd) |
| Baltimore 8, Minnesota 3 | Toronto 6, California 3 (10) |
| Kansas City 3, Cleveland 2 | Seattle 9, Boston 5 |

# NATIONAL

NATIONAL LEAGUE BASEBALL NEWS
FROM USA TODAY'S **NATIONAL NEWS NETWORK**

## STANDINGS

| EAST | W | L | Pct. | GB | Last 10 | Streak | Home | Div. |
|---|---|---|---|---|---|---|---|---|
| New York | 61 | 28 | .685 | — | 6-4 | Won 1 | 32-14 | 30-10 |
| Montreal | 48 | 40 | .545 | 12½ | 5-5 | Lost 2 | 21-21 | 24-19 |
| Philadelphia | 44 | 46 | .489 | 17½ | 4-6 | Won 2 | 22-18 | 19-23 |
| Chicago | 39 | 50 | .438 | 22 | 6-4 | Won 1 | 23-19 | 16-24 |
| St. Louis | 39 | 52 | .429 | 23 | 5-5 | Won 1 | 19-28 | 19-23 |
| Pittsburgh | 38 | 51 | .427 | 23 | 5-5 | Won 3 | 19-27 | 16-25 |

| WEST | W | L | Pct. | GB | Last 10 | Streak | Home | Div. |
|---|---|---|---|---|---|---|---|---|
| Houston | 51 | 42 | .548 | — | 6-4 | Won 4 | 28-20 | 26-19 |
| San Francisco | 50 | 43 | .538 | 1 | 5-5 | Lost 1 | 28-21 | 25-20 |
| San Diego | 46 | 47 | .495 | 5 | 3-7 | Lost 4 | 28-22 | 24-20 |
| Cincinnati | 43 | 46 | .483 | 6 | 7-3 | Lost 2 | 18-22 | 18-24 |
| Atlanta | 43 | 49 | .467 | 7½ | 2-8 | Lost 1 | 22-21 | 22-22 |
| Los Angeles | 42 | 50 | .457 | 8½ | 5-5 | Won 1 | 29-22 | 17-27 |

## MONDAY'S RESULTS

| | WP | LP |
|---|---|---|
| Chicago 6, San Diego 1 | Moyer (2-2) | Hoyt (5-5) |
| Philadelphia 3, Atlanta 1 | Tekulve (3-1) | Dedmon (3-5) |
| St. Louis 8, San Fran. 3 | Mathews (5-2) | Carlton (4-10) |
| New York 4, Cincinnati 2 | Aguilera (3-3) | Soto (3-8) |
| Houston 8, Montreal 7 | Kerfeld (7-1) | Reardon (6-5) |
| Only games scheduled | | |

## TUESDAY'S PITCHING LINE

| Teams | Pitchers | W-L | 1986 season IP | ERA | Career W-L | vs. opp. 85-86 W-L | vs. opp. IP | ERA |
|---|---|---|---|---|---|---|---|---|
| San Diego at Chicago | McCullers (R) Lynch (R) | 5-3 1-1 | 69.0 24.0 | 2.09 1.88 | 0-0 1-4 | 0-0 0-0 | 10.0 7.0 | 0.00 1.29 |
| Los Angeles at Pittsburgh | Pena (R) Rhoden (R) | 1-1 9-6 | 29.0 139.2 | 4.97 2.45 | 4-2 7-6 | 0-0 1-0 | 3.2 14.0 | 4.91 3.86 |
| New York at Cincinnati | Ojeda (L) Terry (R) | 11-2 0-2 | 122.1 38.2 | 2.13 6.28 | 2-0 0-0 | 2-0 0-0 | 15.0 2.0 | 0.60 4.50 |
| Philadelphia at Atlanta | K. Gross (R) Mahler (R) | 6-7 10-9 | 132.2 140.0 | 4.21 5.14 | 2-5 1-1 | 2-1 1-1 | 18.0 11.1 | 5.00 7.94 |
| San Francisco at St. Louis | Blue (L) Tudor (L) | 7-4 6-5 | 71.2 148.2 | 3.27 2.66 | 5-4 3-1 | 0-0 0-0 | 6.0 7.1 | 6.00 4.91 |
| Montreal at Houston | Youmans (R) Ryan (R) | 10-5 6-7 | 113.2 101.1 | 4.04 4.35 | 2-1 12-8 | 1-1 1-0 | 15.2 13.0 | 4.02 2.08 |

Source for standings and statistics: Elias Sports Bureau.

## WEDNESDAY'S GAMES

| | |
|---|---|
| San Diego at Chicago | Los Angeles at Pittsburgh |
| Montreal at Houston | Philadelphia at Atlanta |
| New York at Cincinnati | San Francisco at St. Louis |

## SUNDAY'S RESULTS

| | |
|---|---|
| Pittsburgh 4, San Diego 2 | Los Angeles 7, St. Louis 2 |
| Philadelphia 9, Cincinnati 3 | Houston 9, New York 8 (15) |
| San Francisco 5, Chicago 4 | Atlanta at Montreal, ppd., rain |

## TUESDAY IN BASEBALL

**1905:** Weldon Henley of the Philadelphia Athletics hurled a no-hitter defeating the St. Louis Browns 6-0 in the first game of a doubleheader. It was the highlight of Henley's 5-12 season.

**1906:** Bob Ewing pitched the Cincinnati Reds to a 10-3 victory over the Philadelphia Phillies without a single assist registered by his teammates.

**1926:** Cincinnati had four triples in an 11-run second inning as the Reds beat the Boston Braves 13-1. Curt Walker hit two in the inning to tie a National League record for most triples in an inning.

```
A's . . . . . . . . . . . 5
Red Sox. . . . . . . . 2
```

| BOSTON | ab | r | h | bi | OAKLAND | ab | r | h | bi |
|---|---|---|---|---|---|---|---|---|---|
| Barrett 2b | 3 | 0 | 1 | 0 | Phillips 2b | 4 | 1 | 1 | 1 |
| Boggs 3b | 3 | 0 | 0 | 0 | Griffin ss | 4 | 0 | 1 | 0 |
| Buckner dh | 4 | 0 | 0 | 0 | Canseco lf | 4 | 0 | 0 | 0 |
| Baylor lf | 3 | 1 | 0 | 0 | Kingman dh | 4 | 1 | 1 | 1 |
| Evans rf | 4 | 1 | 1 | 2 | Lansford 1b | 3 | 2 | 3 | 0 |
| Stapleton 1b | 3 | 0 | 0 | 0 | Baker rf | 3 | 0 | 0 | 0 |
| Stenhous ph | 0 | 0 | 0 | 0 | Davis rf | 0 | 0 | 0 | 0 |
| Quinones ss | 3 | 0 | 0 | 0 | Murphy cf | 3 | 1 | 1 | 1 |
| Sullivan c | 3 | 0 | 0 | 0 | Hill 3b | 4 | 0 | 1 | 0 |
| Romine cf | 2 | 0 | 1 | 0 | Tettleton c | 4 | 0 | 1 | 1 |
| Totals | 28 | 2 | 3 | 2 | Totals | 33 | 5 | 9 | 4 |

| Boston | 000 000 002— 2 |
|---|---|
| Oakland | 010 211 00x— 5 |

**Game-winning RBI: None.**
E: Sullivan. DP: Boston 1, Oakland 1. LOB: Boston 5, Oakland 8. 2B: Tettleton. 3B: Lansford. HR: Kingman (22), Phillips (5), Evans (13). SB: Romine (2). Caught stealing: Barrett, Boggs. Struck out: Red Sox (Buckner, Stapleton, Quinones, Boggs); A's (Canseco 2, Hill, Baker, Murphy, Tettleton).

|  | IP | H | R | ER | BB | SO |
|---|---|---|---|---|---|---|
| **Boston** | | | | | | |
| Hurst L,5-4 | 5 1-3 | 7 | 5 | 4 | 3 | 2 |
| Schiraldi | 2 2-3 | 2 | 0 | 0 | 1 | 4 |
| **Oakland** | | | | | | |
| Young W,7-6 | 8 2-3 | 3 | 2 | 2 | 5 | 4 |
| Bair | 1-3 | 0 | 0 | 0 | 1 | 0 |

WP: Young. T: 2:29. A: 19,267. Umpires: HP-Roe; 1B-Hirschbeck; 2B-Tschida; 3B-Bremigan.

From the Red Sox–A's box:

The A's controlled the entire game, holding the Red Sox scoreless until Boston entered the 9th behind, 5–0. Then the Sox scored their two runs on one pitch, a homer by Dwight Evans.

First baseman Carney Lansford had a big game for Oakland, going 3-for-3.

League-leading hitter Wade Boggs was hitless, like his pursuer Mattingly.

Rookie pitcher Young stifled the Sox completely, needing last-out help to end the game. He allowed only three hits, but his control was weak. Veteran Hurst, who has been having a good season and was the leading American League starter scheduled to work that day, was ineffective *and* had poor control.

From the Angels–Brewers box:

Milwaukee pitcher Wegman, who has had a less-than-mediocre year, certainly shut down California, even though they hit the ball regularly (he didn't strike people out.) California only mustered some offence after they were down, 5–0.

Milwaukee's Top 10 hitter, Robin Yount, modestly improved his .328 average by going 1-for-3 (which is .333.)

While the Mets continued to win and increase their big lead as the Expos lost, the Astros – known as a pitching-and-defence team – scored a slugfest victory to gain a game on their three closest pursuers.

```
Brewers. . . . . . . . 5
Angels. . . . . . . . . 3
```

| MILWAUKEE | ab | r | h | bi | CALIFORNIA | ab | r | h | bi |
|---|---|---|---|---|---|---|---|---|---|
| Molitor dh | 4 | 0 | 0 | 0 | Jones rf | 3 | 0 | 0 | 0 |
| Yount cf | 4 | 1 | 1 | 0 | Hendrick rf | 0 | 0 | 0 | 1 |
| Cooper 1b | 3 | 1 | 0 | 0 | Wilfong 2b | 3 | 0 | 1 | 0 |
| Oglivie | 4 | 0 | 1 | 0 | Grich 2b | 1 | 0 | 0 | 0 |
| Manninf lf | 0 | 0 | 0 | 0 | Joyner 1b | 4 | 0 | 0 | 0 |
| Lyle ss | 3 | 1 | 1 | 0 | Downing lf | 4 | 0 | 0 | 0 |
| Deer rf | 4 | 2 | 2 | 2 | Jackson dh | 4 | 0 | 0 | 0 |
| Sveum 3b | 4 | 0 | 2 | 2 | DeCinces 3b | 3 | 1 | 2 | 0 |
| Gantner 2b | 4 | 0 | 2 | 1 | Schofield ss | 4 | 1 | 1 | 0 |
| Moore c | 4 | 0 | 0 | 0 | Pettis cf | 3 | 1 | 1 | 1 |
| | | | | | Boone c | 1 | 0 | 0 | 1 |
| | | | | | Howell ph | 1 | 0 | 1 | 0 |
| | | | | | Narron c | 0 | 0 | 0 | 0 |
| Totals | 34 | 5 | 9 | 5 | Totals | 31 | 3 | 6 | 3 |

| Milwaukee | 014 000 000— 5 |
|---|---|
| California | 000 020 010— 3 |

**Game-winning RBI: Gantner (2).**
DP: California 1. LOB: Milwaukee 4, California 4. 2B: Sveum, Oglivie, Schofield. SF: Boone, Hendrick. Caught stealing: None. Struck out: Brewers (Riles, Deer, Sveum); Angels (Downing 2, Jones, Jackson).

|  | IP | H | R | ER | BB | SO |
|---|---|---|---|---|---|---|
| **Milwaukee** | | | | | | |
| Wegman W,3-8 | 7 | 5 | 3 | 3 | 1 | 2 |
| Plesac S,8 | 2 | 1 | 0 | 0 | 0 | 2 |
| **California** | | | | | | |
| Romanick L,5-8 | 4 2-3 | 8 | 5 | 5 | 2 | 0 |
| Lucas | 4 1-3 | 1 | 0 | 0 | 0 | 3 |

Wegman pitched to 2 batters in 8th.
T: 2:33. A: 22,449. Umpires: HP-Coble; 1B-McClelland; 2B-Young; 3B-Reilly.

## Mets......... 4
## Reds......... 2

```
NEW YORK              CINCINNATI
         ab r h bi             ab r h bi
Dykstra cf  4 0 1 0   Daniels lf  3 0 1 0
Backman 2b  4 1 2 1   Perez ph    1 0 0 0
Hernandz 1b 4 1 1 0   Rose 1b     4 0 0 0
Strawbrry rf 3 1 1 1  Parker rf   3 0 1 0
Carter c    5 0 1 2   Davis cf    4 1 1 0
Heep lf     1 0 0 0   Bell 3b     4 0 2 0
Mitchell lf 3 0 1 0   Rowdon ss   4 1 1 0
Orosco p    0 0 0 0   Butera c    3 0 0 0
Knight 3b   3 1 1 0   Venable ph  0 0 0 0
Santana ss  3 0 1 0   Oester 2b   4 0 1 1
Aguilera p  3 0 0 0   Soto p      1 0 0 0
Wilson lf   0 0 0 0   Murphy p    0 0 0 0
                      Milner ph   1 0 0 0
                      Willis p    0 0 0 0
                      Stillwell ph 1 0 1 0
                      Power p     0 0 0 0
                      Esasky ph   1 0 0 0
Totals     33 4 9 4   Totals     34 2 8 1
```

| | | | |
|---|---|---|---|
| New York | | 002 011 000— | 4 |
| Cincinnati | | 010 000 010— | 2 |

Game-winning RBI: Carter (10).
E: Knight, Daniels. DP: New York 1, Cincinnati 1. LOB: New York 11, Cincinnati 8. 2B: Strawberry, Daniels, Rowdon, Parker. 3B: Oester. S: Backman, Aguilera. SF: Strawberry. Caught stealing: None. Struck out: Mets (Carter, Heep); Reds (Daniels, Davis, Rowdon, Butera 2, Oester 2, Soto).

```
              IP  H  R ER BB SO
New York
Aguilera W,3-3 8  8  2  1  1  9
Orosco S,13    1  0  0  0  1  0
Cincinnati
Soto L,3-8     4  6  3  3  3  1
Murphy         1  0  0  0  0  0
Willis         2  3  1  1  3  0
Power          2  0  0  0  0  0
```

Soto pitched to 2 batters in 5th.
HBP: Daniels (by Aguilera). T: 3:07. A: 23,827. Umpires: HP-Gregg; 1B-Davis; 2B-Harvey; 3B-DeMuth.

From the Mets–Reds box:

Rick Aguilera had an overpowering game, striking out nine in eight innings. One of the two runs scored against him was due to Ray Knight's error (it was unearned; there are no other causes for an unearned run in the box score.)

Gary Carter has been a league leader in RBIs all year with a low batting average; he continued making his hits count, driving in two runs while going 1-for-5.

Note that in the National League, the pitcher is in the batting order, almost always in the 9th spot. Clearly, Mookie Wilson hit for Aguilera in the top of the 9th and then went into the game in leftfield. Kevin Mitchell had replaced Danny Heep, the starting leftfielder, probably as a pinch-hitter when lefty Murphy replaced righty Soto in the 5th inning. When Wilson went into the game, relief pitcher Orosco was slotted into the 6th spot in the batting order.

From the Astros–Expos box:

It was a great day for veteran Houston leftfielder Jose Cruz, 4-for-5 including a double and a home run, with the Game-Winner among three RBIs.

Starter Knudson pitched well for Houston until he ran out of gas; he is not a regular starter. He obviously started to tire in the 5th and collapsed in the 7th.

Since the big production was from the top of Montreal's order; 7 hits from the first three hitters, the chances are Knudson got through the 6th because he was facing the weaker hitters and the top of the order got to him twice in consecutive appearances. (NB: It is rare to spot such a mistake, but note that the Montreal individual hit totals add up to '11'. Since the hitting summary and pitching summary *both* say '12', chances are somebody was credited with a hit mistakenly not reported in the box.)

The game see-sawed. Montreal finally overcame an early Houston lead in the 7th and recaptured the lead after the Astros tied it. Houston won the game in their last at-bat.

Relief pitchers failed throughout this game, but Montreal ace Jeff Reardon had the worst day of all. After getting out the side in the 8th, he failed to retire any of five batters faced in the 9th.

Houston relief pitcher Kerfeld gave up the lead run to Montreal in the 8th, but was

## Astros......... 8
## Expos ......... 7

| MONTREAL | | | | | HOUSTON | | | | |
|---|---|---|---|---|---|---|---|---|---|
| | ab | r | h | bi | | ab | r | h | bi |
| Raines lf | 5 | 2 | 2 | 3 | Doran 2b | 4 | 1 | 0 | 0 |
| Webster cf | 5 | 2 | 3 | 0 | Hatcher cf | 5 | 3 | 4 | 0 |
| Dawson rf | 3 | 0 | 2 | 3 | Garner 3b | 3 | 0 | 1 | 1 |
| Wallach 3b | 5 | 0 | 1 | 0 | Walling 3b | 1 | 1 | 0 | 0 |
| Krnchick 1b | 4 | 1 | 1 | 0 | Davis 1b | 4 | 1 | 3 | 3 |
| Fitzgerald c | 2 | 0 | 0 | 0 | Bass rf | 4 | 0 | 0 | 0 |
| Bilardello c | 1 | 0 | 0 | 0 | Kerfeld p | 0 | 0 | 0 | 0 |
| Gonzales ss | 4 | 0 | 0 | 0 | Pankovits ph | 1 | 0 | 1 | 0 |
| Newman 2b | 3 | 1 | 1 | 0 | Cruz lf | 5 | 2 | 4 | 3 |
| Schatzeder p | 1 | 0 | 0 | 0 | Ashby c | 4 | 0 | 3 | 1 |
| McGaffigan p | 0 | 0 | 0 | 0 | Walker pr | 0 | 0 | 0 | 0 |
| Wright ph | 1 | 0 | 0 | 0 | Mizerock c | 0 | 0 | 0 | 0 |
| St.Claire p | 0 | 0 | 0 | 0 | Thon ss | 2 | 0 | 0 | 0 |
| Wohlford ph | 1 | 1 | 1 | 0 | Reynolds ss | 2 | 0 | 0 | 0 |
| Burke p | 0 | 0 | 0 | 0 | Knudson p | 3 | 0 | 0 | 0 |
| Moore ph | 1 | 0 | 0 | 0 | Andersen p | 0 | 0 | 0 | 0 |
| Reardon p | 0 | 0 | 0 | 0 | Gainey rf | 0 | 0 | 0 | 0 |
| Totals | 36 | 7 | 12 | 6 | Totals | 38 | 8 | 16 | 7 |

| Montreal | 000 030 310— 7 |
|---|---|
| Houston | 200 201 102— 8 |

None out when winning run scored.
Game-winning RBI: Cruz (8).
E: Wallach, McGaffigan, Ashby, Reynolds. DP: Montreal 2, Houston 2. LOB: Montreal 6, Houston 10. 2B: Hatcher, Cruz. 3B: Webster. HR: Cruz (2), Raines (7). SB: Wallach (6), Newman (11), Raines (44), Webster 2 (24), Walker (8), Hatcher 2 (23). Caught stealing: None. S: Bilardello. SF: Davis. Struck out: Expos (Raines, Wright, Moore), Astros (Knudson, Reynolds, Cruz).

| | IP | H | R | ER | BB | SO |
|---|---|---|---|---|---|---|
| **Montreal** | | | | | | |
| Schatzeder | 3 1-3 | 5 | 4 | 3 | 1 | 0 |
| McGaffigan | 2-3 | 0 | 0 | 0 | 0 | 1 |
| St. Claire | 2 | 4 | 1 | 1 | 0 | 1 |
| Burke | 1 | 2 | 1 | 1 | 0 | 1 |
| Reardon L,6-5 | 1 | 5 | 2 | 2 | 2 | 0 |
| **Houston** | | | | | | |
| Knudson | 6 1-3 | 6 | 4 | 4 | 2 | 2 |
| Andersen | 2-3 | 3 | 2 | 2 | 0 | 0 |
| Kerfeld W,7-1 | 2 | 3 | 1 | 1 | 1 | 1 |

Reardon pitched to 5 batters in 9th.
T: 3:03. A: 13,753. Umpires: HP-Crawford; 1B-C.Williams; 2B-Wendelstedt; 3B-Bonin.

turned from a loser to a winner by the last-ditch Houston rally.

Despite a tied-for-first-place team and a tough opponent, the Astros drew only 13,753 fans: the average required to draw a million for the season. Not enough.

The game between the Giants and the Cardinals was close until the Cardinals broke it open in the 7th inning. The Giants, behind veteran lefty Steve Carlton trying to salvage a few more wins in the twilight of his career, took an early lead. St Louis chipped away at Carlton, got the lead from him, and made him the losing pitcher. But they bombed his relief help.

From the Giants–Cardinals box:

To demonstrate the importance to baseball managers of statistical evidence over recent performance, Carlton was hit for in the top of the 7th, even though he drove in the Giant runs with a homer in the 2nd inning.

## Cardinals....... 8
## Giants ......... 3

| SAN FRANCISCO | | | | | ST. LOUIS | | | | |
|---|---|---|---|---|---|---|---|---|---|
| | ab | r | h | bi | | ab | r | h | bi |
| Kutcher cf | 4 | 0 | 0 | 0 | Coleman lf | 4 | 1 | 1 | 1 |
| Thompsn 2b | 3 | 0 | 1 | 0 | Smith ss | 3 | 1 | 0 | 0 |
| Leonard lf | 3 | 0 | 0 | 0 | McGee cf | 3 | 3 | 2 | 3 |
| Davis rf | 4 | 0 | 0 | 0 | Knicely 1b | 3 | 1 | 1 | 0 |
| Brown 3b | 3 | 0 | 0 | 0 | Ford rf | 1 | 0 | 1 | 3 |
| Brenly 1b | 3 | 1 | 0 | 0 | Herr 2b | 3 | 0 | 1 | 1 |
| Melvin c | 4 | 1 | 2 | 0 | Van Slyke rf | 4 | 0 | 1 | 0 |
| Uribe ss | 3 | 0 | 0 | 0 | Lawless 3b | 2 | 0 | 1 | 0 |
| Spilman ph | 1 | 0 | 0 | 0 | Pendleton 3b | 2 | 1 | 1 | 0 |
| Carlton p | 2 | 1 | 1 | 3 | Lavalliere c | 3 | 0 | 0 | 0 |
| Youngbld ph | 1 | 0 | 0 | 0 | Mathews p | 2 | 0 | 0 | 0 |
| Robinson p | 0 | 0 | 0 | 0 | Forsch pr | 0 | 1 | 0 | 0 |
| Minton p | 0 | 0 | 0 | 0 | Soff p | 1 | 0 | 0 | 0 |
| Totals | 31 | 3 | 4 | 3 | Totals | 31 | 8 | 9 | 8 |

| San Francisco | 030 000 000— 3 |
|---|---|
| St. Louis | 100 201 40x— 8 |

Game-winning RBI: Herr (5).
E: Lawless, Leonard. LOB: San Francisco 5, St. Louis 4. 2B: Melvin, Knicely, Ford. HR: McGee 2 (6), Carlton (1). SB: Leonard (16). Caught stealing: Brown. S: Herr. Struck out: Giants (Uribe, Thompson, Leonard, Brown, Spilman); Cardinals (Smith, Soff).

| | IP | H | R | ER | BB | SO |
|---|---|---|---|---|---|---|
| **San Francisco** | | | | | | |
| Carlton L,4-10 | 6 | 5 | 4 | 3 | 1 | 1 |
| Robinson | 1-3 | 2 | 3 | 3 | 0 | 0 |
| Minton | 1 2-3 | 2 | 1 | 1 | 2 | 1 |
| **St. Louis** | | | | | | |
| Mathews W,5-2 | 7 | 4 | 3 | 3 | 2 | 3 |
| Soff | 2 | 0 | 0 | 0 | 1 | 2 |

HBP: Brown, Robinson (by Mathews). T: 2:32. A: 23,340. Umpires: HP-Marsh; 1B-Davidson; 2B-McSherry; 3B-Hallion.

Willie McGee was the leader on the Cardinal championship team of 1985 but was having a terrible year in 1986. A game like this one – two home runs in three at-bats – can be a spark to get a player going.

Cardinal rookie pitcher Mathews was extremely successful, allowing only 7 baserunners in 7 innings (4 hits, 2 walks, 1 hit batsman.)

Giant third baseman Chris Brown – effectively entering the action as the league's leading hitter since Hubie Brooks of Montreal is out for the year – was 0-for-3. He has certainly been passed by Montreal's Tim Raines, who was 2-for-5, and perhaps by other close pursuers as well.

In the States, the Sunday editions of newspapers carry the 'Major League Averages' (known as the 'Sunday averages'), complete through the preceding Friday for all the players who have played approximately half-time or more. The Sunday listings go deeper than the qualifiers for the batting title (appearance is based on charged at-bats) or, for the pitchers, the ERA crown (appearances are actually based on *total decisions*).

In its generally expansive baseball coverage, *USA TODAY* introduced a weekly summary, by each team, of the statistical performance of *all* the players on the roster. In slightly abbreviated form, this summary appears each week in the International Edition as well.

For batters, listed in the order of their batting average, the chart shows at-bats, runs, hits, homers, RBIs, and the batting average. For pitchers it lists the won-lost record, innings pitched, walks allowed, strikeouts recorded, saves, and earned run average.

The illustrations show that information as it appeared in the International Edition of *USA TODAY* on Wednesday, 23 July 1986, for the Red Sox and the Yankees.

Note that both teams rely for hitters with low averages for a lot of run production (runs scored and RBIs): particularly Baylor and Buckner for the Red Sox and Winfield for the Yankees.

Note that Roger Clemens has, by far, the outstanding pitching statistics on either team for anybody having pitched a significant number of innings. At this point in the season, he is striking out more than one man for each inning pitched. No other starter on either team allows fewer than 3 earned runs per game.

Note that Rickey Henderson of the Yankees scores a lot more runs per at-bat or per hit than any other player on either team. This *could* be a statistical anomaly if Henderson *walked* an outrageous percentage of the time. He walks a lot, but he also scores a disproportionate share of the time.

## RED SOX

| Batting | AB | R | H | HR | RBI | AVG |
|---|---|---|---|---|---|---|
| Boggs | 321 | 59 | 116 | 5 | 44 | .361 |
| Rice | 362 | 57 | 120 | 9 | 60 | .331 |
| Barrett | 368 | 52 | 106 | 2 | 28 | .288 |
| Armas | 193 | 18 | 53 | 4 | 19 | .275 |
| Gedman | 270 | 23 | 73 | 5 | 32 | .270 |
| Evans | 323 | 50 | 85 | 13 | 63 | .263 |
| Hoffman | 19 | 1 | 5 | 0 | 1 | .263 |
| Buckner | 375 | 43 | 95 | 10 | 53 | .253 |
| Quinones | 162 | 22 | 40 | 2 | 15 | .247 |
| Baylor | 340 | 56 | 82 | 16 | 59 | .241 |
| Romine | 26 | 4 | 6 | 0 | 2 | .231 |
| Romero | 149 | 25 | 33 | 0 | 16 | .221 |
| Sullivan | 73 | 9 | 14 | 1 | 10 | .192 |
| Stapleton | 17 | 4 | 3 | 0 | 1 | .176 |
| Stenhouse | 15 | 1 | 2 | 0 | 1 | .133 |
| Tarver | 15 | 2 | 2 | 0 | 1 | .133 |

| Pitching | W-L | IP | BB | SO | SV | ERA |
|---|---|---|---|---|---|---|
| Stewart | 3-1 | 26.1 | 16 | 22 | 0 | 1.71 |
| Schiraldi | 0-0 | 5.0 | 2 | 7 | 0 | 1.80 |
| Clemens | 16-2 | 153.0 | 37 | 154 | 0 | 2.59 |
| Hurst | 5-4 | 82.2 | 23 | 91 | 0 | 3.05 |
| Sambito | 1-0 | 29.2 | 8 | 20 | 9 | 3.64 |
| Boyd | 11-6 | 128.2 | 30 | 70 | 0 | 3.71 |
| Crawford | 0-0 | 39.1 | 13 | 24 | 3 | 3.89 |
| Seaver | 4-7 | 98.2 | 32 | 47 | 0 | 4.01 |
| Stanley | 5-3 | 52.2 | 15 | 37 | 14 | 4.10 |
| Sellers | 3-5 | 59.1 | 30 | 34 | 0 | 4.25 |
| Nipper | 4-6 | 88.1 | 25 | 47 | 0 | 4.79 |
| Lollar | 2-0 | 34.1 | 29 | 25 | 0 | 5.24 |

| YANKEES | | | | | | |
|---|---|---|---|---|---|---|
| Batting | AB | R | H | HR | RBI | AVG |
| Mattingly | 400 | 64 | 136 | 16 | 68 | .340 |
| Easler | 313 | 43 | 105 | 8 | 49 | .335 |
| Roenicke | 105 | 11 | 32 | 3 | 16 | .305 |
| Hassey | 177 | 23 | 53 | 6 | 27 | .299 |
| Pasqua | 113 | 17 | 33 | 8 | 18 | .292 |
| Henderson | 371 | 88 | 104 | 16 | 52 | .280 |
| Washington | 50 | 9 | 14 | 3 | 7 | .280 |
| Pagliarulo | 305 | 53 | 84 | 23 | 56 | .275 |
| Randolph | 329 | 47 | 85 | 1 | 35 | .258 |
| Fischlin | 52 | 6 | 13 | 0 | 1 | .250 |
| Berra | 100 | 10 | 24 | 2 | 13 | .240 |
| Winfield | 319 | 54 | 75 | 13 | 57 | .235 |
| Wynegar | 175 | 18 | 38 | 7 | 28 | .217 |
| Zuvella | 39 | 2 | 4 | 0 | 2 | .103 |

| Pitching | W-L | IP | BB | SO | SV | ERA |
|---|---|---|---|---|---|---|
| Montefusco | 0-0 | 12.1 | 5 | 3 | 0 | 2.19 |
| Scurry | 0-1 | 14.0 | 10 | 11 | 2 | 2.57 |
| Stoddard | 0-0 | 10.0 | 1 | 6 | 0 | 2.70 |
| Righetti | 6-4 | 57.0 | 24 | 45 | 22 | 3.32 |
| Rasmussen | 11-2 | 124.1 | 51 | 87 | 0 | 3.40 |
| Tewksbury | 6-4 | 92.2 | 18 | 34 | 0 | 3.59 |
| Holland | 1-0 | 25.0 | 5 | 24 | 0 | 3.60 |
| John | 3-1 | 37.1 | 9 | 12 | 0 | 3.62 |
| Guidry | 4-8 | 106.2 | 23 | 76 | 0 | 4.05 |
| Nielsen | 2-1 | 21.1 | 5 | 10 | 0 | 4.22 |
| Niekro | 8-6 | 96.1 | 43 | 46 | 0 | 4.39 |
| Fisher | 4-5 | 56.2 | 27 | 36 | 4 | 4.92 |
| Drabek | 2-2 | 48.1 | 21 | 25 | 0 | 5.21 |
| Shirley | 0-4 | 66.0 | 28 | 42 | 1 | 6.14 |

decisions miles away and hours after a game.

When somebody talking baseball in an American bar says, 'Did you see that no-hitter Mike Witt pitched last night?', he usually means: 'Did you see the box score?'

## GETTING EVEN MORE STATISTICAL DATA

Although *USA TODAY* and other daily newspapers in the US provide a plethora of information, the most dedicated baseball fans also read *The Sporting News*, a 100-year-old weekly publication which has the most complete baseball coverage available. *TSN* has reports each week from correspondents covering each club for a local daily, and its statistical review exceeds what is available from any other source. A dedicated British fan would be well advised to subscribe to *TSN*, to augment the coverage in *USA TODAY*.

## GREAT INDIVIDUAL PERFORMANCES, MORE BOX SCORE INSIGHT

The important individual game records of baseball, established as they have been over a long period of time, are seldom broken.

Last year, Roger Clemens of Boston struck out 20 Seattle Mariners in a 9-innings game, breaking the record of 19 previously held by Tom Seaver and Steve Carlton. That was unusual.

The record for home runs in a game by one hitter is *four*, first done in 1897 in the pre-Modern era, achieved for the first time in the twentieth century by Lou Gehrig in the 1930s, most recently by Bob Horner of the Braves last year. Even in an extra-inning game, nobody has hit more.

A pitcher can throw a **shutout** (allowing no runs) fairly often; the league leader will have 4–6; a pitcher with 10 in a season is hitting

## YOU DON'T HAVE TO SEE THE GAMES

A lot of games in the States are televised, but most fans get most of their fun following baseball through the standings, box scores, and Sunday averages. No matter how elaborate the satellite hook-up, or how sophisticated the VCR, or how many hours available to watch, nobody can watch 13 Major League games a day.

But everybody can follow 26 teams, 600–650 players, every day. From their numbers in the box scores, the fans will know them. A fan can spot a rising young star without ever laying eyes on him; see that a pitcher is losing his fastball without watching him pitch; and read between the lines of a manager's strategic numbers more reminiscent of the Dead Ball Era, when shutout records were set that still stand. He can throw a **no-hitter**, allowing no hits while gathering the 27 outs. There are usually 1–3 no-hitters in a Major League season of over 2000 games.

The **perfect game** is achieved by a pitcher allowing no baserunners in a game. This requires the cooperation of the defence; an error spoils a perfect game as much as a walk or a hit.

No batter has ever had more than 7 hits in a game.

The record for **total bases** in a game is *18* – the astounding number achieved by Joe Adcock of the 1954 Milwaukee Braves when he hit four home runs and a double against the Dodgers.

The fan using the box scores as the morning eye-opener will find it extra-strong coffee the day of a pitching perfecto or the first 5-homer game.

# APPENDICES

## READER'S GUIDE TO APPENDICES

The team introductions and player profiles that follow were written for *Baseball Explained* by Bob Carroll.

The team write-ups review history, but also detail the team's current prospects. A little of the information will change before you read it, but the historical report retains its value. Season stats in parentheses refer to the 1986 records.

The all-star profiles start with a statistical summary similar to what is on the back of an American baseball card (sold with sticks of gum, they are often a youngster's first introduction to higher mathematics). All of the headings for the statistical summary are explained in the book.

Bob touches on two post-season awards that are not covered in the text. The **Cy Young Award**, named for the biggest winner in baseball history, is awarded each year to the top pitcher in each league as voted by the sportswriters. The **Most Valuable Player Award** (MVP), also goes to a player designated by the writers covering the league. Nobody is exactly sure what a 'most valuable player' is, but players who have good seasons while their teams win tend to do well in the voting.

In the interests of ready reference, teams and players are listed in alphabetical order within their respective leagues.

The table at the back of the book lists the pennant winners and World Champions of the 'modern' (post-1901) era.

# 1 THE AMERICAN LEAGUE

## BALTIMORE ORIOLES

The Orioles have enough big bats to fill Dracula's attic but their pitching needs new blood.

This franchise was originally the St Louis Browns, a charter member of the American League from the turn of the century. The Browns were legendary losers whose fan base atrophied in a market with the perennially successful Cardinals. In 1954, the franchise moved to Baltimore and became the Orioles, taking the name as well as the place of a longstanding minor league team in that Maryland city.

By the 1960s, the Orioles had contending teams on a regular basis. Led by Brooks Robinson – one of the best-fielding third basemen in baseball history – Frank Robinson and Boog Powell, they had a vicious home run attack. And the Baltimore farm system regularly yielded outstanding young pitchers: Wally Bunker, Dave McNally, Milt Pappas, Chuck Estrada, Jack Fisher, Steve Barber. When the Orioles beat the Dodgers in four straight games to take the 1966 World Series, they reached the pinnacle and, until last year, have stayed pretty close to it ever since.

The Orioles were the American League's most successful team during the 1970s because they always had more pitching than anyone else. One year they paraded out four 20-game winners. Now their great righthander Jim Palmer has retired to a TV announcer's booth. Mike Cueller, Dave McNally and the others who used to foil the opposition have also hung up their spikes.

In 1987, the Orioles started the season without their longtime manager, feisty and combative Earl Weaver, who has retired. Veteran Coach Cal Ripkin Sr, takes over. The new field boss has no worries about his shortstop, the AL's best – a hard-hitting fellow named Cal Ripkin Jr. Young Cal had an off-year in 1986, but still totalled 25 home runs, 81 RBIs, and a .282 BA. There's not another shortstop in either league who wouldn't take those figures and ask for a raise. Moreover, the kid can field as well as anyone and hasn't missed an inning in four seasons.

At first base, Eddie Murray (17 HR, 84 RBI, .305) missed a lot of innings last year with injuries. Healthy, Murray joins Cal Jr for a potent one-two punch. Centrefielder Fred Lynn (23, 67, .287) seems ALWAYS to be injured. Lee Lacy (11, 47, .287) in rightfield is healthy but 38 years old. Baltimore traded during the winter to add another power hitter, catcher Terry Kennedy (12, 57, .264), but had to give up a much-needed pitcher to get him.

The current Baltimore slabmen resemble the former greats the way an armadillo resembles an Eskimo. Mike Flanagan (11-13, 4.24 ERA) and Scott McGregor (11-15, 4.52) look about three or four years past their best days. Ken Dixon (11-13, 4.58) may never blossom. Mike Boddicker was 14-12 but his 4.70 ERA inspires confidence only in opponents. Relief man Don Aase had 34 saves before overwork made him ineffective in September.

If the Orioles could resurrect the pitchers of a decade ago and graft them to this year's lineup, they'd destroy the rest of the league. As it is, they can only hope some of the young pitchers in the farm system grow up fast.

## BOSTON RED SOX

In legend, the Boston Red Sox are always loaded with lumbering righthanded power hitters and lots of people who can't pitch. That's because the 'Green Monster,' Fenway Park's infamous 40-foot leftfield wall, sits invitingly a mere 315 feet from home plate (most pitchers say closer). It's true the Monster makes righty powderpuff hitters into awesome sluggers and sends pitchers' ERAs into the red zone. And it's true that over the years the Sox front office sometimes let Sox pitching go hang and collected righthanded hitters the way the Gabors collect husbands.

It's also true that in their 86 summers (74 in Fenway) the Red Sox nevertheless have employed plenty of excellent pitchers and that most of their best hitters have batted lefthanded. You just can't trust those legends anymore. The best batsman ever to play for Boston – maybe the best to play anywhere – was Ted Williams, the last major leaguer to hit over .400 – .406 in 1941. From 1939 through 1960, Ted averaged .344 and popped 521 home runs, while winning six batting championships. Carl Yastrzemski took over Ted's leftfield spot in '61 and stayed until 1983, winning a couple of batting titles himself and totalling 452 home runs. Both batted lefthanded.

So does current Red Sox batting leader Wade Boggs, a third baseman who wrapped up his third batting crown in five years with a .357 mark in 1986. He knocked 207 basehits and walked 105 times, putting him on base more often than chalk.

Boston has been blessed with many fearsome sluggers in their history: twice batting champ Pete Runnels, slugging shortstop Vern Stephens, Hall of Fame second baseman Bobby Doerr, and, more recently, Tony Conigliaro, Rico Petrocelli, Jim Rice, Dwight Evans, and the young Fred Lynn.

The Red Sox have a long, illustrious history: full of great ballplayers and very few championships. They've lost 7-game World Series three times since World War II, in 1946, 1967, and 1986. The last time they won it all was in 1918, when their star pitcher was the future home run king, Babe Ruth.

The Wall at Fenway, looming over the leftfielder's back, entices righthanded hitters, but it hasn't stopped the Red Sox from featuring some great lefty pitchers, most notably the immortal Lefty Grove and Mel Parnell. Righthander Jim Lonborg was the pitching leader of the 1967 A.L. Championship team, but his career was shortened by a knee injury in a skiing accident.

As for current pitching, there just wasn't anybody better last year than fireballing Roger Clemens, who took the A.L. Cy Young Award and Most Valuable Player Trophy with league leading 24-4 and 2.48 stats. More important, he paced Boston into the World Series.

He holds the key to their '87 hopes again, but this time he may get more help from lefty Bruce Hurst (13-8, 2.99) and Oil Can Boyd (16-10, 3.78). Hurst came on strong at the end of the season, but Boyd is as erratic as the pendulum in a funhouse clock.

Big Jim Rice (20, 110, .324), Dwight Evans (26, 97, .259), and Don Baylor (31, 94, .238) are righthanded hitters to take advantage of the Green Monster. They'll spend the summer driving in Boggs and pesky second baseman Marty Barrett (4, 60, .288).

The Red Sox command New England; they regularly pile up high attendance figures despite playing in the smallest park in the majors: Fenway's seating capacity of about 33,000 is about 40 per cent less than most other major league parks. The 1987 Sox are fighting a jinx. No team has repeated as A.L. East champ since 1981.

## CALIFORNIA ANGELS

Last season the Angels were only one strike away from their first American League pennant. Ahead in the League Championship Series three games to one, with a comfortable ninth-inning lead in the fifth game, the Angels somehow gave up a pair of two-run homers, lost in extra innings, and then dropped two more games by one-sided scores to earn the right to watch the World Series on television. For Manager Gene Mauch, who has spent a quarter century as one of baseball's most respected skippers yet never won a pennant, 1986 capped a frustrating career.

The California (né Los Angeles) Angels were formed in the first major league expansion, when the American League went from 8 to 10 teams in 1961. After a season in a former minor league park, Wrigley Field, and two sharing Dodger Stadium with its owners, they moved to their present home in Anaheim, a city of 100,000 just south of L.A., and to a spanking new stadium usually referred to as 'The Big A'.

The early Angels featured a few solid ballplayers: shortstop Jim Fregosi was a star, as was righthander Dean Chance – who had a spectacular season in 1964 (20–9, 1.65 ERA). Lefty Bo Belinsky pitched a no-hitter for the early Angels, but his career was more renowned for the starlets he dated than the games he won.

In the mid-1970s, when players won free agency and the right to sell their services to the highest bidder, Angel owner (ex-movie cowboy star) Gene Autry opened his cheque book and brought star after star to Anaheim: Bobby Grich, Don Baylor, Bob Boone, Reggie Jackson, and Rod Carew, among others. All this investment has brought the Angels close – a couple of division championships – but they have yet to make the World Series.

For 1987, the Angels abandoned their traditional persona of aging free agent sluggers, in hopes of finally winning it all with a nice mix of experience, youth and pitching. Jackson was released and Grich has retired. First baseman Wally Joyner (22 HR, 100 RBI, .290) – only 25 – provides the power, and 29-year-old centrefielder Gary Pettis (50 SB) gives them speed. Young Dick Schofield (13 HR, .249) established himself as one of the league's better shortstops in 1986. Veterans like outfielder Brian Downing (20 HR, 95 RBI) and third baseman Doug DeCinces (26, 96) lend a steadying hand.

The team's real strength is in its pitching. Six-foot-seven stringbean Mike Witt (18–10, 208 SO) is the ace of the staff at 28. Smooth lefty John Candelaria (10–2, 2.55 ERA), only a whit shorter than Witt at six-foot-six, appears to be over the arm trouble that held him back for a couple of seasons. The third starter is Kirk McCaskill (17–10, 202 SO). Crafty Don Sutton is 42 this year but has shown he can still pitch. He was 15–11 in 1986 to move his career total to 310 wins.

## CHICAGO WHITE SOX

Fans of the South Side Sox are not as famous for their suffering as North Side Cubs masochists, but in many ways they have more cause to parade their anguish. In the last sixty-seven years, the White Sox have struggled to only one lonely pennant. And then they lost the World Series. Worse, at ancient Comiskey Park (built in 1910, making it the oldest in the majors) Sox fans can't regularly bask in the summer sunshine. The Sox play mostly at night – the better to hide their inadequacies. A brand new park is promised for 1990; fans pray it won't be host to S.O.S. – Same Old Sox.

The White Sox entered the American League as a charter member under the ownership of Charles A. Comiskey, whose family owned the team until the 1950s. In their first years, the Sox were an up-and-down team, often finishing with a losing record, but winning a couple of early pennants.

Around World War I, the White Sox had the best team in baseball. Then seven of their players took bribes to lose the 1919 World Series and became for ever branded 'the Black Sox'. As a result, Judge Kenesaw Mountain Landis was installed as the first strong Commissioner of Baseball to govern the game. His irrevocable expulsion of the crooked seven (and an eighth who kept silent despite his knowledge of the fix) has kept baseball free of similar incidents since.

In 1920, to win back the game's shaken popularity, the baseball establishment 'juiced up' (made more lively) the baseball, making home runs easier. The popularity returned, but the Black Sox remain infamous, and nearly every summer the White Sox do public penance by allowing themselves to be flogged by most of the American League.

The Sox didn't win another pennant until 1959, despite some great players in their line-up. Long-time shortstop Luke Appling could hit .300 as easily as most men brush their teeth. Pitcher Ted Lyons was a consistent winner for twenty-one seasons despite inconsistent support.

The 1959 Sox featured a Go-Go attack: not many home runs but a lot of hits, bunts and basestealing. The leaders were shortstop and basestealing king Luis Aparicio, Most Valuable Player and second baseman Nellie Fox, catcher Sherm Lollar, and a pitching staff that featured Hall of Famer Early Wynn in his last twenty-win year. The pennant interrupted the Yankees' string of nine flags in ten years, but the Sox dropped a 6-game World Series to the Dodgers.

The Pale Hose have a few fine players today. Outfielder Harold Baines (.296, 21 HR, 88 RBI in 1986) is an All-Star and first baseman Greg Walker had 13 home runs and 55 RBIs before a wrist injury put him out halfway through the 1986 season. Shortstop Ozzie Guillen was A.L. Rookie of the Year in 1985.

Until they come up with a half dozen more like these, they'll languish in the cellar.

## CLEVELAND INDIANS

It's been a long dry spell for the Indians, another charter American League team. In 1948 they drew a then-record 2.8 million fans while winning a pennant and World Series. Six years later, in 1954, they won a league-record 111 games. They haven't had a pennant since.

Cleveland's Municipal Stadium is right next to Lake Erie and has long been called 'the mistake on the lake'. It can hold 80,000 people without splitting a gut, but when the crowd is small it's lonesome as an arctic night. For the past two decades the stadium was getting lonesomer every year. The wonder was the loyal few who turned out to watch the tired menagerie of has-beens and never-would-bes that the front office pretended were major league ballplayers.

In their first sixty-plus years, Cleveland had many great players. From Tris Speaker in the early years (the leader of the World Championship team in 1920), to sluggers Hal Trosky and Earl Averill in the 1930s, to 'boy wonder' playing-manager Lou Boudreau and Bob Feller – the great strikeout pitcher whose career flanked World War II – the Tribe marshalled some outstanding stars on generally competitive teams. The 1950s Indians, who usually finished second to the Yankees, featured a great assembly of starting pitchers: Early Wynn, Bob Lemon, and Mike Garcia, joined by the aging Feller. And the late 1950s teams had Rocky Colavito, an outstanding home run slugger.

When Colavito was traded away in 1960, the team started on a downward trail that included poor performances, a near-empty park, and ownership threats of moving the franchise. Fans said the team couldn't be moved but might be extradited.

All that has changed with the arrival of a pride of exciting young lions who have Clevelanders seriously thinking pennant for the first time since the 1950s. Last season Cleveland bottoms wiped dust off seats that hadn't been used since Eisenhower was president. The feeling is the Indians will win it all pretty soon.

Fiery shortstop Julio Franco (10, 74, .306 in 1986) may never earn a Golden Glove, but his bat more than makes up for any fielding flaws. Big Joe Carter (29, 121, .302) is an emerging superstar in the outfield. Versatile Cory Snyder (24, 69, .272) proved in only two-thirds of the 1986 season that he deserves a regular spot in the line-up. Third baseman Brook Jacoby (17, 80, .288), outfielder Mel Hall (18, 76, .296), and second baseman Tony Bernazard (17, 73, .301) had fine years. All up and down the line-up there's speed and power.

The Tribe's pitching leaves something to be desired. At 48, knuckleballer Phil Niekro (11–11, 4.32) is something of a national monument, but even monuments eventually crumble. Tom Candiotti (16–12, 3.57), another knuckler, is the ace. Ken Schrom (14–7, 4.54) won more often than he deserved to. The main hope is 22-year-old Greg Swindell who was 5–2 in September.

The 1954 team, built on pitching, won a lot of 1–0 and 2–1 games. The 1987 Indians will win them 9–8 and 14–12.

## DETROIT TIGERS

When the Tigers won the 1984 World Series, their fans went slightly crazy. The championship was a glorious moment for a city long-famous as America's automobile manufacturing capital but more recently deep in the economic doldrums.

Cozy Tiger Stadium, hard by downtown Detroit, is one of the oldest and best-for-fans parks in the big leagues. It's a hitter's ballpark and the Bengals have traditionally played an exciting kind of baseball: lots of good hitting, with power featured over speed. In their eighty-six years, the Tigers have had 8 league home run leaders, 15 RBI leaders, and 21 batting champions.

The Tigers' first great star was the legendary Ty Cobb, who played in Detroit from 1905 to 1926, led the A.L. in batting average twelve times, and finished his career with a breathtaking .367 BA. Some oldtimers still rate him as the best player ever. He was joined by fellow outfielder Sam Crawford, famed for his ability to hit triples, as the Tigers won three early pennants.

Outfielder Harry Heilmann led the league in hitting four times in the 1920s and finished at .342. 1930s first baseman Hank Greenberg blasted 331 homers on top of a .313 average. The team won two 1930s pennants under player-manager Mickey Cochrane, whose catching career was tragically ended when he was nearly killed by a pitch.

The Tigers of the post-war era have enjoyed occasional success: the 1968 American League champs were led by the last 30-game winner in the majors, righthander Denny McLain. He was joined on the mound by lefty Mickey Lolich and backed by a cast of hitters including Hall of Famer Al Kaline, slugging catcher Bill Freehan, and first baseman Norman Cash.

Tiger fans keep expecting current rightfielder Kirk Gibson (28, 86, .268) to turn into a superstar. He hits tape measure home runs but strikes out too much. First baseman Darrell Evans (20, 86, .273) is nearly 40 and may be phased out. Centrefielder Chet Lemon (12, 53, .251), second baseman Lou Whitaker (20, 73, .269), and shortstop Alan Trammell (21, 75, .277) are key men.

Catcher Lance Parrish (22, 62, .257) did not return. He's opted for free agency and signed with the Phillies.

Also testing the free agent waters was pitching ace Jack Morris (21–8, 3.27). When his price tag was too high for other teams, he went into arbitration with the Tigers and came out with nearly 2 million dollars. Veteran lefty Frank Tanana (12–9, 4.16), Walt Terrell (15–12, 4.56), and Eric King (11–4, 3.51) are useful starters, but Morris is the leader. Reliever Willie Hernandez (8–7, 24 saves) was only okay in 1986.

## KANSAS CITY ROYALS

The Royals fell from the heights of their 1985 World Championship to also-ran status in 1986. Injuries were much of the cause. Righthander Bret Saberhagen, the Cy Young Award winner in 1985, collapsed to 7–12 thanks to an aching elbow. Top hitter George Brett, who missed nearly 40 games, slumped to .290 – 26 points below his career average – and only 16 home runs after 30 the year before.

The Royals need all the hitting they can get. Centrefielder Willie Wilson, the A.L.'s batting leader in 1982, struggled with a .269 batting average. Catcher Jim Sundberg hit a feeble .212. First baseman Steve Balboni blasted 29 home runs but his BA was only .229 and his career is threatened by a bad back. Slick fielding second baseman Frank White had a good year at .272 and 20 homers, but he'll be 37 before October 1987.

*Willie Wilson is a switch-hitter; here he bats lefthanded.*

## THE AMERICAN LEAGUE

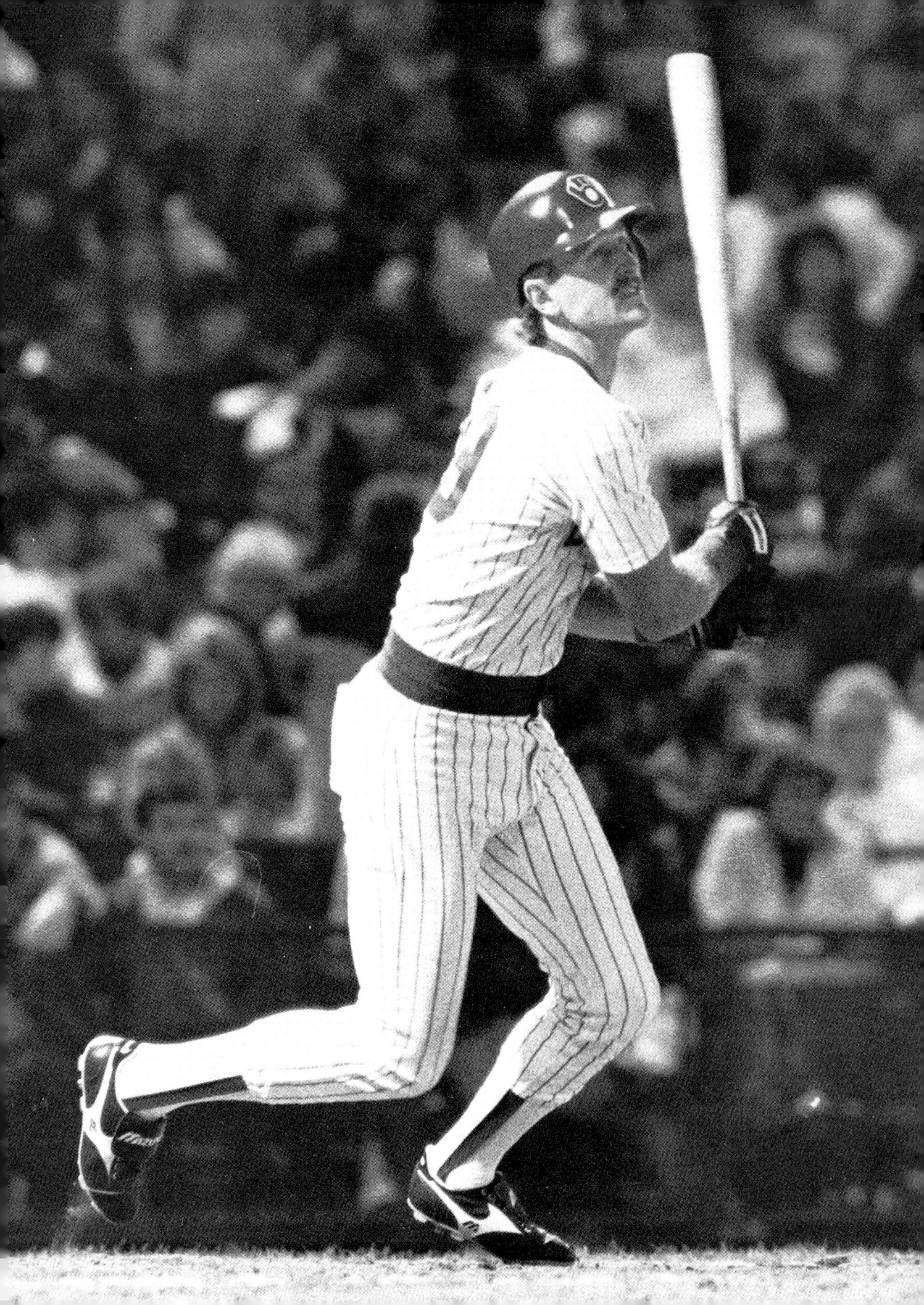

During the off-season the Royals moved to improve run production by trading for young outfielder Danny Tartabull who cracked 25 home runs last year at Seattle. Former college football star Bo Jackson has been promoted to the major leagues.

The Royals were formed in the expansion preceding the 1969 season, when the two major leagues went from 10 teams to 12. They play in the most beautiful and fan-friendly of the modern, symmetrical ballparks. When they regularly reached the top of their division by 1976–77–78, they became arguably the most quickly-successful expansion team in baseball history.

Brett has been the bellwether for over a decade. When he hit a sky-high .390 in 1980, he came the closest anybody has to .400 since Ted Williams topped that mark in 1941. But, because they play on artificial turf with long outfield fences, the Royals are successful with pitching and speed, not power.

With Saberhagen back to top form, the pitching is strong again. Lefty Charlie Leibrandt (14–11) and Mark Gubicza (12–6) are reliable starters. Young Danny Jackson pitched better than his 11–12 record. Longtime relief ace Dan Quisenberry slipped badly in 1985, but the Royals are deep in the bullpen.

The Royals aren't so confident that Brett can play up to his old all-star standard. A serious shoulder injury in 1986 hampered him both at bat and in the field. He's bounced back from injuries before but, at 34, the old resiliency may be gone.

## MILWAUKEE BREWERS

The good people of Milwaukee love to come out to County Stadium on a Sunday afternoon, sip good Milwaukee beer and chomp bratwurst at tailgate parties in the parking lot,

*Robin Yount was the first of a new generation of powerhitting shortstops; a shoulder injury has chased him to the outfield.*

and then go in and watch their Brewers win. In 1987, the beer and bratwurst are plentiful, and the wins more frequent than in recent seasons.

The Brewers were born as the Seattle Pilots in the 1969 expansion and, after one season there, moved to Milwaukee. County Stadium was originally built for the Braves, who'd come to Milwaukee from Boston in 1953 and moved on to Atlanta in 1965.

One thing the Brewers have going for them is the best Mexican-born, lefthanded pitcher in the American League. Teddy Higuera (20–11, 2.79 ERA) may challenge the Dodgers' Valenzuela as the best portsider in baseball in 1987. He needs help. Juan Nieves (11–12, 4.92) has shown promise on occasion, but the occasions must become more common.

Despite a .232 BA, outfielder Rob Deer is considered the club's big gun off 33 home runs and 86 RBIs. The Brewers' greatest star since their arrival has been Robin Yount (.312, 9, 46), who was the A.L.'s MVP shortstop before a bum shoulder forced him into the outfield. He still hits for average, but his power has deserted him. First baseman Cecil Cooper (.258, 12, 75) may be ready for the farm at 37. Jim Gantner (.274, 7, 38), and Paul Molitor (.281, 9, 59) anchor an acceptable infield, and Molitor has exhibited some sting with his bat. Rookie outfielder Glenn Braggs adds punch to the attack.

Only five years ago, the Brewers under then-manager Harvey Kuenn had so many long-ball hitters they were known as 'Harvey's Wallbangers'. Then, age and injury turned them into light wine. 1987 is the year Brewer fans glimpse a better future.

## MINNESOTA TWINS

If your taste is for home runs, spend a summer at the Hubert H. Humphrey Metrodome, the enclosed stadium hosting the baseball team 'shared' by the twin cities of Minneapolis and St Paul, and their surrounding communities. Baseballs fly into the grandstand with such monotonous regularity there that the ballpark is universally known as the 'Homerdome'.

For their first two decades-plus, the Twins played on a grass field in suburban Bloomington. They had plenty of legitimate sluggers but in 1982, with the completion of HHH Metrodome, the home runs really started flying.

In 1986, for example, Twins' centrefielder Kirby Puckett registered 31 four-baggers (and 96 RBIs with a .328 BA), third baseman Gary Gaetti cracked 34, outfielder Tom Brunansky bopped 23, first baseman Kent Hrbek 29 (in an off year!), and DH Roy Smalley 20. These are all accomplished hitters, but in the Homerdome the peanut vendors could sock a few over the fences. Unfortunately for the Twins, they play half their games on the road in ballparks where their Minnesota homers are only long fly-outs.

Worse, at home or away the other teams get to bat just as often as the Minnesotans. And for all the Twins' home runs, their pitchers give up even more. Staff ace Bert Blyleven (17–14) possesses as good a curve ball as there is in baseball, but when it hangs it's Bye-Bye Bly. He hung a record 50 in 1986. Stylish lefty Frank Viola (16–13) and righthander Mike Smithson (13–14) were both tagged too often for ERA health. The rest of the pitching staff could have got rich if they were paid by the pounding. The Twins sent four players to Montreal during the winter for relief ace Jeff Rearden (35 saves), and he is a busy man in 1987.

Originally, the Twins were the Washington Senators, a charter American League franchise. When they left there in 1961 when the American League expanded, a new team was placed in the nation's capital. As the Senators, they earned the cynical description: 'Washington – first in war, first in peace, and last in the American League.'

That wasn't always true. The great righthander Walter Johnson won 416 games in a Senator uniform. Outfielder 'Goose' Goslin hit his way into the Hall of Fame. All told, they won three pennants. Since arriving in 'the Land of a Thousand Lakes' they took a pennant in 1965 and division titles in 1969 and 1970.

That 1965 pennant came on a combination of stars the Twins brought with them from Washington (Harmon Killebrew, the fifth leading homer hitter of all time with a career total of 573; slugger Bob Allison, pitchers Camilio Pasqual and Jim Kaat), young players who started in Minnesota (shortstop Zoilo Versalles, outfielder Jim Hall) and some veteran acquisitions (catcher Earl Battey, pitcher Mudcat Grant). The Dodgers nipped them in a 7-game World Series.

## NEW YORK YANKEES

There was a time – a long time, in fact – when the Yankees winning the American League pennant was almost like Death and Taxes. Almost every year, they had the best pitching and fielding, but their trademark was the home run. Fans called them the 'Bronx Bombers,' after the borough in New York housing Yankee Stadium.

In the 1920s they had Babe Ruth hitting monster home runs in monstrous numbers and Lou Gehrig hitting almost as many home runs and they won six pennants.

Then in the 1930s Joe DiMaggio showed everyone how centrefield REALLY should be played. He and Gehrig hit a ton as the Yankees won five pennants. In the 1940s they still had DiMaggio and they won five more flags.

Along came the 1950s. Mickey Mantle hit home runs as long as Ruth and almost as often. Catcher Yogi Berra made everyone laugh with his malaprops but no rival smiled when he batted. Whitey Ford was the smoothest and bestest lefthander in baseball. They won eight pennants and people talked about the then-8-team American League as 'Snow Yankees and the Seven Dwarfs'.

The A.L. expanded in the 1960s, but the Yankees started in winning the first five pennants. In 1961, Roger Maris even out-homered Ruth with 61 round trippers. New

## THE AMERICAN LEAGUE

York fans loved the Bombers; most other fans hated them. They were called 'Damn Yankees' so often that some children grew up thinking the team came from a city named Damn.

After an uncharacteristic dry spell, the Yanks found an aggressive owner in George Steinbrenner, who spread dollars like gravel in hiring free agent sluggers such as Reggie Jackson and Dave Winfield to hit his home runs and who changed his manager as often as most men change their socks. Steinbrenner's tactics turned many people off, but his Yankees won four more pennants for him.

It's a surprise to realize the Yankees haven't won a flag since 1981. With the Mets' success, a lot of New Yorkers are beginning to think of the Yanks as the city's 'other' team. Fans around the league have forgotten why they used to hate them.

No one remembers how many managers the Yankees have had since their last pennant. The present temporary is Lou Piniella who manages with a line-up card in one pocket and a train schedule in the other. When he comes to Yankee Stadium, the first thing he does is look to see if his name is still on the locker. Then, he sits down and wonders why the Yankees don't win as in days of yore.

Certainly they have home run hitters. First baseman Don Mattingly (31 HR, 113 RBI, .352) is the best hitter in baseball. He'll lead the league in homers, RBIs, batting average, or all three just about any year that has an eight in it. Outfielder Dave Winfield (24, 104, .262) feuds with Steinbrenner but plays great for him.

*Dave Winfield is one of baseball's highest-paid superstars, earning about $2 million a year.*

Third baseman Mike Pagliarulo (28, 71, .238) and part-timers Don Pasqua (16, 45, .293) and Ron Kittle (21, 60, .218) add to the carnage. Even centrefielder Rickey Henderson, the best leadoff hitter in the world with 130 runs scored, chipped in 28 homers. It's not the hitting that separates these Yankees from the Olde Damn Yankees.

They don't field like they used to. Pagliarulo had 19 errors at third in 1986 and Willie Randolph 20 at second base. Until Wayne Tolleson took over shortstop, that position was a shambles. Tolleson would make a fine utility man; as a regular he's just adequate. In the outfield, even Henderson's speed can't make anyone forget DiMaggio. The catching has Yankee fans longing for the days of Berra.

And they don't pitch like they used to. Lefty Dennis Rasmussen (18–6, 3.88) did his part, and reliever Dave Righetti (46 saves) did everyone else's. After that, the staff was either unproved, unreliable, unwell, or un-young. In the latter two categories are Joe Niekro, 42 (9–10, 4.87), and Tommy John, 44 (5–3, 2.93). Steinbrenner improved that situation by trading for veteran Rick Rhoden who won 15 games for the last-place N.L. Pirates and acquiring Charles Hudson for the Phillies.

## OAKLAND ATHLETICS

The Oakland Athletics enter the 1987 season rated as the California team least likely to wind up in a World Series. They hope to combine home run power with underrated pitching to surprise the experts.

The A's are a charter American League franchise. They started as the Philadelphia A's, owned and managed for the first half of the century by Connie Mack. Mack twice built powerful championship teams (in the early 1910s and the early 1930s) and then was forced by economics to sell off his best players, doom-

*Willie Randolph is the most veteran Yankee, having covered second base for them since 1976.*

ing his teams to a dizzying drop in the standings. The dismantling of the 1930s champions; shedding outfielder Al Simmons, first baseman Jimmie Foxx, catcher Mickey Cochrane, and pitcher Lefty Grove (ALL Hall of Famers); was not overcome until forty years (and two cities) later.

In 1955, like the American pioneers of the 1800s, the Athletics pulled up stakes and headed for the golden west. After a decade of mediocrity in Kansas City, the A's were moved to Oakland, California, the blue-collar city across the bay from San Francisco, by the flamboyant, anti-establishment owner Charlie Finley in 1968.

And in the early 1970s, the A's became great champions again, winning the Series three consecutive years ('72, '73, '74), a feat unmatched by anybody except the Yankees in the post-World War II era. The aggressive, moustachioed A's featured great pitching (Jim 'Catfish' Hunter, Vida Blue, Ken Holtzman, and reliever Rollie Fingers) and great hitting (third baseman Sal Bando, outfielders Reggie Jackson and Joe Rudi) and a catalytic manager named Dick Williams.

The 1987 A's boast a pair of impressive young home run hitters in outfielders Jose Canseco (33 HR, 117 RBI) and Mike Davis (19 HR, 55 RBI). Neither hits for a high batting average, but when they connect the ball goes into orbit. Third baseman Carney Lansford (19 HR, .284) is a solid hitter. Reggie Jackson returns to Oakland as a free agent bringing his home run bat for what will probably be his final season. Second-year lefty Curt Young bulwarks a pitching staff with potential.

## SEATTLE MARINERS

Although famous nationwide for its rainy weather, Seattle, Washington, prides itself on looking towards a blue-sky future. Just as well! Its baseball team has a short, dismal past. The sun has never shone on the baseball nine representing the half million optimists of this northwest American coast city. Since 1977 when the Seattle Mariners joined the American League in the last expansion, they've never had a winning season. But hope springs eternal; certainly it does in Seattle.

This year's Mariner team is stocked with exciting, young sluggers, including third baseman Jim Presley (27 HR, 107 RBI), first baseman Alvin Davis (18 HR, 72 RBI), and centrefielder Phil Bradley (.310 BA). To some extent, those marks are illusory; the Mariners' indoor home – the 59,438-seat Kingdome – lends itself to hefty hitting. Nonetheless, many other teams would be happy to have youngsters like these on the payroll.

The Mariners have boasted good hitting before; they've always been short on pitching. Last year's staff ace Mark Langston led the A.L. in strikeouts, but won only 12 games with an overblown 4.85 ERA.

## TORONTO BLUE JAYS

The Blue Jays won the A.L. East in 1985 and might have won in 1986 if they hadn't staggered out of the starting gate like an arthritic tortoise. By the time they looked up, Boston was too far out front to be caught.

Much of the reason for last year's slow start was the ineffective pitching of long-time ace Dave Stieb (7–12, 4.74). He's been an all-star but for a while he couldn't put the cat out, much less major league hitters. He doesn't figure highly in Toronto plans and anything they get out of him will be gravy.

Jim Clancy was 14–14 (3.94) and pitched even better than that. Jimmy Key (14–11, 3.57) has become one of the league's top lefthanders. If Stieb doesn't come back, Manager Jimmy Williams can pick and choose from a half dozen other good young arms for the other starters. Mark Eichorn (14–6, 10 saves) and Tom Henke (9–5, 27 saves) make a formidable bullpen and there are several more to back them.

Every other team salivates at the Jays' out-

*Carney Lansford won a batting championship in 1981.*

## THE AMERICAN LEAGUE

*Jose Canseco was the American League's premier new player in 1986, winning the 'Rookie of the Year' honor awarded to the top newcomer.*

field. Jesse Barfield (40, 108, .289) led the league in home runs. He's improved his stats every year he's been in the majors. George Bell (31, 108, .309) has been one of baseball's best-kept secrets for a couple of seasons. He runs, throws, fields, hits for average, hits for power, and no doubt shelters stray animals. Centrefielder Lloyd Moseby (21, 86, .253) fell off a little at bat in 1986 but catches everything hit even vaguely in his direction. All three stars are 28.

Another player who's got better every year is shortstop Tony Fernandez (10, 65, .310), who won a Gold Glove and deserved one of platinum. He's probably the team's MVP. The rest of the infield doesn't come up to his level – few can – but they're not weak spots either.

The Blue Jays have been in the majors only since the last expansion in 1977. Their fans saw them loyally through a few rough seasons while the front office built wisely. Now it all seems to be peaking. When they win the pennant – no one says 'if' in Toronto – they'll be the first non-USA team ever to compete in the 'World' Series.

## TEXAS RANGERS

The Texas Rangers were formed in the 1961 expansion as the second version of the Washington Senators. In Washington, they were known more for their managers than for winning: Gil Hodges went from Senators' manager to the Mets, where he led the 'Impossible Dream' team to the 1969 world title, and legendary Ted Williams came out of retirement to take the helm for the team's last years in Washington and their first seasons in Texas.

Perennial also-rans since their 1972 arrival in the Dallas–Fort Worth area after a dozen sparse Washington years, the Rangers seldom have been more than tired punching bags for the American league's pennant contenders. But, under bright young manager Bobby Valentine, the Rangers hope to parlay an exciting outfield, long on power and potential, and a youthful but strong-armed flock of pitchers into a Texas pennant.

Texans sometimes boast a molehill into a mountain but they have every reason to brag when they talk about the Rangers' outfield. Powerful rightfielder Pete Incaviglia crunched the ball last year for 30 home runs and 88 RBIs. Centrefielder Oddibe McDowell combined 18 home runs with 33 stolen bases as a leadoff man with punch. Leftfielder Ruben Sierra arrived at midseason to post 16 home runs and 55 RBIs. All are under 25 years old, with their best years ahead of them. First baseman Pete O'Brien added 23 homers and 90 RBIs, and designated hitter Larry Parrish chipped in with 28 home runs and 94 RBIs. Almost unnoticed amidst all that power, smooth shortstop Scott Fletcher hit an even .300 and was 'our MVP,' according to Valentine.

Veteran knuckleballer Charlie Hough (17-10) was the top Texas pitcher last year and one of the best in the league. But Hough is pushing 40, and the Rangers' hopes ride on the young arms of Edwin Correa, Jose Guzman, Mike Loynd, Mike Mason and Bobby Witt. Together, they were only 41-53 with ERAs in the 4.00 and 5.00 range in 1986 but Mason at 28 was the only one not a rookie. The other four are all under 25.

The Rangers' past is grim as forty miles 'tween waterholes, but with all those youngsters whooping it up, the future looks as happy as a heifer in tall grass.

# 2 THE NATIONAL LEAGUE

BASEBALL EXPLAINED

## ATLANTA BRAVES

The Atlanta Braves are one of the most-watched baseball teams in America: owner Ted Turner's Superstation WTBS–TV takes their games, via satellite, all over the country. Had they been a network show last season, they would have been cancelled – if not for ratings, for standards.

For example, there was the Excessive Violence done to their pitchers. Righthander Rick Mahler was the staff workhorse, but his 14-18, 4.88 ERA, left plenty to be desired. David Palmer (11-10, 3.65) has made a career out of nursing his sore arm. No one else won in double figures – or deserved to.

The batting attack had a good pair of leads. Dale Murphy (29, 83, .265) was about 20 per cent off his MVP performances of 1982 and 1983, but remains one of baseball's best. Big Bob Horner (27, 87, .273) kept his weight below his batting average and had four home runs in a single game. But Horner has opted for free agency, and left the Braves to play in Japan.

Optimist Chuck Tanner manages with an encouraging word and a pat on the back, but his promos are strained in 1987.

The Braves are the longest running act in baseball. They started in Boston five years before the National League was formed and joined the N.L. as a charter member in 1876. They were a power in the last century, winning pennants, and featuring such stars as Hugh Duffy, whose .438 batting average in 1894 is still the higest ever.

The first half of the twentieth century was far less kind. The Braves pulled one 'Miracle Finish' in 1914. Led by fiery second baseman Johnny Evers and happy-go-lucky shortstop Rabbit Maranville, they came from last place in late August to win the World Championship. There was another pennant in 1948 but mostly there were second division finishes. Along the way, they lost Boston to the Red Sox.

In 1953 they made the first major league franchise shift in fifty years when they moved to Milwaukee. In their first years there, the Braves set attendance records with an exciting team featuring Eddie Mathews, who had more than 500 career home runs, and the all-around play of Hammerin' Hank Aaron. Hall of Fame lefty Warren Spahn and tricky righthander Lew Burdette were great pitchers. In 1957 Burdette won three World Series games, as they topped the Yankees in a 7-game classic.

When attendance slipped in the mid-1960s, the Braves' owners asked permission of the league to move to Atlanta. The league forced them to remain through the 1965 season, but bitter Milwaukee fans considered them dead. Several 'crowds' numbered fewer than a thousand.

The Braves have been better known for home runs than for victories since arriving in Atlanta. Until the Hubert H. Humphrey Metrodome opened in Minnesota, Atlanta–Fulton County Stadium was considered the most homer-friendly ballpark in the majors. Most fans refer to it as 'The Launching Pad'.

On perhaps the most famous night in Atlanta's brief baseball history, Aaron broke Babe Ruth's 'unbreakable' career home run mark. Before a standing-room-only crowd of 53,775, he blasted number 715 at 9:07 p.m. on 8 April 1974. When he retired two years later, he'd raised his total to 755.

## CHICAGO CUBS

The Cubs are another team whose games are regularly telecast across the nation. Because venerable Wrigley Field is the only major league ballpark without lights, WGN–TV's satellite network beams afternoon Cubbie home games to an audience more accustomed to soap operas at that viewing time. The baseball team is distinguishable from the soaps primarily because it brings more tears to viewers' eyes.

The 'Bleacher Bums' who loyally pack the open outfield stands bask in both afternoon sun and aftergame blues. Though they often ap-

*Centerfielder Dale Murphy has hit for average and power for the Atlanta Braves for many years.*

pear shirtless on the TV screen, in reality they wear the hairshirts of martyrs. They have willingly – even gladly – chosen to root for baseball's most frustrating franchise.

The Cubs haven't won a pennant since 1945. Yet, in the National League's first sixty years, they were its most successful team. Not only did they take the league's first pennant in 1876, but they added five more before the turn of the century.

From 1906 to 1910, they took four more flags with the famous 'Tinker-to-Evers-to-Chance' double-play combo. Shortstop Joe Tinker and second baseman Johnny Evers feuded with each other but played brilliantly under manager and first baseman Frank Chance. Mordecai 'Three-Finger' Brown used his damaged digits to put an unusual spin on the ball; it made him a Hall of Fame pitcher.

Well into the 1930s, the Cubs challenged each year for the pennant and won four times. Brilliant catcher Gabby Hartnett and slugger Hack Wilson, who set the N.L. single season home run mark with 56 in 1929, were two of their stars.

Since the end of World War II, Wrigley Field (built in 1914) has been the 'House of Heartache'. Despite the presence of such Hall of Fame batsmen as Billy Williams and Ernie Banks, the top homer hitter among shortstops, the Cubbies have seldom been in the race by September.

Three years ago, in their best postwar effort, they won the N.L. eastern division, but lost the League Championship Series. The pitchers who led them in 1984 earned handsome raises then but few wins since. Once more, the Cubbies are rebuilding.

They have a nucleus. Ryne Sandberg (14, 76, .284), the 1984 league MVP, is still an outstanding second baseman. Young Shawon Dunstan (17, 68, .260) may be the best power-hitting shortstop since Banks but must cut down on his 32 errors. The baseman Keith Moreland (12, 79, .271) and catcher Jody Davis (21, 74, .250) have handy bats and they signed ex-Expo star Andre Dawson to play rightfield.

But, unless the pitchers make a mass comeback, the Bleacher Bums can only look forward to suntans at Wrigley this summer.

## CINCINNATI REDS

Reds fans looked forward to the 1987 season with more anticipation than at any time since the 1970s when 'The Big Red Machine' annually rolled over National League opponents. Pete Rose, once Cincinnati's greatest player, is now the manager. As he teaches a couple of his younger players any of the savvy that earned him an all-time high of 4,256 basehits, happy days return to the Rhineland.

Cincinnati's long baseball history has had its ups and downs ever since the independent Red Stockings toured the country as the first fully professional team in 1869. Although the city was a charter member of the National League in 1876, they dropped out after the 1880 season and did not return until 1890. In the interim, a Cincinnati team played in the then-major league American Association. The Reds did not win their first N.L. pennant until 1919. While that club went on to victory in the World Series, the win was tainted when it was revealed that their opponents – the 'Black Sox' – had been bribed by gamblers.

After lulling in the second division for twenty years, the Reds hit the heights again in 1939 with a team led by pitchers Bucky Walters and Paul Derringer, and slow-footed but power-hitting catcher Ernie Lombardi. They lost the 1939 Series to the Yankees, but returned the following year to win against Detroit.

More down-years followed. Then, in the mid-1950s, the Reds began building a home run line-up featuring Frank Robinson and Vada Pinson. They slugged their way to a pennant in 1961 but again lost to the Yankees in the World Series.

Having found the secret of success, the Reds put together an awesome line-up for the 1970s, one that was perfect for Riverfront Stadium, the

*Versatile Keith Moreland plays outfield, third base, and catcher for the Cubs; he hits with power regardless of where he plays in the field.*

team's symmetrical, carpeted home park since 1970. The 'Machine' ran on basehits by Rose and second sacker Joe Morgan, followed by the home runs of Johnny Bench, Lee May, and Tony Perez. They won six division titles, four pennants, and two world championships during the decade.

Rose's current Reds boast veterans Dave Parker (31, 116, .273) and Buddy Bell (20, 75, .278). The keys to the future will be the performances of Young Eric Davis (27, 71, .277) and shortstop Barry Larkin (.283 in 41 games at season's end). Both are touted as future greats by Cincy partisans.

Pitching leader Tom Browning slumped to 14-13 after a 20-win year in 1985. He's expected to bounce back, and the bullpen is deep.

## HOUSTON ASTROS

When baseball's first domed, indoor stadium, the Houston Astrodome, opened in April of 1965, it was hailed as the 'Eighth Wonder of the World'. The ballclub, which had laboured under the awkward name of 'Houston Colt 45's' since its 1962 origin as a National League expansion team, moved in and changed its handle to the more euphonious 'Houston Astros'. Fans and critics quickly split on the benefits and follies of playing baseball inside.

There would be no more rainouts, everyone agreed, but the air-conditioned atmosphere inside the dome turned potential home runs into long fly-outs. That, coupled with cavernous power alleys, made the dome a 'pitcher's paradise'. Early Astro power-hitter Jimmy Wynn hit 37 homers one year, but that was the exception.

One major problem soon developed; the grass died. The following year, a ninth wonder was introduced: artificial grass. Because of the peculiarities of the Astrodome, the team has always been geared towards speed and pitching and lacked a home run threat.

Although the Astros were first in domes and first in carpets, they have never been first in the National League. In 1980, a team predicated on pitching got as far as the League Championship Series before bowing to Philadelphia in an exciting set of games. The 1986 Astros again made it to the LCS only to be shoved aside by the all-conquering Mets.

The 1987 Astros have more hitting than in previous years. First baseman Glenn Davis (31, 101, .265) might have been league MVP had he not tailed off in September. Kevin Bass (20, 79, .311), Jose Cruz (10, 72, .278), and Denny Walling (13, 58, .312) are proven hitters.

The pitching is strong as always. Mike Scott (18-10, 2.22, and 306 strikeouts) won the 1986 N.L. Cy Young Award and clinched the western division title for his team with a no-hitter. Lefty Bob Knepper (17-12, 3.14), and aging fireballer Nolan Ryan (12-8, 3.34) are other quality starters. Dave Smith (4-7, 33 saves) leads an admirable bullpen.

## LOS ANGELES DODGERS

Even today, nearly thirty years after the Dodgers moved all the way across the continent in 1958, a few oldtime baseball fans slip and call them the BROOKLYN Dodgers. No team was ever so associated with its city as the Dodgers in their Brooklyn days. From the time they entered the National League in 1890 (and won that year's pennant), they were the fans' darlings. The team was even named after the fans who supposedly dodged trolleys on their way to the ballpark.

Although the Dodgers won pennants in 1899, 1900, 1916 and 1920, their image – particularly between the World Wars – was one of lovable bumblers. Dodger fans flocking to Ebbets Field affectionately referred to the team as 'Dem Bums' and always warned 'Wait till next year.' Such free spirits as Babe Herman, the only man ever to triple into a triple play, or eccentric pitcher Van Lingle Mungo, could always ruin the best efforts of Hall of Famers Zach Wheat and Dazzy Vance.

When Branch Rickey took over the Dodger

# THE NATIONAL LEAGUE

front office shortly after World War II, the image began to change. With a revitalized farm system and clever trades, Rickey built the 'Bums' into winners. The 1941 pennant was a herald of things to come.

In the years following the war, the Dodgers were second only to the A.L. Yankees as consistent winners. In 1947, Rickey revolutionized baseball when he brought in Jackie Robinson, the first black in major league baseball since the 1880s, thus opening baseball's doors to a flood of talented black stars. Robinson, a brilliant second baseman, teamed with smooth shortstop Pee Wee Reese in a legendary double-play combination. Duke Snider, Gil Hodges, and Roy Campanella were powerful home run hitters. Brooklyn won pennants in 1947, 1949, 1952, 1953, 1955, and 1956. The 1955 team won the World Series, defeating the Yankees.

Then, in 1958, the baseball world was shocked to learn that the Dodgers were moving to Los Angeles. At the same time, the Giants relocated in San Francisco, thus depriving the New York metropolitan area of two baseball teams in one fell swoop. Though the attendance in Brooklyn was among the best in the majors, team owner Walter O'Malley recognized the bonanza awaiting him on the untapped west coast.

For their first four west coast years, the Dodgers played in the L.A. Memorial Coliseum, a converted football stadium with a 440-foot power alley in right and a laughable 251-foot left field. Outfielder Wally Moon, a lefthanded batter, became adept at slapping 'Moon Shots' over the 40-foot screen in left. Despite its absurd dimensions, the Coliseum could seat enormous crowds. Opening day in 1958 drew 78,672; a World Series game the next year set a record at 92,706.

In 1962, the club moved into Dodger Stadium, a beautiful, symmetrical park built for baseball only. Although its capacity is only a little more than half that of the Coliseum, its easy freeway access combined with excellent Dodger teams to put the average attendance per game at over 40,000. In 1982, the Dodgers drew 3,608,881.

The Dodgers have continued as one of the N.L.'s strongest teams, winning ten division titles, eight pennants, and four world championships since arriving in Los Angeles. Their hallmark has been outstanding pitching: Hall of Famers Sandy Koufax and Don Drysdale were the aces in the early L.A. years.

Mexico's Fernando Valenzuela (21-11, 3.14), baseball's best lefthander, leads the present staff. Other excellent hurlers are Rick Honeycutt (11-9, 3.32) and Orel Hershiser (14-14, 3.85), but the pitching isn't as deep as usual.

Also returning is the usual Dodger firepower. Steve Sax (6, 56, .332) is coming off his best year, and Mike Marshall (19, 53, .233) can be counted on for an occasional home run. Pedro Guerrero (5, 10, .246) tore up his leg in the spring of 1986 and was virtually no help the whole season. This year he is back in good form.

## MONTREAL EXPOS

For years, Montreal Expos ace Steve Rogers was known as 'the best pitcher never to win twenty games'. He retired without winning away that reputation for nonfulfilment, and his disappointments mirror those of the Expos. The team has been frustratingly 'on the verge' for a decade.

The Expos joined the National League in the expansion of 1969 when both major leagues jumped from 10 to 12 teams each. After the usual growing pains at Jarry Park, a temporary home, they moved into the stadium built for the 1976 Olympics and became 'a team on the rise'. Somehow, they have never risen quite high enough to fly a pennant at Olympic Stadium. They've wallowed in potential. They've even come close. But, never a cigar.

The 1987 Expos have some possibilities: Young Floyd Youmans (13-12, 3.53) may be ready to blossom into an outstanding pitcher. If shortstop Hubie Brooks (14, 58, .340) can

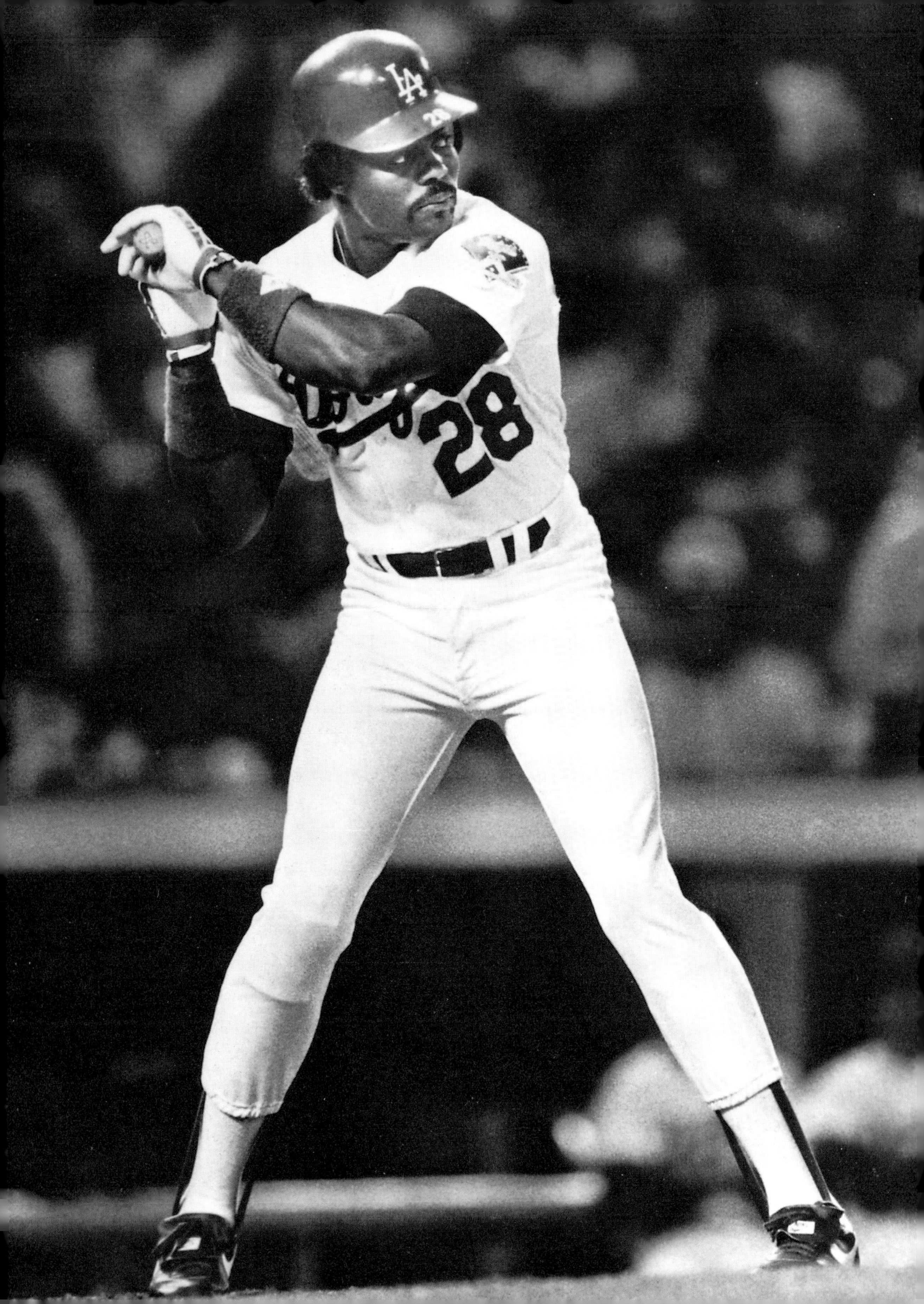
LA
28

escape the kind of injury that put him on the shelf for half a season, he may actually justify the controversial trade that sent all-star catcher Gary Carter to the Mets two years ago. Andres Galarraga (10, 42, .271) is touted by many as a coming home run hitter.

However, the front office seems bent on economizing. Relief ace Jeff Reardon (7-9, 35 saves) was dealt to Minnesota for a flock of lesser salaries. Both of last year's top hitters – Tim Raines (9, 62, .334) and Andre Dawson (20, 78, .280) – opted for free agency and Dawson didn't come back. Raines, the best lead-off man in the N.L., won the batting crown in 1986, and Dawson was regarded by many as the top player in the league a couple of years ago before injuries slowed him.

Taking a step back from 'almost-but-not-quite' and rebuilding may be a smart way to go. Just so long as no one tags this new bunch of Expos 'a team on the rise'.

## NEW YORK METS

The Mets have undergone an image transplant.

Back in 1962, when they were born as a New York expansion team to replace the departed Dodgers and Giants, they were wonderfully awful. They were so bad that America fell in love with them as the ultimate underdog. Across the nation, fans rooted for their home team first and the Mets second. 'Marvellous Marv' Throneberry, the good-natured Met first baseman, became a folk hero, not because of his occasional home runs, but for his more common strikeouts. Always good for a laugh, the Mets were Curly, Larry, and Moe in spikes. Through 1968, they never finished above ninth in a 10-team league, and there were seasons they could have finished fourteenth.

A really funny thing happened in 1969. The Mets won the World Championship. Manager Gil Hodges had a pair of great young starting pitchers in Tom Seaver and Jerry Koosman, a good reliever in Tug McGraw, and an essentially starless regular line-up. But the team got hot near the end of the season, roared from behind for a division title, and then took the pennant in the first League Championship Series. When they beat Baltimore four games to one in the World Series, the accomplishment was termed 'The Impossible Dream' and 'The Miracle of Flushing Meadow' (the site of Shea Stadium, the Mets' ballpark).

After a couple of lovably mediocre seasons, the Mets had another miracle of sorts in 1973. With Seaver brilliant as ever and McGraw yelling 'Ya gotta believe!' every time he saved another win, the team again came from behind to take their division and then trash heavily-favoured Cincinatti in the LCS. The magic ran out when Oakland won the 7-game World Series.

Those two pennants did nothing to harm the country's affection for the Mets. The scrappy, off-the-floor way they'd won helped. So did the public perception that only unassuming Tom Seaver was a real talent; the rest of the Mets were ordinary guys who got together to play some ball. And, except for those two isolated moments of glory, the team could usually be counted on for an inoffensive season of also-running.

Then came 1986.

While no one was looking, New York built an un-Metlike team of all-stars. The assembled powerhouse won 108 games – easily. Rather than coming from behind, this bunch was out in front so far and so early that, in looking back, it seemed like they'd clinched the division by the third inning on opening day. The LCS and World Series were accomplished with less ease, but accomplished they were.

The list of Met goodies starts with the pitching: Dwight Gooden (17-6, 2.84), Bobby Ojeda (18-5, 2.57), Sid Fernandez (16-6, 3.52), and Ron Darling (15-6, 2.81), Roger McDowell (14-9, 22 saves), Jesse Orosco (8-6, 21 saves). And there

*Pedro Guerrero's 1986 injury crippled the Dodger's chances; they hope he's back at his power-hitting best in 1987.*

are some other good Met pitchers who just never get much chance to be seen.

Gary Carter (24, 105, .255) is both the best catcher and the best-hitting catcher in baseball. Keith Hernandez (13, 83, .310) is baseball's best fielding first baseman and a top clutch hitter. Rightfielder Darryl Strawberry (27, 93, .259) is a star nearing superstardom. The rest of the line-up is sprinkled with good, better, and best.

Everyone loves a winner, right? Well, not quite. New York still loves the Mets, but the rest of the country is having second thoughts. In those areas where 'New York' has always been somewhat of an epithet, fans feel that the Mets win perhaps a little too easily and noisily. That they take a few too many bows after their home runs. That they tend to rub their opponents' noses in the dirt. The adjective 'arrogant' is heard.

Fans outside New York used to make a religion out of hating the Yankees, but that team has vitiated much of the old loathing by losing opportunely and often looking pretty silly doing it. It's hard to see how the present Mets could take that road to regain their previous popularity. They'll win most of their games and probably the pennant. If they could only learn to say, 'Aw, shucks,' and look a bit humble ...

## PHILADELPHIA PHILLIES

Philadelphia fans are the most notorious faultfinders in baseball. At symmetrical Veterans' Stadium, they'd boo Mom on Mother's Day. They've even booed long-time third baseman Mike Schmidt, which borders on sacrilegious considering that Mike has been the best player in baseball for much of the past decade. Last year was another typical Schmidt year: 37 HRs, 119 RBIs, .290, and the MVP Award, his third.

Just why are Phillie fans so hard to please? Perhaps because over the years they've had so many bad ballclubs, they can only rail, Prometheus-like, against their unfriendly gods. From 1883 to 1979, they won exactly two pennants: in 1915 and 1950. Both of those seasons were keyed by Hall of Fame pitchers; first Grover Cleveland Alexander and later Robin Roberts. In most other years, they had excellent hitters, dreadful pitching, and bottom-of-the-league finishes. In 1930, they had a team batting average in excess of .300 and still wound up dead last! One of their pitchers was nicknamed 'Boom-Boom' because of the sound his pitches made when opposing hitters blasted them off outfield walls.

In 1980, after ninety-eight years, the Phillies won a World Championship, besting Kansas City four games to two in the World Series. Schmidt, of course, had his usual MVP year, but the team sailed home on the best left arm in the solar system, that of Steve Carlton. Both were around to win another pennant in 1983, although Baltimore took the World Series.

Lefty Carlton may have moved on to eventual Hall of Fame enshrinement. The history of Phillie baseball seems to prove they can only win with a great pitcher in the stable. The history of 1986 seems to prove they don't have one.

Schmidt has help in the slugging department. Von Hayes (19, 98, .305), Juan Samuel (16, 78, .266), and Glenn Wilson (15, 84, .271) will put runs on the scoreboard. The Phils added powerful catcher Lance Parrish. The question is, can any of the young pitchers the Phils have hung their hopes on keep the opposition from scoring more?

## PITTSBURGH PIRATES

Before the 1891 season, when the Pittsburgh Alleghenys had been members of the National League for only four years, the club took advantage of a clerical error to acquire second baseman Louis Bierbauer, formerly of the then-major American Association. The Association did not take the slick-but-legal transaction in good grace and termed the

## THE NATIONAL LEAGUE

*The Phillies traded five players to Cleveland for Von Hayes, a solid hitter.*

Pittsburghers 'Pirates!' And they've been the Pittsburgh Pirates ever since.

However, before last season – their hundredth in the N.L. – it seemed likely they would become the New Orleans or Louisville Pirates. Because of a perceived lackadaisical attitude among its veterans and the sense that ownership was past caring, the ballclub was not just ignored by Pittsburgh fans – it was actively disliked. At Three Rivers Stadium (so named because it sits where the Allegheny and Monongehela Rivers join to form the Ohio), attendance was so poor the vendors sometimes outnumbered the paying customers.

Back at the turn of the century, when Pittsburgh was the nation's steelmaker and the smoke was so heavy they turned lights on at noon, the Pirates won pennants from 1901 to 1903, playing in the first World Series in 1903 and losing to the Red Sox. In 1909, they won the World Championship. Bow-legged, long-armed shortstop Honus Wagner was the league's best hitter, fielder, and base stealer. Eventually he became one of the first five men named to the Hall of Fame.

In the 1920s, Pittsburgh was still Smoke City and the Pirates won a couple of pennants with hard hitters Kiki Cuyler, Paul Waner, and Pie Traynor cracking basehits into the smoky air. After World War II, pollution reforms began making Pittsburgh air breathable. The ballclub was weak, but home run slugger Ralph Kiner brought out large crowds. In 1960, after years of rebuilding, the Pirates defeated the Yankees on a dramatic ninth-inning home run by Bill Mazeroski, a second baseman better known for his fielding.

Sharp-hitting Roberto Clemente helped keep the club a contender through the 1960s and led them to a World Series win in 1971. In 1979, aging slugger Willie Stargell helped bring another title to Pittsburgh.

Then, in the early 1980s, just as years of cleanup bore fruit with Pittsburgh being named 'America's Most Livable City', the ballclub alienated the fans. The popular Stargell retired; fans accused the remaining veterans of loafing and the management of pinching pennies. It seemed only a matter of time before the Pirates would move or be ridden out of town on a rail.

In 1986, Pittsburgh moved bravely to save the franchise; with the help of local corporations, the city bought the ballclub. The new ownership lopped off the most offending veterans, put hustling young players on the field, and sailed forth into dead last place with easily the worst team in the major leagues. But they won back the fans. Attendance reached a million on the last day of the 1986 season. The team was typified by young outfielder Barry Bonds (16, 48, .223), who showed flashes of brilliance amid many strikeouts and rookie mistakes.

## ST LOUIS CARDINALS

From 1892 to 1925, the Cardinals made barely a ripple on the National League pond. Then, in 1926, with young player-manager Rogers Hornsby hitting up a storm and ancient Grover Alexander weathering a few on the mound, the Cards won their first pennant and topped the Yankees of Babe Ruth in a thrill-packed World Series. Once they tried post-season play, the Cardinals liked it. They've been regular World Series participants ever since with 14 pennants and 9 World Championships to date.

Although the 'Gashouse Gang,' the mid-1930s Cards, claim only one of those championships, they are perhaps the most famous team ever to represent St Louis. With free-spirits Ducky Medwick, Pepper Martin, and Rip Collins as regulars and unpredictable Dizzy Dean as their pitching star, the Gang drove opponents and their own player-manager Frankie Frisch to distraction with enough bizarre antics to fill a couple of books. But they won.

The far more successful Cardinals of the 1940s (four pennants) were less colourful. Such Hall of Famers as Stan Musial, undoubtedly the best player the Cards ever had, and Enos

*Jack Clark, Cardinals outfielder-first baseman.*

*Vince Coleman, Cardinals outfielder and National League basestealing leader.*

Slaughter could be routinely depended upon to show up on time, lash out basehits, and win.

In the 1960s, the record base-stealing of Lou Brock and the fireball hurling of pitcher Bob Gibson added three more pennants to the St Louis stock. In 1966, the Cards moved into the newly-built Busch Stadium after forty-seven seasons in historic Sportsman's Park. Busch's 380-plus power alleys and the addition of a very fast artificial carpet in 1970 meant successful Cardinal teams would have to stress speed and pitching rather than home runs.

By following that blueprint in the 1980s under manager Whitey Herzog, the Cards have won two pennants and one world title. But the 1986 team total of only 58 home runs and a team batting average fourteen points below any other club left St Louis gasping for runs. Even their league-topping 262 stolen bases couldn't lift them higher than a distant third in the N.L. East.

Acrobatic shortstop Ozzie Smith (0, 54, .280) is an all-star, but centrefielder Willie McGee (1, 24, .256) saw his batting average drop nearly a hundred points from 1985. Rapid Vince Coleman (0, 29, .232) stole 107 bases but couldn't steal first. Jack Clark (9, 23, .237), the only Card home run threat, was laid up most of the year with an injury.

The pitchers also slumped slightly. Veteran Bob Forsch (14-10, 3.25) ended as the top starter when lefty John Tudor (13-7, 2.92) and big Danny Cox (12-13, 2.90) were inconsistent. A few more runs behind them would help. Young Todd Worrell (9-10, 36 saves) was the league's best relief pitcher..

## SAN DIEGO PADRES

A recently-traded former Padre referred to the situation in San Diego as 'a mess'. That's a bit harsh. The Padres are rebuilding.

Of course, the Padres have been rebuilding almost from the moment they entered the National League as an expansion team in 1969. And things have seldom broken right for this beleaguered team from the beautiful southern California city. Jack Murphy Stadium, San Diego's ballpark, has traditionally been a great place to see natural grass, symmetrical fences, and a Padre loss.

The one shining exception came in 1984 when a largely veteran team surprised everyone with a division title and astonished all by beating the Cubs in the LCS. The Tigers knocked them off in the World Series, but the Padres expected a few more years of winning. Instead, as though frightened by their success, the team dived back to the familiar bottom of the standings.

Some of the veterans who brought that 1984 pennant are gone. Others, like Steve Garvey (21, 81, .255) and reliever Goose Gossage (5-7, 21 saves), are a couple of years older and wiser but not better.

The Padres' future chances depend on a few legitimate stars and a lot of unproved youngsters. The stars include Garvey, Gossage, reliable outfielder Tony Gwynn (14, 59, .329) and erratic shortstop Garry Templeton (2, 44, .247). All of them have performed better than they did last year. The youngsters include most of the pitchers and catcher Benito Santiago, who is expected to add a home run bat to the line-up.

New manager Larry Bowa was a fiery competitor as a player; he hopes to light a fire under this continually disappointing team.

## SAN FRANCISCO GIANTS

When they were the New York Giants, they had the ballpark with the strangest contours. As the San Francisco Giants, they simply have a strange ballpark. Candlestick Park, their home since two seasons after they moved (along with the Dodgers) to the west coast in 1958, has the strongest and coldest winds in the major leagues. Fans bring coats and sweaters to afternoon games in August. One day in 1961 – before they enclosed the park – Giant relief pitcher Stu Miller went into his windup and was

*Steve Garvey of the Padres making contact.*

*Third baseman Chris Brown emerged as a hitting star for the Giants in 1986.*

literally blown off the mound for a balk. Shortstops have started back for pop flies that the wind blew into home runs. Blasts that looked like homers when struck have been caught by second basemen. Not even Fenway's Green Monster has such a quirky bearing on games as the weird winds of Candlestick.

According to legend, the New York team that joined the National League in 1883 had acquired a large number of very tall players by the time they won the 1888 pennant. Hence: Giants. In the early twentieth century, under manager John McGraw, the team fielded some of the 'biggest' stars in baseball. Perhaps the greatest was pitcher Christy Mathewson who won 373 games during his career.

In 1911, the Giants moved into the Polo Grounds, a ballpark with foul lines under 280 feet but a centrefield wall nearly 500 feet from home plate. Giant batters learned to take advantage of the field's idiosyncratic shape by pulling or slapping the ball down the lines. Two of the greatest Giant hitters were Bill Terry, who hit .401 in 1930, and Mel Ott, who cracked 511 career home runs. Both managed the Giants after McGraw's long tenure ended in 1932. McGraw, Ott, Terry, and lefthander Carl Hubbell are among the nearly three-dozen former Giants enshrined in the Hall of Fame.

After World War II, in perhaps the franchise's most thrilling exploit, the Giants came from $13\frac{1}{2}$ games back on 12 August 1951, to catch the Dodgers at the wire. The teams split two play-off games, but in the decider New York trailed by 4–1 in the ninth inning yet won on Bobby Thomson's 'shot heard 'round the world' homer. Although they lost the World Series that year to the Yankees, the Giants pulled a real post-season shocker in 1954 when, in four straight, they defeated Cleveland, a team that had won a record 111 games (out of 154). Memorable from that Series was centrefielder Willie Mays' unbelievable over-the-shoulder catch of a Cleveland drive in the deepest reaches of the Polo Grounds.

Since arriving on the west coast, the Giants have not been as successful either on the field or at the gate as have been the Dodgers to the south. Despite the presence of such greats as the supremely talented Mays, home run slugger Willie McCovey, and high-kicking righthander Juan Marichal, one pennant in 1962 and one division title in 1971 are all they can show for nearly thirty years. The often-sparse attendance is usually blamed on the bitter winds of Candlestick Park, unanimously rated the majors' least comfortable ballpark.

Much is expected of the present Giants. Veteran Mike Krukow (20-9, 3.05) heads a pitching staff stocked mostly by youngsters. Chili Davis (13, 70, .278) and Candy Maldonado (18, 85, .252) provide power in the outfield. Third baseman Chris Brown (7, 49, .317) and first sacker Will Clark (11, 41, .287) have their best seasons ahead of them.

With just a little luck there could soon be a World Series at Candlestick in October. Brrrrr!

# 3 NATIONAL LEAGUE ALL-STARS

## HUBIE BROOKS – SS, Montreal Expos

Born: 9/24/56, Los Angeles, California

Hgt: 6–0    Wgt: 178 Bats: Right Throws: Right

|  | G | AB | R | H | 2B | 3B | HR | RBI | SB | BA |
|---|---|---|---|---|---|---|---|---|---|---|
| Career – 7 yrs | 787 | 2954 | 313 | 822 | 137 | 23 | 55 | 377 | 38 | .278 |
| 1986 | 80 | 306 | 50 | 104 | 18 | 5 | 14 | 58 | 4 | .340 |

Brooks once made three errors in one inning as a Met third baseman, but since switching to shortstop in 1984, he's become a solid fielder. Traded to Montreal in 1985, he had an even hundred RBIs. He was enjoying an all-star year in 1986 until a wrist injury put him out for the second half of the season.

## GARY CARTER – C, New York Mets

Born: 4/8/54, Culver City, California

Hgt: 6–2    Wgt: 215 Bats: Right Throws: Right

|  | G | AB | R | H | 2B | 3B | HR | RBI | SB | BA |
|---|---|---|---|---|---|---|---|---|---|---|
| Career – 13 yrs | 1689 | 6063 | 847 | 1646 | 287 | 26 | 271 | 999 | 36 | .271 |
| 1986 | 132 | 490 | 81 | 125 | 14 | 2 | 24 | 105 | 1 | .255 |

Carter has been recognized as the game's top catcher for years. A thumb injury that put him out of the line-up for a couple of weeks may have cost him the 1986 MVP Award. He still tied for the league lead in game-winning RBIs, and his handling of the Mets' pitchers was given much of the credit for their league-leading effectiveness.

## VINCE COLEMAN – LF, St Louis Cardinals

Born: 9/22/61, Jacksonville, Florida

Hgt: 6–0    Wgt: 170 Bats: Both Throws: Right

|  | G | AB | R | H | 2B | 3B | HR | RBI | SB | BA |
|---|---|---|---|---|---|---|---|---|---|---|
| Career – 2 yrs | 305 | 1236 | 201 | 309 | 33 | 18 | 1 | 69 | 217 | .250 |
| 1986 | 154 | 600 | 94 | 139 | 13 | 8 | 0 | 29 | 107 | .232 |

Although Coleman led the N.L. with more than a hundred stolen bases again in 1986, the season wasn't a success for the '85 Rookie of the Year. His batting average dropped 35 points. Once on first, he's a nearly-impossible-to-stop blur, but he must improve his on-base average to make the Cards' Go-Go offence work.

## NATIONAL LEAGUE ALL-STARS

### ERIC DAVIS – CF, Cincinnati Reds

Born: 5/29/62, Los Angeles, California

Hgt: 6–3    Wgt: 175 Bats: Right Throws: Right

|  | G | AB | R | H | 2B | 3B | HR | RBI | SB | BA |
|---|---|---|---|---|---|---|---|---|---|---|
| Career – 3 yrs | 245 | 711 | 156 | 184 | 28 | 7 | 45 | 119 | 106 | .259 |
| 1986 | 132 | 415 | 97 | 115 | 15 | 3 | 27 | 71 | 80 | .277 |

The pressure is on Davis. With only one full season in the majors, he's being universally hailed as a budding superstar. One preseason magazine called him 'The next Willie Mays.' As only the third major leaguer in history to enter the '20–60 club' – at least 20 homers and 60 stolen bases – he's shown he has the tools.

### GLENN DAVIS – 1B, Houston Astros

Born: 3/28/61, Jacksonville, Florida

Hgt: 6–0    Wgt: 210 Bats: Right Throws: Right

|  | G | AB | R | H | 2B | 3B | HR | RBI | SB | BA |
|---|---|---|---|---|---|---|---|---|---|---|
| Career – 3 yrs | 276 | 985 | 148 | 260 | 48 | 3 | 53 | 173 | 3 | .264 |
| 1986 | 158 | 574 | 91 | 152 | 32 | 3 | 31 | 101 | 3 | .265 |

The Astros expect superstardom for the power-hitting Davis, who finished second in the N.L. MVP voting last year. He set a torrid early pace to put Houston out front in the division scramble, and, though he fell off at the end, he still tied for the league lead in game-winning RBIs with 16.

### DWIGHT GOODEN – RHP, New York Mets

Born: 11/16/64, Tampa, Florida

Hgt: 6–2    Wgt: 190 Bats: Right Throws: Right

|  | G | IP | W | L | Pct. | SO | BB | ERA | SVS |
|---|---|---|---|---|---|---|---|---|---|
| Career – 3 yrs | 99 | 744.2 | 58 | 19 | .753 | 744 | 222 | 2.28 | 0 |
| 1986 | 33 | 250 | 17 | 6 | .739 | 200 | 80 | 2.84 | 0 |

'Dr K' went from god-like (24-4, 1.53 ERA) in 1985 to simply very good in 1986. When he didn't repeat his Cy Young season, some picky fans suggested he'd lost a foot off his fastball. He still has enough speed (along with a great curve and fine control) to win a mantleful of Cy Youngs before he's done.

## PEDRO GUERRERO – LF, Los Angeles Dodgers

Born: 6/29/56, San Pedro de Marcoris, Dominican Republic

Hgt: 5-11    Wgt: 190  Bats: Both  Throws: Right

|  | G | AB | R | H | 2B | 3B | HR | RBI | SB | BA |
|---|---|---|---|---|---|---|---|---|---|---|
| Career – 9 yrs | 825 | 2842 | 448 | 865 | 137 | 21 | 139 | 461 | 75 | .304 |
| 1986 | 31 | 61 | 7 | 15 | 3 | 0 | 5 | 10 | 0 | .246 |

When Guerrero tore up his leg in 1986, the Dodgers' chances went on the shelf along with him. He tried to come back late in the season but was obviously not nearly ready. In the past, a healthy Guerrero has carried the team for weeks at a time with his hefty slugging.

## TONY GWYNN – RF, San Diego Padres

Born: 5/9/60, Los Angeles, California

Hgt: 5-11    Wgt: 185  Bats: Left  Throws: Left

|  | G | AB | R | H | 2B | 3B | HR | RBI | SB | BA |
|---|---|---|---|---|---|---|---|---|---|---|
| Career – 5 yrs | 612 | 2364 | 252 | 770 | 107 | 24 | 27 | 230 | 99 | .326 |
| 1986 | 160 | 642 | 107 | 211 | 33 | 7 | 14 | 59 | 37 | .329 |

Gwynn won the N.L. batting title in '84 with a .351 average, and was third last year. He's a good bet to add several more crowns before he's done. His power stats were up last season, but the Padres pay him to get on base so others can knock him home. On a strong team he'd be a possible MVP.

## VON HAYES – 1B, Philadelphia Phillies

Born: 8/31/58, Stockton, California

Hgt: 6-2    Wgt: 190  Bats: Left  Throws: Right

|  | G | AB | R | H | 2B | 3B | HR | RBI | SB | BA |
|---|---|---|---|---|---|---|---|---|---|---|
| Career – 6 yrs | 779 | 2728 | 299 | 753 | 145 | 22 | 69 | 366 | 153 | .276 |
| 1986 | 158 | 610 | 107 | 186 | 46 | 2 | 19 | 98 | 24 | .305 |

After several disappointing seasons with the Phillies, during which he was a favourite target of the Philadelphia boo-birds, Hayes emerged in 1986 as a first-rate slugger. Hayes' strong season meant opponents couldn't pitch around MVP Mike Schmidt.

*Lefthanded hitter Tony Gwynn is the Padres' leading player.*

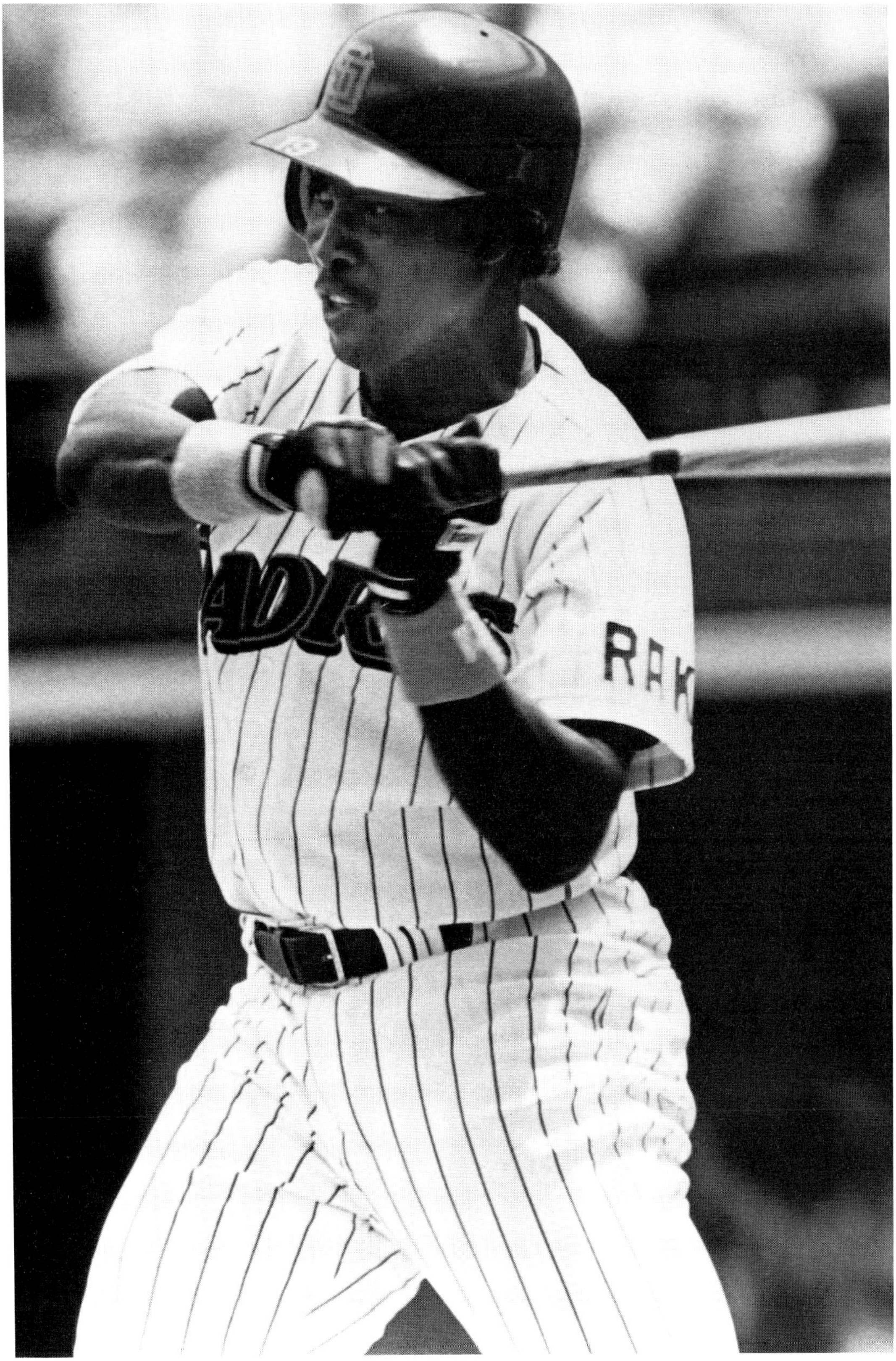
RAK

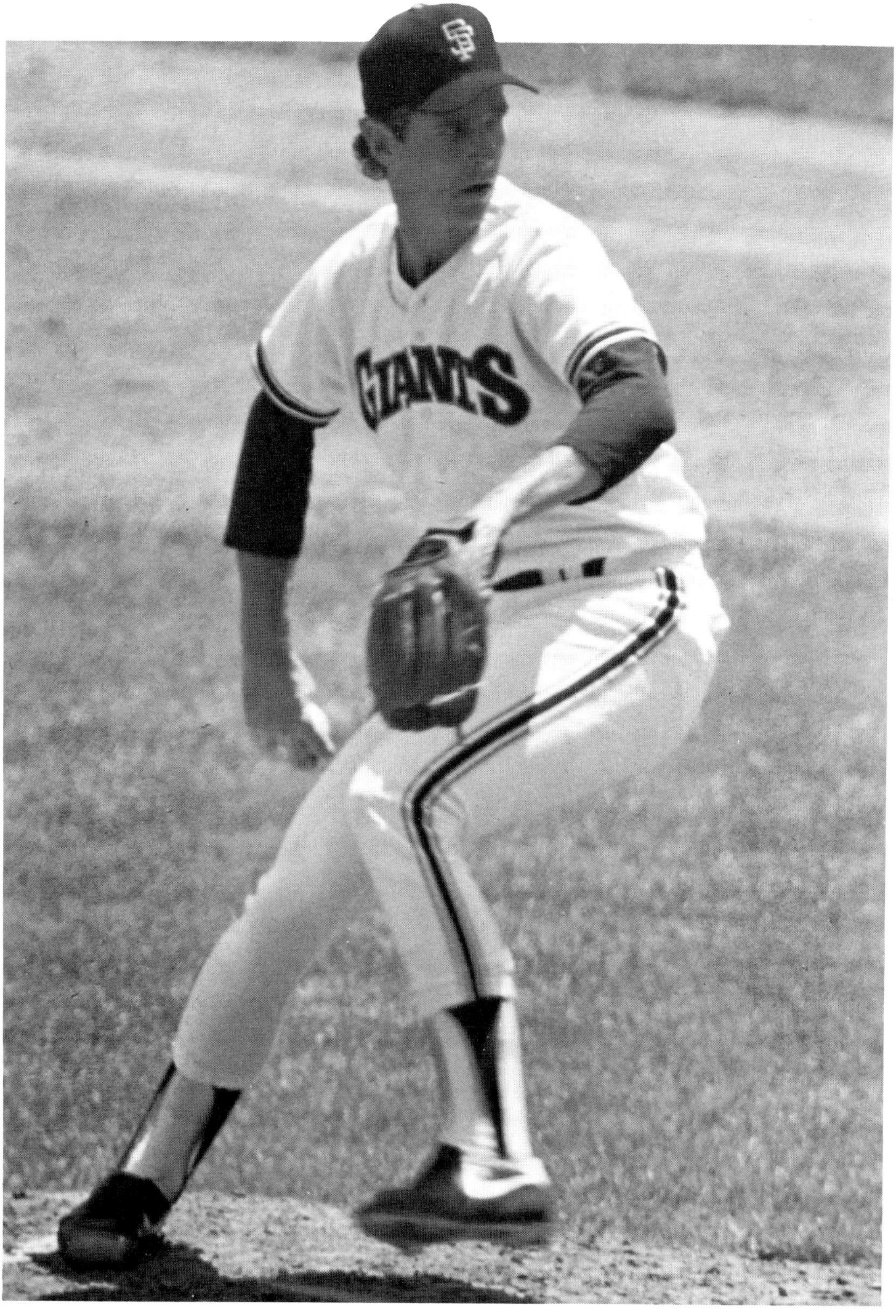
GIANTS

# NATIONAL LEAGUE ALL-STARS

## KEITH HERNANDEZ – 1B, New York Mets

Born: 10/20/53, San Francisco, California

Hgt: 6–0    Wgt: 185 Bats: Left Throws: Left

|  | G | AB | R | H | 2B | 3B | HR | RBI | SB | BA |
|---|---|---|---|---|---|---|---|---|---|---|
| Career – 13 yrs | 1721 | 6090 | 969 | 1840 | 372 | 58 | 128 | 900 | 96 | .302 |
| 1986 | 149 | 551 | 94 | 171 | 34 | 1 | 13 | 83 | 2 | .310 |

Although Hernandez led the N.L. in batting with a .344 mark in 1979 (when he was co-MVP), it's his fielding that sets him apart from other first basemen, traditionally a position reserved for lumbering sluggers. His lightning reactions, quickness, and grace make him certainly the top fielding first sacker today, and perhaps the best ever.

## MIKE KRUKOW – RHP, San Francisco Giants

Born: 1/21/52, Long Beach, California

Hgt: 6–4    Wgt: 205 Bats: Right Throws: Right

|  | G | IP | W | L | Pct. | SO | BB | ERA | SVS |
|---|---|---|---|---|---|---|---|---|---|
| Career – 11 yrs | 311 | 1859 | 108 | 104 | .509 | 1281 | 672 | 3.84 | 1 |
| 1986 | 34 | 245 | 20 | 9 | .690 | 178 | 55 | 3.05 | 0 |

Krukow credits adding a split-finger fastball to his explosive curve with turning him from a journeyman pitcher into a 20-game winner in 1986. Better support didn't hurt either. In his first decade of major league work (for mostly losing teams), he'd never won more than 13.

## DALE MURPHY – CF, Atlanta Braves

Born: 3/12/56, Portland, Oregon

Hgt: 6–4    Wgt: 215 Bats: Right Throws: Right

|  | G | AB | R | H | 2B | 3B | HR | RBI | SB | BA |
|---|---|---|---|---|---|---|---|---|---|---|
| Career – 11 yrs | 1360 | 5017 | 813 | 1388 | 214 | 32 | 256 | 822 | 129 | .277 |
| 1986 | 160 | 614 | 89 | 163 | 29 | 7 | 29 | 83 | 7 | .265 |

Likeable, hardworking Murphy had back-to-back MVP years in 1982 and 1983, then led the N.L. in homers the next two seasons. Last year was a bit off his usual production, in part because teams pitched around him. A former catcher, he's become an outstanding centrefielder.

*Righthander Mike Krukow learned a new pitch, the split-fingered fastball, in 1986 and won 20 games for the first time in his career.*

## DAVE PARKER – RF, Cincinnati Reds

Born: 6/9/51, Jackson, Mississippi

Hgt: 6–5    Wgt: 225 Bats: Left Throws: Right

|  | G | AB | R | H | 2B | 3B | HR | RBI | SB | BA |
|---|---|---|---|---|---|---|---|---|---|---|
| Career – 14 yrs | 1779 | 6727 | 978 | 2024 | 397 | 69 | 247 | 1093 | 140 | .301 |
| 1986 | 162 | 637 | 89 | 174 | 31 | 3 | 31 | 116 | 1 | .273 |

With Pittsburgh in the 1970s, Parker won batting crowns in 1977 and 1978 and was MVP in the latter year. He combined speed, power, and the best throwing arm of any outfielder in baseball. Injuries and personal problems nearly ended his career, but since coming to Cincinnati in 1984, he's regained his old form.

## LANCE PARRISH – C, Philadelphia Phillies

Born: 6/15/56, McKeesport, Pennsylvania

Hgt: 6–3    Wgt: 210 Bats: Right Throws: Right

|  | G | AB | R | H | 2B | 3B | HR | RBI | SB | BA |
|---|---|---|---|---|---|---|---|---|---|---|
| Career – 10 yrs | 1146 | 4273 | 577 | 1123 | 201 | 23 | 212 | 700 | 22 | .263 |
| 1986 | 91 | 327 | 53 | 84 | 6 | 1 | 22 | 62 | 0 | .257 |

From 1983 to 1985, the strong-armed Parrish averaged nearly 30 homers and over a hundred RBIs. Although slowed by a bad back much of last year, he was still a dangerous home run threat when in the line-up. His defence remained superb.

## TONY PENA – C, St Louis Cardinals

Born: 6/4/57, Monty Christy, Dominican Republic

Hgt: 5–11    Wgt: 175 Bats: Right Throws: Right

|  | G | AB | R | H | 2B | 3B | HR | RBI | SB | BA |
|---|---|---|---|---|---|---|---|---|---|---|
| Career – 7 yrs | 801 | 2873 | 307 | 821 | 140 | 15 | 63 | 340 | 42 | .286 |
| 1986 | 144 | 510 | 56 | 147 | 26 | 2 | 10 | 52 | 9 | .288 |

Despite the Pirates' dismal play of the last couple of seasons, their hustling catcher kept his star status. Now with St Louis, he is a line drive hitter with occasional power, he really shines on defence where his remarkable throwing makes him the most difficult N.L. catcher for base stealers to run on.

*Tim Raines, the NL's leading batter in 1986, a great basestealer and outfielder as well.*

NATIONAL LEAGUE ALL-STARS

## BASEBALL EXPLAINED

### TIM RAINES – LF, Montreal Expos

Born: 9/16/59, Sanford, Florida

Hgt: 5–8    Wgt: 175  Bats: Both  Throws: Right

|  | G | AB | R | H | 2B | 3B | HR | RBI | SB | BA |
|---|---|---|---|---|---|---|---|---|---|---|
| Career – 8 yrs | 882 | 3372 | 604 | 1028 | 180 | 55 | 48 | 419 | 471 | .305 |
| 1986 | 151 | 580 | 91 | 194 | 35 | 10 | 9 | 62 | 70 | .334 |

Raines led the N.L. in stolen bases in each of his first four seasons as a regular (1981–84), but he's far more than just a fast runner. An excellent flyhawk, his batting average has consistently topped .300, and in 1986 his .334 gave him his first batting crown.

### NOLAN RYAN – RHP, Houston Astros

Born: 1/31/47, Refugio, Texas

Hgt: 6–2    Wgt: 195  Bats: Right  Throws: Right

|  | G | IP | W | L | Pct. | SO | BB | ERA | SVS |
|---|---|---|---|---|---|---|---|---|---|
| Career – 20 yrs | 611 | 4114.2 | 253 | 226 | .528 | 4277 | 2268 | 3.15 | 3 |
| 1986 | 30 | 178 | 12 | 8 | .600 | 194 | 82 | 3.34 | 0 |

Ryan added nearly 200 more strikeouts to his all-time major league record total in 1986, proving that he still has the blazing fastball that earned him the nickname 'Von Ryan's Express'. Seven different seasons he's led his league in K's. Among his 253 lifetime victories are five no-hitters.

### RYNE SANDBERG – 2B, Chicago Cubs

Born: 9/18/59, Spokane, Washington

Hgt: 6–1    Wgt: 175  Bats: Right  Throws: Right

|  | G | AB | R | H | 2B | 3B | HR | RBI | SB | BA |
|---|---|---|---|---|---|---|---|---|---|---|
| Career – 6 yrs | 790 | 3146 | 494 | 902 | 153 | 45 | 74 | 345 | 189 | .287 |
| 1986 | 154 | 627 | 68 | 178 | 28 | 5 | 14 | 76 | 34 | .284 |

Sandberg's 1986 stats were down some from his MVP performance of 1984 and equally impressive 1985, but he remains the Cubs' most valuable asset. A shortstop early in his career, he broke in with the Cubs as a third baseman. Adding to his defensive versatility, he combines excellent speed with good power on offence.

*Ryne Sandberg, Chicago Cubs star second baseman.*

NATIONAL LEAGUE ALL-STARS

*Steve Sax, righthanded second baseman of the Dodgers.*

*Mike Schmidt, who hit his 500th home run in 1987, is the leading power hitter of his generation.*

## STEVE SAX – 2B, Los Angeles Dodgers

Born: 1/20/60, Sacramento, California

Hgt: 5-11    Wgt: 185 Bats: Right Throws: Right

|                | G   | AB   | R   | H   | 2B  | 3B | HR | RBI | SB  | BA   |
|----------------|-----|------|-----|-----|-----|----|----|-----|-----|------|
| Career – 6 yrs | 774 | 3070 | 420 | 872 | 118 | 24 | 19 | 230 | 211 | .284 |
| 1986           | 157 | 633  | 91  | 210 | 43  | 4  | 6  | 56  | 40  | .332 |

Although Sax was named N.L. Rookie of the Year in 1982, his career lay in jeopardy the next season when he developed a bad problem with wild throws on the simplest plays. His hitting suffered. Hard work seems to have solved his fielding lapses, and 1986 was his best.

## MIKE SCHMIDT – 3B, Philadelphia Phillies

Born: 9/27/49, Dayton, Ohio

Hgt: 6-2    Wgt: 203 Bats: Right Throws: Right

|                   | G    | AB   | R    | H    | 2B  | 3B | HR  | RBI  | SB  | BA   |
|-------------------|------|------|------|------|-----|----|-----|------|-----|------|
| Career – 15 years | 2107 | 7292 | 1347 | 1954 | 352 | 54 | 495 | 1392 | 169 | .268 |
| 1986              | 160  | 552  | 97   | 160  | 29  | 1  | 37  | 119  | 1   | .290 |

When Schmidt won his third MVP Award in 1986 (the first two were in 1980 and 1981), he joined an exclusive group: only five other players – all of them Hall of Famers – have earned three and no one has ever taken four. Early in the 1987 season, Schmidt passed 500 career homers and 1400 RBIs.

## MIKE SCOTT – RHP, Houston Astros

Born: 4/26/55, Santa Monica, California

Hgt: 6-3    Wgt: 215 Bats: Right Throws: Right

|                | G   | IP    | W  | L  | Pct. | SO  | BB  | ERA  | SVS |
|----------------|-----|-------|----|----|------|-----|-----|------|-----|
| Career – 8 yrs | 212 | 1160  | 65 | 62 | .512 | 750 | 363 | 3.70 | 3   |
| 1986           | 37  | 275.1 | 18 | 10 | .643 | 306 | 72  | 2.22 | 0   |

Scott's split-finger fastball dips so precipitously that opponents constantly accuse him of doctoring the ball. However he does it, he led the league in ERA and strikeouts and, on 25 September 1986, tossed a no-hitter to wrap up Houston's division title. It all earned him the N.L.'s Cy Young Award.

*Mike Scott became a dominant pitcher in 1986 with the split-fingered fastball.*

## NATIONAL LEAGUE ALL-STARS

## OZZIE SMITH – SS, St Louis Cardinals

Born: 12/26/54, Mobile, Alabama

Hgt: 5–10     Wgt: 150 Bats: Both Throws: Right

|  | G | AB | R | H | 2B | 3B | HR | RBI | SB | BA |
|---|---|---|---|---|---|---|---|---|---|---|
| Career – 9 yrs | 1317 | 4739 | 583 | 1169 | 179 | 38 | 13 | 374 | 303 | .247 |
| 1986 | 153 | 514 | 67 | 144 | 19 | 4 | 0 | 54 | 31 | .280 |

When St Louis signed Smith to a 2-million-dollar contract, some critics looked askance at his so-so batting average. But the Cards simply realized that at the key defensive position, nobody does it better than 'The Wizard of Oz'. Wide-ranging, sure-handed, acrobatic, and with a gun for an arm, he's one of the top shortstops of all time.

## DARRYL STRAWBERRY – RF, New York Mets

Born: 3/12/62, Los Angeles, California

Hgt: 6–6     Wgt: 190 Bats: Left Throws: Left

|  | G | AB | R | H | 2B | 3B | HR | RBI | SB | BA |
|---|---|---|---|---|---|---|---|---|---|---|
| Career – 4 yrs | 516 | 1810 | 292 | 471 | 84 | 20 | 108 | 343 | 100 | .260 |
| 1986 | 136 | 475 | 76 | 123 | 27 | 5 | 27 | 93 | 28 | .259 |

The Mets' tallest star has been in rightfield for four years, so critics tend to forget he won't be 25 until the 1987 season. Most of the knocks boil down to the fact that he has not yet reincarnated Babe Ruth. He does strike out too often, but he was second in the league in slugging average in 1986 and his best is to come.

## JOHN TUDOR – LHP, St Louis Cardinals

Born: 2/2/54, Schenectady, New York

Hgt: 6–0     Wgt: 185 Bats: Left Throws: Left

|  | G | IP | W | L | Pct. | SO | BB | ERA | SVS |
|---|---|---|---|---|---|---|---|---|---|
| Career – 8 yrs | 204 | 1343 | 85 | 58 | .594 | 775 | 366 | 3.24 | 1 |
| 1986 | 30 | 219 | 13 | 7 | .650 | 107 | 53 | 2.92 | 0 |

Tudor has always been a winner, usually under difficult circumstances. After five years in lefty-killing Fenway Park, he was traded to the last-place Pirates. Finally, in 1985, a trade to St Louis let him show what he could do with a contending team: 21-8, 1.93 ERA. But in 1986 the Cards' offence collapsed and Tudor was back pitching in hard luck, which continued with a freak injury in 1987.

*Ozzie Smith is the slickest-fielding shortstop in the game, nicknamed the 'Wizzard of Oz.'*

NATIONAL LEAGUE ALL-STARS

## FERNANDO VALENZUELA – LHP, Los Angeles Dodgers

Born: 11/1/60, Sonora, Mexico

Hgt: 5–11      Wgt: 200 Bats: Left Throws: Left

|  | G | IP | W | L | Pct. | SO | BB | ERA | SVS |
|---|---|---|---|---|---|---|---|---|---|
| Career – 7 yrs | 210 | 1555 | 99 | 68 | .593 | 1274 | 540 | 2.93 | 1 |
| 1986 | 34 | 269.1 | 21 | 11 | .656 | 242 | 85 | 3.14 | 0 |

Ever since he took both the Rookie of the Year and the Cy Young Awards in 1981, Valenzuela – Mexico's most popular athlete – has been regarded as baseball's top lefty. He wins with fine control of a wide assortment of pitches, including a baffling screwball. Last year, while other Dodgers stumbled, he had his best season.

ABOVE: *John Tudor, one of the NL's top lefty pitchers.* RIGHT: *Fernando Valenzuela, the best pitcher in baseball in the 1980s.*

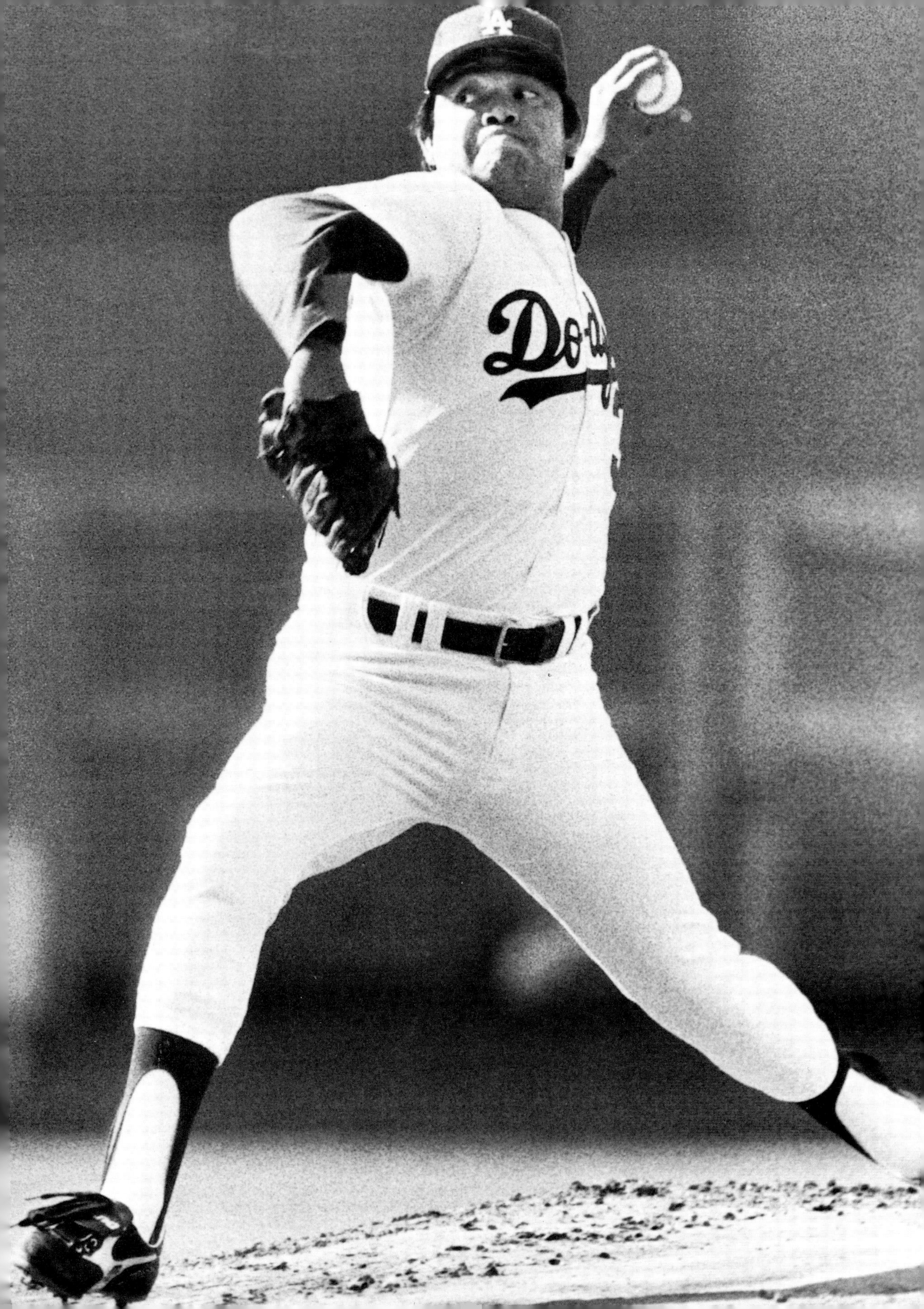
LA

*Todd Worrell of the Cardinals emerged in 1986 as a dominant relief pitcher.*

### TODD WORRELL – Relief Pitcher, St Louis Cardinals

| Born: 9/28/59, Arcadia, California | | | | | | | | | |
|---|---|---|---|---|---|---|---|---|---|
| Hgt: 6–5 | Wgt: 200 Bats: Right Throws: Right | | | | | | | | |
| | G | IP | W | L | Pct. | SO | BB | ERA | SVS |
| Career – 2 yrs | 91 | 125.1 | 12 | 10 | .545 | 90 | 48 | 2.23 | 41 |
| 1986 | 74 | 103.2 | 9 | 10 | .474 | 73 | 41 | 2.08 | 36 |

Although he pitched a few clutch games down the stretch in 1985 to help win a Cardinal pennant, Worrell was still a rookie in 1986. That allowed him to break a twenty-five-year-old record for rookie relievers with his 36 saves. The hard-throwing righthander was an ineffective starter in the minors.

# 4 AMERICAN LEAGUE ALL-STARS

## JESSE BARFIELD – RF, Toronto Blue Jays

Born: 10/29/59, Joliet, Illinois

Hgt: 6-1    Wgt: 180 Bats: Right Throws: Right

|  | G | AB | R | H | 2B | 3B | HR | RBI | SB | BA |
|---|---|---|---|---|---|---|---|---|---|---|
| Career – 6 yrs | 716 | 2325 | 371 | 634 | 112 | 19 | 128 | 376 | 129 | .273 |
| 1986 | 158 | 589 | 107 | 170 | 35 | 2 | 40 | 108 | 8 | .289 |

Barfield's 40 homers led the majors in 1986, and he was second in the A.L. in slugging average. Together with George Bell, he gives the Blue Jays one of baseball's top one-two punches. A streak hitter, when he's hot he's HOT! His throwing arm is one of the best.

## GEORGE BELL – LF, Toronto Blue Jays

Born: 10/21/59, San Pedro de Macoris, Dominican Republic

Hgt: 6-1    Wgt: 185 Bats: Right Throws: Right

|  | G | AB | R | H | 2B | 3B | HR | RBI | SB | BA |
|---|---|---|---|---|---|---|---|---|---|---|
| Career – 5 yrs | 574 | 2129 | 297 | 610 | 112 | 21 | 92 | 319 | 43 | .287 |
| 1986 | 159 | 641 | 101 | 198 | 38 | 6 | 31 | 108 | 7 | .309 |

Bell can do it all: run, hit, hit with power, field, and throw. After several years as the American League's best-kept secret, he is finally getting recognition as one of baseball's best young stars. 1986 saw him post personal highs in runs, hits, homers, RBIs, and average.

## WADE BOGGS – 3B, Boston Red Sox

Born: 6/15/58, Omaha, Nebraska

Hgt: 6-2    Wgt: 185 Bats: Left Throws: Right

|  | G | AB | R | H | 2B | 3B | HR | RBI | SB | BA |
|---|---|---|---|---|---|---|---|---|---|---|
| Career – 5 yrs | 725 | 2778 | 473 | 978 | 222 | 29 | 71 | 322 | 9 | .352 |
| 1986 | 149 | 580 | 107 | 207 | 47 | 2 | 8 | 71 | 0 | .357 |

Only three players in baseball history have finished their careers with higher lifetime batting averages than Boggs' current .352. In 1986 he notched his third A.L. batting title in four years. He's topped 200 hits for four years in a row, with a high of 240 in 1985. Part of his secret is his discriminating eye; he walked 105 times in 1986.

# AMERICAN LEAGUE ALL-STARS

## GEORGE BRETT – 3B, Kansas City Royals

Born: 5/15/53, Moundsville, West Virginia

Hgt: 6-0    Wgt: 200 Bats: Left Throws: Right

|  | G | AB | R | H | 2B | 3B | HR | RBI | SB | BA |
|---|---|---|---|---|---|---|---|---|---|---|
| Career – 14 yrs | 1741 | 6675 | 1072 | 2095 | 428 | 112 | 209 | 1050 | 141 | .314 |
| 1986 | 124 | 441 | 70 | 128 | 28 | 4 | 16 | 73 | 1 | .290 |

For Brett, 1986 was a poor season. Injuries held him to an un-Brett-like, below-.300 batting average. In 1980, when he was the A.L. MVP, he flirted with .400 all summer and finished at .390, the highest major league mark in forty years. 1986's 16 home runs were off his normal pace, too; he's had as many as 30.

## JOE CARTER – RF, Cleveland Indians

Born: 3/7/60, Oklahoma City, Oklahoma

Hgt: 6-3    Wgt: 215 Bats: Right Throws: Right

|  | G | AB | R | H | 2B | 3B | HR | RBI | SB | BA |
|---|---|---|---|---|---|---|---|---|---|---|
| Career – 4 yrs | 394 | 1447 | 210 | 404 | 70 | 11 | 57 | 222 | 56 | .279 |
| 1986 | 162 | 663 | 108 | 200 | 36 | 9 | 29 | 121 | 29 | .302 |

To get Carter, Cleveland traded ace pitcher Rick Sutcliffe to the Cubs in 1984. Sutcliffe won a Cy Young, but the Indians have no regrets. Carter's big bat had fans pouring into Cleveland's Municipal Stadium. His 121 RBIs were the majors' top figure. Only an ordinary outfielder, he can also play first base or DH.

## ROGER CLEMENS – RHP, Boston Red Sox

Born: 8/4/62, Dayton, Ohio

Hgt: 6-4    Wgt: 205 Bats: Right Throws: Right

|  | G | IP | W | L | Pct. | SO | BB | ERA | SVS |
|---|---|---|---|---|---|---|---|---|---|
| Career – 3 yrs | 69 | 485.2 | 40 | 13 | .755 | 438 | 133 | 3.15 | 0 |
| 1986 | 33 | 254 | 24 | 4 | .857 | 238 | 67 | 2.48 | 0 |

When Clemens was named MVP in 1986, on top of his Cy Young Award, it set off a debate about whether a pitcher (who plays only every four or five days) can be the most valuable player on a team. One thing's certain: the Red Sox wouldn't have won their pennant without his exceptional contribution.

BASEBALL EXPLAINED

## TONY FERNANDEZ – SS, Toronto Blue Jays

Born: 8/6/62, San Pedro de Macoris, Dominican Republic

Hgt: 6–1     Wgt: 160  Bats: Both  Throws: Right

|                | G   | AB   | R   | H   | 2B | 3B | HR | RBI | SB | BA   |
|----------------|-----|------|-----|-----|----|----|----|-----|----|------|
| Career – 4 yrs | 427 | 1518 | 204 | 448 | 70 | 22 | 17 | 137 | 43 | .295 |
| 1986           | 163 | 687  | 91  | 213 | 33 | 9  | 10 | 65  | 25 | .310 |

The little town of San Pedro de Macoris in the Dominican Republic has produced a half dozen current major league shortstops, but Fernandez is the best. Possessed of fine speed and a sharp bat, his extraordinary range in the field made him the A.L. Golden Glove shortstop in 1986.

## JULIO FRANCO – SS, Cleveland Indians

Born: San Pedro de Macoris, Dominican Republic

Hgt: 5–11    Wgt: 175  Bats: Right  Throws: Right

|                | G   | AB   | R   | H   | 2B  | 3B | HR | RBI | SB | BA   |
|----------------|-----|------|-----|-----|-----|----|----|-----|----|------|
| Career – 5 yrs | 634 | 2482 | 330 | 715 | 110 | 22 | 27 | 326 | 74 | .288 |
| 1986           | 149 | 599  | 80  | 183 | 30  | 5  | 10 | 74  | 10 | .306 |

Franco is another San Pedro de Macoris shortstop. He came to the Indians in a controversial trade with the Phillies for Von Hayes. Although the sometimes-moody infielder is adequate with his glove, his most important contributions to Cleveland victories are with his bat.

## KIRK GIBSON – RF, Detroit Tigers

Born: 5/28/57, Pontiac, Michigan

Hgt: 6–3     Wgt: 215  Bats: Left  Throws: Left

|                | G   | AB   | R   | H   | 2B  | 3B | HR  | RBI | SB  | BA   |
|----------------|-----|------|-----|-----|-----|----|-----|-----|-----|------|
| Career – 8 yrs | 765 | 2723 | 433 | 750 | 115 | 32 | 126 | 420 | 140 | .275 |
| 1986           | 119 | 441  | 84  | 118 | 11  | 2  | 28  | 86  | 34  | .268 |

Gibson leads the league in long, long home runs, but he doesn't hit them often enough to qualify as the superstar they expect him to be in Detroit. An ex-football player, he spends too much time on the bench injured. When he's healthy and hot, he can carry a team.

*Grizzled outfielder Kirk Gibson of the Tigers was a college football star and could have played in the National Football League; the Tigers are glad he chose baseball.*

## AMERICAN LEAGUE ALL-STARS

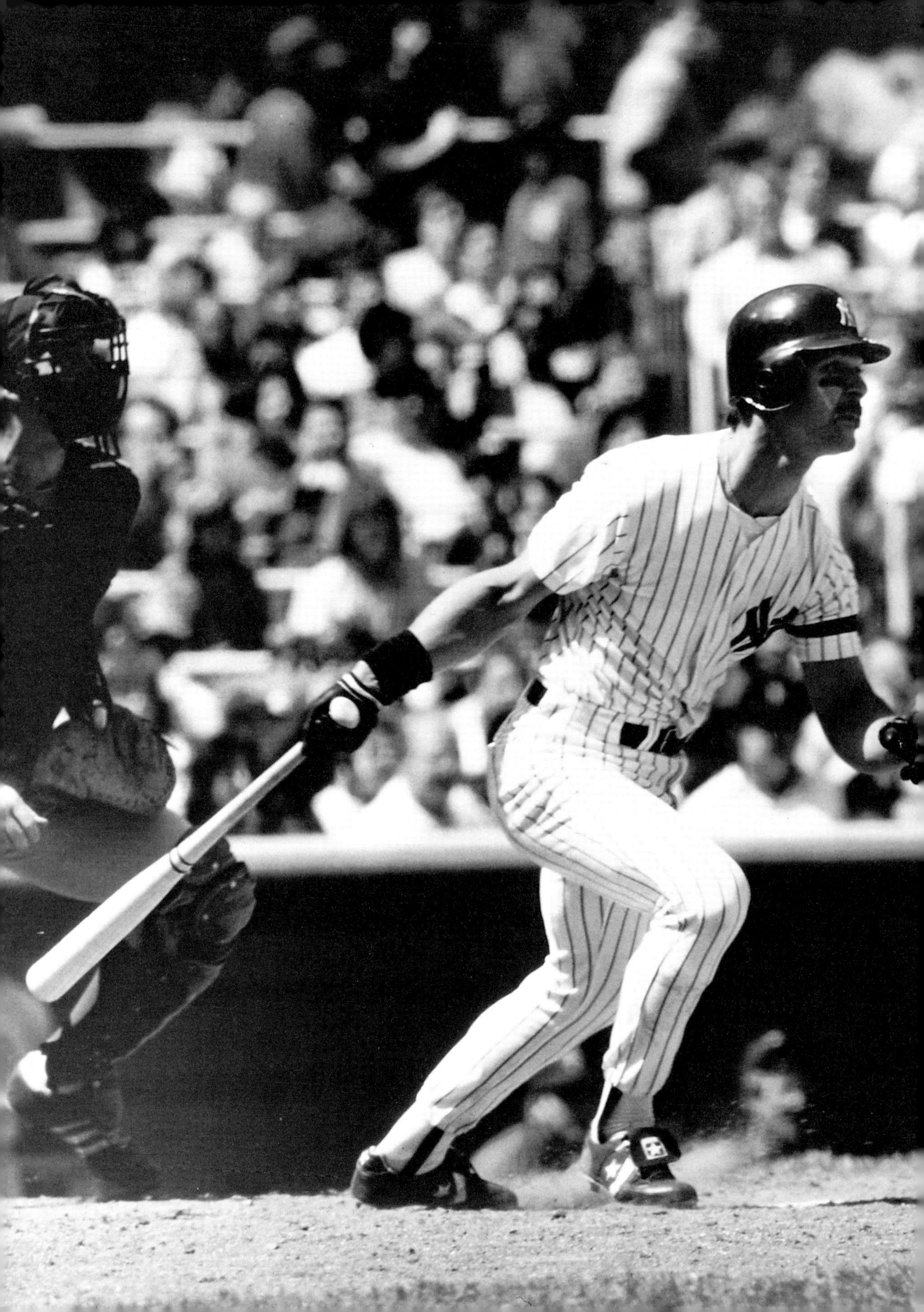

## AMERICAN LEAGUE ALL-STARS

### RICKEY HENDERSON – CF, New York Yankees

Born: 12/25/58, Chicago, Illinois

Hgt: 5-10    Wgt: 180 Bats: Right Throws: Left

|  | G | AB | R | H | 2B | 3B | HR | RBI | SB | BA |
|---|---|---|---|---|---|---|---|---|---|---|
| Career – 8 yrs | 987 | 4071 | 862 | 1182 | 188 | 39 | 103 | 417 | 660 | .290 |
| 1986 | 153 | 608 | 130 | 160 | 31 | 5 | 28 | 74 | 87 | .263 |

Henderson has now led the American League in stolen bases seven straight years, swiping an all-time major league record 130 in 1982. Called by many baseball's best lead-off man, his batting average was down a bit in 1986, perhaps because he pushed his home run swing.

### TED HIGUERA – LHP, Milwaukee Brewers

Born: 11/9/58, Los Mochis, Sinaloa, Mexico

Hgt: 5-10    Wgt: 178 Bats: Switch Throws: Left

|  | G | IP | W | L | Pct. | SO | BB | ERA | SVS |
|---|---|---|---|---|---|---|---|---|---|
| Career – 2 yrs | 66 | 460.2 | 35 | 19 | .648 | 334 | 137 | 3.30 | 0 |
| 1986 | 34 | 248.1 | 20 | 11 | .645 | 207 | 74 | 2.79 | 0 |

After six years in the Mexican League, Higuera was purchased by the Brewers and moved up quickly. The A.L.'s top rookie pitcher in 1985, he was the league's winningest lefty in 1986. His fine control, 90-m.p.h. fastball, wicked slider, and surprise screwball make him nearly unhittable.

### DON MATTINGLY – 1B, New York Yankees

Born: 4/20/61, Evansville, Indiana

Hgt: 5-11    Wgt: 185 Bats: Left Throws: Left

|  | G | AB | R | H | 2B | 3B | HR | RBI | SB | BA |
|---|---|---|---|---|---|---|---|---|---|---|
| Career – 5 yrs | 572 | 2223 | 349 | 737 | 160 | 11 | 93 | 401 | 3 | .332 |
| 1986 | 162 | 677 | 117 | 238 | 53 | 2 | 31 | 113 | 0 | .352 |

In only three full seasons, Mattingly has established himself as the premier all-around hitter in baseball. So far, the hard-working over-achiever has led the American League in batting (1984), RBIs (1985), hits (1984 and 1986), and doubles (1984, 1985, and 1986). His 238 basehits in 1986 was the 15th highest in baseball history. A.L. MVP in 1985, he finished second in 1986.

*Don Mattingly shows the form which has made him the top hitter in baseball today.*

## JACK MORRIS – RHP, Detroit Tigers

Born: 5/16/56, St Paul, Minnesota

Hgt: 6–3    Wgt: 195 Bats: Right Throws: Right

|                  | G   | IP     | W   | L  | Pct.  | SO   | BB  | ERA  | SVS |
|------------------|-----|--------|-----|----|-------|------|-----|------|-----|
| Career – 10 yrs  | 302 | 2122.1 | 144 | 94 | .605  | 1327 | 754 | 3.57 | 0   |
| 1986             | 35  | 267    | 21  | 8  | .724  | 223  | 82  | 3.27 | 0   |

Morris is not so spectacular as such pitchers as Gooden or Clemens. His stats are usually good, rather than great. He's never led in ERA and only once in K's. All he does is win. He's the winningest pitcher in the majors during the 1980s, particularly effective during the warmest part of each summer.

## EDDIE MURRAY – 1B, BaltimoreColts

Born: 2/24/56, Los Angeles, California

Hgt: 6–2    Wgt: 200 Bats: Both Throws: Right

|                  | G    | AB   | R   | H    | 2B  | 3B | HR  | RBI  | SB | BA   |
|------------------|------|------|-----|------|-----|----|-----|------|----|------|
| Career – 10 yrs  | 1499 | 5624 | 884 | 1679 | 296 | 20 | 275 | 1015 | 55 | .299 |
| 1986             | 137  | 495  | 61  | 151  | 25  | 1  | 17  | 84   | 3  | .305 |

Until an eye problem cut into his power stats and playing time in 1986, Murray was the model of consistency, hitting about .300 with 30 home runs and 100 RBIs every season. Curiously, the only previous time he failed to approximate those figures was the strike-shortened 1981 season when his 22 homers and 78 RBIs led the league.

## PHIL NIEKRO – RHP, Cleveland Indians

Born: 4/1/39, Blaine, Ohio

Hgt: 6–1    Wgt: 195 Bats: Right Throws: Right

|                  | G   | IP    | W   | L   | Pct. | SO   | BB   | ERA  | SVS |
|------------------|-----|-------|-----|-----|------|------|------|------|-----|
| Career – 23 yrs  | 838 | 5265  | 311 | 261 | .544 | 3278 | 1743 | 3.27 | 10  |
| 1986             | 34  | 210.1 | 11  | 11  | .500 | 81   | 95   | 4.32 | 0   |

Niekro has pitched in the major leagues during the administrations of five US Presidents. Some day he may walk off the mound and go straight to the old folks' home, but right now he can still pitch. His secret is simple: the knuckleball puts almost no strain on the arm and Niekro throws the best ever.

## AMERICAN LEAGUE ALL-STARS

### KIRBY PUCKETT – CF, Minnesota Twins

Born: 3/14/61, Chicago, Illinois

Hgt: 5–8    Wgt: 175 Bats: Right Throws: Right

|               | G   | AB   | R   | H   | 2B | 3B | HR | RBI | SB | BA   |
|---------------|-----|------|-----|-----|----|----|----|-----|----|------|
| Career – 3 yrs| 450 | 1928 | 262 | 587 | 78 | 24 | 35 | 201 | 55 | .304 |
| 1986          | 161 | 680  | 119 | 223 | 37 | 6  | 31 | 96  | 20 | .328 |

Until 1986, Puckett had averaged a home run every 312 at bats. In 1986, he hit one every 22 trips to the plate. His new muscles – coupled with superior defensive skills and a reliable batting eye – moved him into the ranks of baseball's top centrefielders.

### JEFF REARDON – Relief Pitcher, Minnesota Twins

Born: 10/1/55, Dalton, Mississippi

Hgt: 6–1    Wgt: 190 Bats: Right Throws: Right

|               | G   | IP    | W  | L  | Pct. | SO  | BB  | ERA  | SVS |
|---------------|-----|-------|----|----|------|-----|-----|------|-----|
| Career – 8 yrs| 456 | 665.2 | 42 | 46 | .477 | 537 | 246 | 2.80 | 162 |
| 1986          | 62  | 89    | 7  | 9  | .438 | 67  | 26  | 3.94 | 35  |

As the Expos fireman, Reardon led the N.L. in saves with 41 in 1985 and followed with 35 in 1986. The Twins, desperate for a bullpen, traded a load of youngsters for him. The flip side is, his ERA has been going up and his strikeout per inning average has been going down.

### JIM RICE – LF, Boston Red Sox

Born: 3/8/53, Anderson, South Carolina

Hgt: 6–2    Wgt: 205 Bats: Right Throws: Right

|                | G    | AB   | R    | H    | 2B  | 3B | HR  | RBI  | SB | BA   |
|----------------|------|------|------|------|-----|----|-----|------|----|------|
| Career – 13 yrs| 1790 | 7127 | 1104 | 2163 | 331 | 74 | 351 | 1289 | 55 | .303 |
| 1986           | 157  | 618  | 98   | 200  | 39  | 2  | 20  | 110  | 0  | .324 |

Although Rice was the A.L. MVP in 1978 while leading in homers and RBIs, some experts feel he was even more effective last season when he helped bring a pennant to Fenway Park. As a righthanded power hitter, he benefits from the Green Monster, but he also plays its odd caroms brilliantly on defence.

ABOVE: *Kirby Puckett, the centerfielder for the Twins.* RIGHT: *Righthanded Red Sox outfielder Jim Rice has been a scourge of American League pitchers since 1975.*

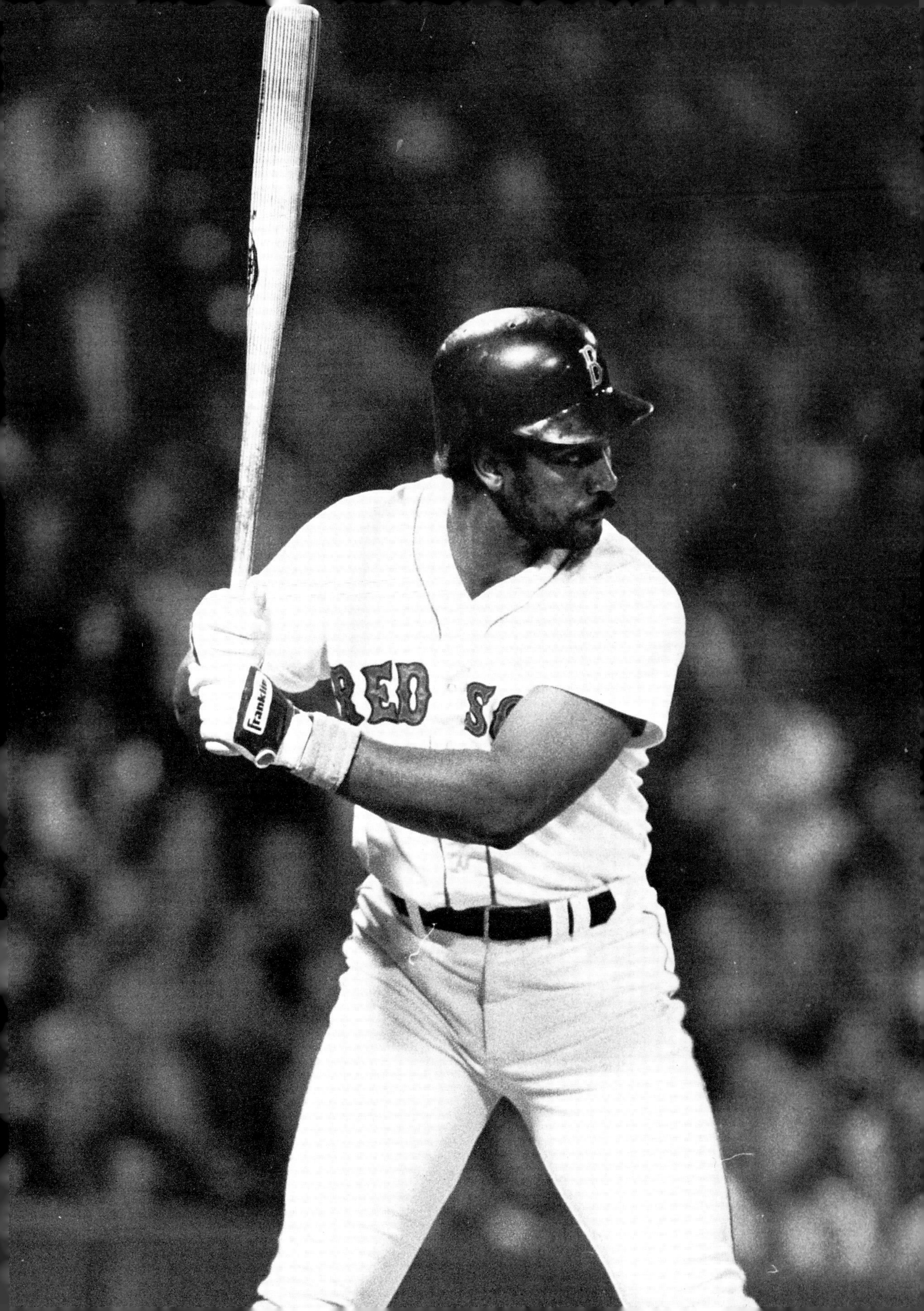
B
RED SO
franklin

BASEBALL EXPLAINED

## DAVE RIGHETTI – Relief Pitcher, New York Yankees

Born: 11/29/58, San Jose, California

Hgt: 6–3  Wgt: 195 Bats: Left Throws: Left

|  | G | IP | W | L | Pct. | SO | BB | ERA | SVS |
|---|---|---|---|---|---|---|---|---|---|
| Career – 7 yrs | 297 | 832 | 58 | 44 | .569 | 699 | 340 | 3.01 | 107 |
| 1986 | 74 | 106.2 | 8 | 8 | .500 | 83 | 35 | 2.45 | 46 |

Righetti was a starter through 1983, usually a little wild but effective. He threw a no-hitter on 4 July of that year. Since switching to the bullpen, he's become the top A.L. fireman. In 1986 he received credit for saves in more than half the Yankee victories, setting the major league record with 46.

## CAL RIPKIN, JR – SS, Baltimore Orioles

Born: 8/24/60, Havre de Grace, Maryland

Hgt: 6–4  Wgt: 200 Bats: Right Throws: Right

|  | G | AB | R | H | 2B | 3B | HR | RBI | SB | BA |
|---|---|---|---|---|---|---|---|---|---|---|
| Career – 6 yrs | 830 | 3210 | 529 | 927 | 183 | 20 | 133 | 472 | 11 | .289 |
| 1986 | 162 | 627 | 98 | 177 | 35 | 1 | 25 | 81 | 4 | .282 |

Ripkin is undoubtedly the best slugging shortstop since Ernie Banks, and his hitting makes the headlines. However, he's a reliable fielder with amazing stamina: he hasn't missed an inning in four years, while playing baseball's most demanding position. A.L. Rookie of the Year in 1982 as a third baseman, he switched to short the next season and was MVP.

## DAVE WINFIELD – RF, New York Yankees

Born: 10/3/51, St Paul, Minnesota

Hgt: 6–6  Wgt: 220 Bats: Right Throws: Right

|  | G | AB | R | H | 2B | 3B | HR | RBI | SB | BA |
|---|---|---|---|---|---|---|---|---|---|---|
| Career – 14 yrs | 1964 | 7287 | 1135 | 2083 | 353 | 71 | 305 | 1234 | 195 | .286 |
| 1986 | 154 | 565 | 90 | 148 | 31 | 5 | 24 | 104 | 6 | .262 |

Big Dave may feud with Yankee owner George Steinbrenner, but when the ballgame starts, he's one of the most feared and valuable sluggers in the game. His excellent arm and loping speed make him a defensive plus. A college star, he came directly to the majors without any minor league experience.

## AMERICAN LEAGUE ALL-STARS

### LOU WHITAKER – 2B, Detroit Tigers

Born: 5/12/57, Brooklyn, New York

Hgt: 5-11   Wgt: 160 Bats: Left Throws: Right

|  | G | AB | R | H | 2B | 3B | HR | RBI | SB | BA |
|---|---|---|---|---|---|---|---|---|---|---|
| Career – 10 yrs | 1283 | 4705 | 724 | 1320 | 202 | 49 | 93 | 522 | 94 | .281 |
| 1986 | 144 | 584 | 95 | 157 | 26 | 6 | 20 | 73 | 13 | .269 |

Teaming with shortstop Alan Trammell, Whitaker gives the Tigers the A.L.'s best double-play combo. Ever since he was selected A.L. Rookie of the Year back in 1978, 'Sweet Lou' has been recognized as a slick, dependable fielder. But, as he's matured, he's added more sock to his bat, smacking 21 and 20 home runs the past two years.

### FRANK WHITE – 2B, Kansas City Royals

Born: 9/4/50, Greenville, Mississippi

Hgt: 5-11   Wgt: 175 Bats: Right Throws: Right

|  | G | AB | R | H | 2B | 3B | HR | RBI | SB | BA |
|---|---|---|---|---|---|---|---|---|---|---|
| Career – 14 yrs | 1803 | 6100 | 743 | 1583 | 314 | 53 | 131 | 693 | 166 | .260 |
| 1986 | 151 | 566 | 76 | 154 | 37 | 3 | 22 | 84 | 4 | .272 |

White was a graduate of Royals Academy, a school created by Kansas City to teach baseball skills to promising athletes. Certainly he deserves a Phi Beta Kappa key. One of the Royals' most reliable hitters, he's best known for his superb fielding, having won more Golden Gloves than any other second baseman in history.

### MIKE WITT – RHP, California Angels

Born: 7/20/60, Fullerton, California

Hgt: 6-7   Wgt: 185 Bats: Right Throws: Right

|  | G | IP | W | L | Pct. | SO | BB | ERA | SVS |
|---|---|---|---|---|---|---|---|---|---|
| Career – 6 yrs | 201 | 1228.2 | 71 | 59 | .546 | 821 | 424 | 3.52 | 5 |
| 1986 | 34 | 269 | 18 | 10 | .643 | 208 | 73 | 2.84 | 0 |

Witt's wide-breaking curve and live fastball would be effective delivered by anyone, but coming at a batter from the unexpected angle his height provides, his stuff is devastating. 1986 was his best season. Particularly notable was his strikeout-to-walk ratio.

# CHAMPIONSHIP TEAMS

| Year | NL Champion | AL Champion | World Series |
|------|-------------|-------------|--------------|
| 1901 | Pittsburgh | Chicago | |
| 1902 | Pittsburgh | Philadelphia | |
| 1903 | Pittsburgh | Boston | Red Sox 5–3 |
| 1904 | New York | Boston | |
| 1905 | New York | Philadelphia | Giants 4–1 |
| 1906 | Chicago | Chicago | White Sox 4–2 |
| 1907 | Chicago | Detroit | Cubs 4–0 |
| 1908 | Chicago | Detroit | Cubs 4–1 |
| 1909 | Pittsburgh | Detroit | Pirates 4–3 |
| 1910 | Chicago | Philadelphia | Athletics 4–1 |
| 1911 | New York | Philadelphia | Athletics 4–2 |
| 1912 | New York | Boston | Red Sox 4–3 |
| 1913 | New York | Philadelphia | Athletics 4–1 |
| 1914 | Boston | Philadelphia | Braves 4–0 |
| 1915 | Philadelphia | Boston | Red Sox 4–1 |
| 1916 | Brooklyn | Boston | Red Sox 4–1 |
| 1917 | New York | Chicago | White Sox 4–2 |
| 1918 | Chicago | Boston | Red Sox 4–2 |
| 1919 | Cincinnati | Chicago | Reds 5–3 |
| 1920 | Brooklyn | Cleveland | Indians 5–2 |
| 1921 | New York | New York | Giants 5–3 |
| 1922 | New York | New York | Giants 4–0 |
| 1923 | New York | New York | Yankees 4–2 |
| 1924 | New York | Washington | Senators 4–3 |
| 1925 | Pittsburgh | Washington | Pirates 4–3 |
| 1926 | St Louis | New York | Cardinals 4–3 |
| 1927 | Pittsburgh | New York | Yankees 4–0 |
| 1928 | St Louis | New York | Yankees 4–0 |
| 1929 | Chicago | Philadelphia | Athletics 4–1 |
| 1930 | St Louis | Philadelphia | Athletics 4–2 |
| 1931 | St Louis | Philadelphia | Cardinals 4–3 |
| 1932 | Chicago | New York | Yankees 4–0 |
| 1933 | New York | Washington | Giants 4–1 |
| 1934 | St Louis | Detroit | Cardinals 4–3 |
| 1935 | Chicago | Detroit | Tigers 4–2 |
| 1936 | New York | New York | Yankees 4–2 |
| 1937 | New York | New York | Yankees 4–1 |
| 1938 | Chicago | New York | Yankees 4–0 |
| 1939 | Cincinnati | New York | Yankees 4–0 |
| 1940 | Cincinnati | Detroit | Reds 4–3 |
| 1941 | Brooklyn | New York | Yankees 4–1 |

| Year | NL | AL | Winner |
|------|-----|-----|--------|
| 1942 | St Louis | New York | Cardinals 4–1 |
| 1943 | St Louis | New York | Yankees 4–1 |
| 1944 | St Louis | St Louis | Cardinals 4–2 |
| 1945 | Chicago | Detroit | Tigers 4–2 |
| 1946 | St Louis | Boston | Cardinals 4–3 |
| 1947 | Brooklyn | New York | Yankees 4–3 |
| 1948 | Boston | Cleveland | Indians 4–2 |
| 1949 | Brooklyn | New York | Yankees 4–1 |
| 1950 | Philadelphia | New York | Yankees 4–0 |
| 1951 | New York | New York | Yankees 4–2 |
| 1952 | Brooklyn | New York | Yankees 4–2 |
| 1953 | Brooklyn | New York | Yankees 4–3 |
| 1954 | New York | Cleveland | Giants 4–0 |
| 1955 | Brooklyn | New York | Dodgers 4–3 |
| 1956 | Brooklyn | New York | Yankees 4–3 |
| 1957 | Milwaukee | New York | Braves 4–3 |
| 1958 | Milwaukee | New York | Yankees 4–3 |
| 1959 | Los Angeles | Chicago | Dodgers 4–2 |
| 1960 | Pittsburgh | New York | Pirates 4–3 |
| 1961 | Cincinnati | New York | Yankees 4–1 |
| 1962 | San Francisco | New York | Yankees 4–3 |
| 1963 | Los Angeles | New York | Dodgers 4–0 |
| 1964 | St Louis | New York | Cardinals 4–3 |
| 1965 | Los Angeles | Minnesota | Dodgers 4–3 |
| 1966 | Los Angeles | Baltimore | Orioles 4–0 |
| 1967 | St Louis | Boston | Cardinals 4–3 |
| 1968 | St Louis | Detroit | Tigers 4–3 |
| 1969 | **NY**/Atlanta | **Baltimore**/Minnesota | Mets 4–1 |
| 1970 | **Cincinnati**/Pgh | **Baltimore**/Minnesota | Orioles 4–1 |
| 1971 | **Pittsburgh**/San Fran | **Baltimore**/Oakland | Pirates 4–3 |
| 1972 | **Cincinnati**/Pgh | **Oakland**/Detroit | A's 4–3 |
| 1973 | **New York**/Cincinnati | **Oakland**/Baltimore | A's 4–3 |
| 1974 | **Los Angeles**/Pgh | **Oakland**/Baltimore | A's 4–1 |
| 1975 | **Cincinnati**/Pgh | **Boston**/Oakland | Reds 4–3 |
| 1976 | **Cincinnati**/Philly | **New York**/KC | Reds 4–0 |
| 1977 | **Los Angeles**/Philly | **New York**/KC | Yankees 4–2 |
| 1978 | **Los Angeles**/Philly | **New York**/KC | Yankees 4–2 |
| 1979 | **Pittsburgh**/Cincy | **Baltimore**/Calif | Pirates 4–3 |
| 1980 | **Philadelphia**/Hou | **Kansas City**/NY | Phillies 4–2 |
| 1981 | **Los Angeles**/Montr | **New York**/Oakland | Dodgers 4–2 |
| 1982 | **St Louis**/Atlanta | **Milwaukee**/Calif | Cardinals 4–3 |
| 1983 | **Philadelphia**/LA | **Baltimore**/Chicago | Orioles 4–1 |
| 1984 | **San Diego**/Chicago | **Detroit**/Kansas City | Tigers 4–1 |
| 1985 | **St Louis**/LA | **Kansas City**/Toronto | Royals 4–3 |
| 1986 | **New York**/Houston | **Boston**/California | Mets 4–2 |

NOTE: The leagues were divided into divisions in 1969. Winners of LCS in bold; losers in roman.

## PHOTO CREDITS

The author and publishers are grateful to the following for permission to reproduce copyright photographs in the book: Atlanta Braves page 100; Boston Red Sox/Peter Travers pages 19, 42, 43, 155; California Angels pages 14, 27, 71; Chicago Cubs pages 48, 111, 135; Detroit Tigers page 149; Houston Astro pages 46, 60, 139; Kansas City Royals pages 31, 55, 97; Los Angeles Dodgers pages 35, 44, 114, 136, 143; Milwaukee Brewers/Larry Stoudt pages 36, 98; Minnesota Twins page 154; Montreal Expos page 133; New York Yankees pages 50, 58, 101, 102, 150; Oakland Athletics pages 104, 105; Philadelphia Phillies pages 117, 137; Pittsburgh Pirates page 47; St Louis Cardinals pages 119, 120, 141, 142, 144; San Diego Padres pages 122, 129; San Francisco Giants pages 123, 130.